The Spirit of Ancient Egypt

The Spirit of Ancient Egypt

Ana Ruiz

Algora Publishing
New York

Algora Publishing, New York
© 2001 by Algora Publishing
All rights reserved. Published 2001.
Printed in the United States of America
ISBN: 1-892941-68-6
Editors@algora.com

Library of Congress Cataloging-in-Publication Data 2001-004087

Ruiz, Ana.
The spirit of Ancient Egypt / by Ana Ruiz.
    p. cm.
ISBN 1-892941-68-6 (alk. paper)
1. Egypt—Civilization—To 332 B.C. I. Title.
DT60 .R89 2001
932—dc21
                              2001004087

New York
www.algora.com

To my parents, Isabel and Manuel

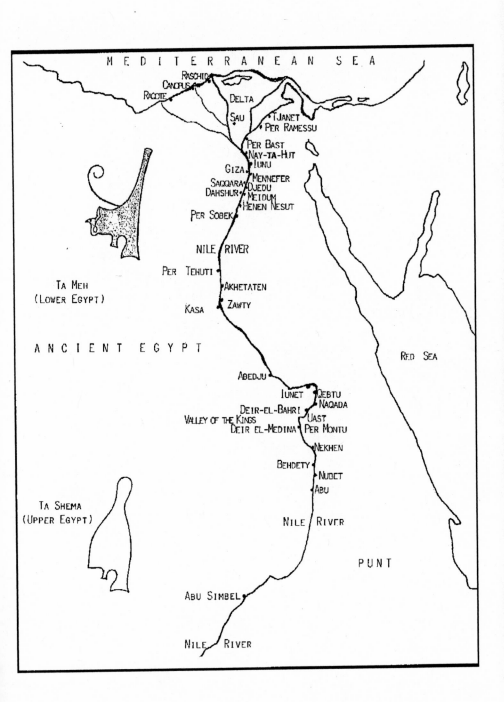

A Chronology of Egypt's Rulers

rly Dynastic or Archaic Period
100- 2700 BC)
Dynasty (3100-2890 BC)
  Narmer, or Menes
  Aha
  Djer
  Djet
  Den
  Anendjib
  Semerkhet
  Qaa

ad Dynasty (2890-2700 BC)
  Hotepsekhemwy
  Raneb
  Nynetjer
  Peribsen
  Khasekhem

ld Kingdom
-d Dynasty (2700-2613 BC)
  Djoser
  Sekhemkhet
  Khaba
  Huni

th Dynasty (2613-2498 BC)
  Sneferu
  Khufu
  Djedefre
  Khafre
  Menkaura
  Shepseskaf

5th Dynasty (2498-2345 BC)
  Userkaf
  Sahure
  Neferirkare
  Shepseskare
  Nyuserre
  Menkauhor
  Djedkare
  Iunas

6th Dynasty (2345-2150 BC)
  Teti
  Userkare
  Pepy I
  Merenre
  Pepy II
  Neitkrety^ſ (on some lists)

1st Intermediate Period
(2150-2050 BC)
7th-10th Dynasties*

Middle Kingdom
11th Dynasty (2050-1991 BC)
  Inyotef I
  Inyotef II
  Inyotef III
  Montuhotep I
  Montuhotep II
  Montuhotep III
  Montuhotep IV

12th Dynasty (1991-1775 BC)
  Amenemhet I
  Senwosret I

  Amenemhet II
  Senwosret II
  Senwosret III
  Amenemhet III
  Amenemhet IV
  Neferu-Sobek^ſ

Second Intermediate Period
Hyksos Invasion, 13th-17th Dynasties
(1775- 1550 BC)
13th Dynasty
  Wegaf
  Amenemhet V
  Sobekhotep I
  Hor
  Amenemhet VI
  Sobekhotep II
  Khendjer
  Sobekhotep III
  Neferhotep I
  Sobekhotep IV
  Sobekhotep V
  Aye
  Neferhotep II

14th-16th Dynasties
Little is known about this period.

17th Dynasty (1640-1550 BC)
  Intef IV
  Sobekemsaf
  Seqenenre Tao I
  Seqenenre Tao II
  Kamose

[Continued]

ſ Denotes ruling queens.
* Many kings ruled, for longer or shorter reigns, during each of the four short-lived dynasties and, according to the
King List of Abydos, 25 kings ruled during the 8th Dynasty, which lasted about 30 years. Scarce evidence has been
found to demarcate any major turning points in this interim, during which the Nomarchs managed to establish
greater independence and strove to take control of Egypt by appointing themselves as pharaohs. This group of
kings" came from Henen-Nesut (Herakleopolis), Beni Hasan (north of Hermopolis) and Qebtu (Coptos). They were
recognized within their own territories but they were not acknowledged throughout the rest of the land.

New Kingdom (1550-1087 BC)
18th Dynasty (1550-1307)
  Ahmose I
  Amenhotep I
  Tuthmose I
  Tuthmose II
  Hatshepsut^f
  Tuthmose III
  Amenhotep II
  Tuthmose IV
  Amenhotep III
  Akhenaten (Amenhotep IV)
  Smenkhare
  Tutankhamen
  Aye
  Horemheb

19th Dynasty (1307-1196 BC)
  Ramses I
  Seti I
  Ramses II
  Merneptah
  Amenmesses
  Seti II
  Siptah
  Twosret^f

20th Dynasty (1196-1087 BC)
  Setnakhte
  Ramses III - XI

3rd Intermediate Period
(1087- 712 BC)
21st Dynasty (1087 -945 BC)
  Smendes
  Amenemnisu
  Psusennes I
  Amenemope
  Osorkon
  Saimun
  Psusennes II

22nd Dynasty (945-712 BC)
  Sheshonq I

Osokron II
Takelot I
Sheshonq II
Osorkon III
Takelot II
Sheshonq III
Pami
Sheshonq IV
Osorkon IV

23rd Dynasty (818-724 BC — dates
overlap previous Dynasty)
  Pedibastet I
  Osorkon V
  Peftjauabaster

24th Dynasty (724-712 BC)
  Tefnakht I
  Bakenrenef

Late Period (712-332 BC)
25th Dynasty (712- 657 BC)
  Piankhi
  Shabaqo
  Shebitku
  Taharqa
  Tanatamen

26th Dynasty (657-525 BC)
  Necho I
  Psamtek I
  Necho II
  Psamtek II
  Wahibre
  Ahmose II
  Psamtek III

27th Dynasty (525-404 BC)
First Persian Period
  Cambyses
  Darius I
  Xerxes I
  Artaxerxes I
  Darius II

28th Dynasty (404-399 BC)
  Amyrateus

29th Dynasty (399- 380 BC)
  Neferites I
  Hakoris
  Neferites II

30th Dynasty (380-343 BC)
  Nectanebo I
  Teos
  Nectanebo II

2nd Persian Period (343-332 BC)
  Artaxerxes III
  Arses
  Darius III

Macedonian Dynasty (332-304
BC)
(or the 31st Dynasty)
  Alexander the Great
  Philip Arrhidaeus
  Alexander IV

Ptolemaic Dynasty (304-30 BC)
(or the 32nd Dynasty)
  Ptolemy I Soter I
  Ptolemy II Philadelphus
  Ptolemy III Eueregetes I
  Ptolemy IV Philopator
  Ptolemy V Epiphanes
  Ptolemy VI Philometor
  Ptolemy VII Neos Philopator
  Ptolemy VIII Eueregetes II
  Ptolemy IX Soter II
  Ptolemy X Alexander I
  Ptolemy XI Alexander II
  Ptolemy XII Auletes
  Berenice^f IV
  Cleopatra^f VII with Ptolemy
  XIII, XIV, XV (Caesarion)

Table of Contents

Egypt's Evolution

A civilization forms along the Nile

Man settled along the banks of the Nile River as long ago as 7000 BC; four millennia later, in this very region, he had learned to read, write, and develop and expand as a community. Over the next 3000 years, Egypt prospered despite hardships, internal conflicts and foreign invasion. Herodotus, the Greek historian who traveled to Egypt in the 5th century BC, called it "the gift of the Nile."

Wind and water

The Nile is the source of all Egyptian life. Without that sacred river, all this land would have been barren, dried by the broiling sun and the wind. Rainfall gradually diminished in the area of Egypt, starting around the beginning of the third millennium BC; over time, it became almost non-existent. People began concentrating along the narrow strip of land on both sides of the river, where they survived by fishing, hunting, gathering, farming and breeding livestock. The remaining region was desert, known as *deshret* ("red land") — an area that was regarded as sinister and perilous, and was often avoided. The black soil and the narrow colonized strip of land alongside the Nile was called *khemet* ("black land"); it provided a sharp contrast to the lifeless "red land."

7

The Nile received its modern name from the Greeks, who referred to the river as "Neilos." The Nile is the longest river in the world — almost 4200 miles long — yet it is only 500 yards wide. Out of Ethiopia rises the Blue Nile and from Uganda comes the White Nile. They converge at Khartoum, Sudan, flowing northward into Egypt, becoming *Iteru Aa* (or "the Great River," as it was known to the ancient Egyptians). The Nile is the only major river to flow north; its many tributaries originate in the mountains south of the equator, and it cuts through hills, deserts and riparian marshes to empty into the Mediterranean Sea or *Wadj Wer* ("the Great Green"). (Both "aa" and "wer" translate into "great.") Thus, Upper Egypt and Deshret are located in the southern region while Lower Egypt, the marsh area and the Delta are situated to the north. Both regions were known as *taui* ("the two lands"). The northernmost area, where the waters fan out into streams in a triangular-shaped region, is known as the Delta; the name of the fourth letter of the Greek alphabet whose shape it resembles.

Each summer, rains from Africa cause the waters of the Nile to rise and temporarily flood the land, depositing a new layer of rich silt — ideal for growing crops. The fertile valley and warm climate afforded an optimal environment for the villagers or *fellahin* to become proficient in the science of agriculture. Ancient Egyptian civilization was based upon the fertility of the soil; seeds were planted that only the Nile could nourish. The annual flooding also left behind immense thickets of papyrus. This versatile reed was converted into myriad necessities including paper, rope, fabric, sandals, baskets, mats, stools and river rafts.

Every year, the settlers watched and waited with anticipation hoping that the waters would rise high enough to ensure irrigation. As the settlements grew, not only in number but in size, the collective effort, the commitment to cultivating the land, required the organization of extensive labor; the expanding irrigation works were an enterprise that had to be performed on a grand scale and this, in turn, became crucial in the development of the community.

Measuring and recording the level of the annual flood was a matter of national importance; the device used for this task was called a "Nilometer". It consisted of simple markings, in the form of a descending staircase leading down into the river; the depth of the rising waters was observed and documented by officials who used this economic predictor to set the level of taxes based on the prospective crops for the coming year. The ideal height for the waters to rise, based on the Nilometer, was about 25 to 30 feet. Low water — anything less than six feet below the target — meant food shortages, and possibly famine. Highs of six feet over the ideal meant disaster as well — the destruction of protective dykes, dams, and mud-brick homes, and the flooding of entire villages.

In successful years, the Nile overflowed during the summer months and flooded the valley, setting the scene for the year ahead. The agricultural cycle consisted of three seasons, based upon the cycle of the Nile. The first and most important was called *Akhet*, the season of inundation that took place from mid-July to mid-November. Akhet was followed by *Peret*, or *Proyet*, the season of emergence or "coming forth," when growth occurred, from mid-November to mid-March. During this time, the farmers worked the fields, and reaped their grain and flax. The third season, when the river was at its lowest, marking the end of the harvest, spanned from mid-March to mid-July; it was called *Shemu* or *Shomu*.

The ancient Egyptians believed the Nile's springs to have originated in paradise — or at the first cataract, near Abu (Elephantine). The water of the Nile was considered to have nutritive value; it not only served as a symbol of purity and renewal but it visibly gave life to Egypt every year, bringing forth abundance. The river was also thought to contain healing properties, and it was frequently used in medicinal prescriptions.

The people of ancient Egypt dedicated many songs to the Nile, such as the "Hymn to the Nile," "Adoration of the Nile" and "Hymn to Hapi." *Hapi* was the androgynous god of the Nile, also known as "Son of the Nile" — and yet, Hapi was not considered to be responsible for the annual inundation. This honor and grave responsibility went to *Khnemu*, the ram-headed god who was worshipped as the "God of Floods." Khnemu was credited with "bringing forth the waters" from the first cataract, where he was believed to dwell. The people of Egypt traditionally expressed profound gratitude to the Nile and its deity for the abundance of crops that provided sufficient food for the coming year.

Kings and chaos

Ancient Egypt emerged from the pre-Dynastic Age in 3100 BC and its civilization of dynasties endured for over three millennia. The enormous task of categorizing Egypt's history was first taken up during the third century BC, by an Egyptian scholar and priest named Manetho, from Tjebneter (Sebennytos). At the request of Kings Ptolemy I and II, he developed a chronological list of past pharaohs and their reigns. Manetho divided Egyptian history into 30 dynasties (successions of related rulers, each of which ended when a pharaoh died without an heir or when outsiders managed to break the sequence). This classification has been maintained throughout the ages by historians who, in turn, have partitioned Manetho's list of kings into three time-periods known as Kingdoms and three more periods of internal political unrest known as Intermediate Periods.

It is important to bear in mind that dates often vary by several hundred years, depending on the historical source one consults, and in some cases dates may overlap as a result of the royal tradition of co-regency.

It is generally accepted that the 1st Dynasty began with the unification of the two lands by King Narmer in 3100 BC, establishing him as the first pharaoh. As king of Upper Egypt, Narmer conquered Lower Egypt, thus uniting the two lands under one ruler for the first time in history. (A competing version holds that this honor went to King Scorpion or King Menes — or that they were one and the same person.) As a unified entity, Egypt would stand to benefit and prosper from cooperation rather than competition.

It is at this time that hieroglyphic writing made its first appearance. As the people amalgamated, improved communication was needed to ensure a prosperous harvest for the growing population and the successful administration and development of the country.

The capital of the newly-unified Egypt was founded at Mennefer (Memphis), meaning "Established and Beautiful." This site was selected because of its strategic position at the apex of the Delta, between Upper and Lower Egypt. Mennefer was also known as Ineb-Hedj ("White Wall," a reference to the white wall enclosing the town's most prominent landmark, the royal palace). Mennefer, or Ineb-Hedj, was the official capital during the 3rd Dynasty and remained an important religious and administrative center throughout ancient Egyptian history. It was here that the pyramids and royal necropolis of Giza and Saqqara were situated.

Egypt flourished during the Old Kingdom, Middle Kingdom and New Kingdom. These empires were separated by periods of strife and decline known as the 1st, 2nd and 3rd Intermediate Periods, when Egypt lacked a strong central government and was racked by internal political turmoil. Foreign trade and contacts with other lands also attracted covetous attention from abroad, resulting in foreign invasion.

The 1st and 2nd Dynasties comprise the Early Dynastic, Archaic or Thinite Period.

The Old Kingdom began during the 3rd Dynasty, c. 2700 BC. This period is known as the Era of Stability, or the Pyramid Age. For 500 years, Egypt experienced tranquility and prosperity, particularly during the 4th Dynasty, where grand achievements were attained in art and architecture in the form of the construction of the pyramids. During this time, an efficient administrative system was established as the government became more centralized. However, a breakdown within the central administration arose as a result of the dispersion of duties and powers. This decline brought about the collapse of the highly-structured society of the Old Kingdom.

The 7th Dynasty gave rise to the 1st Intermediate Period (c. 2150 BC). This was a time of internal conflict, revolution, riots, strikes and civil war that lasted until the 10th Dynasty. Eventually, order and prosperity were restored; battles were fought and won, resulting in the re-unification of the land and paving the way to the 11th Dynasty (c. 2050 BC), inaugurating the Middle Kingdom.

The Middle Kingdom is also known as the Period of Greatness and Rebirth. The finest Egyptian literature and craftsmanship in jewelry and art date back to this period, never to be surpassed. The Middle Kingdom was prosperous, as the administration was reformed and new cities (or *niwty*) were founded. The Egyptians expanded into Nubia and increased their political power, foreign trade and economic strength. A new social class (a middle class) emerged during this period and gained influence, as it comprised a new population that was willing and prepared to work hard for the growth and expansion of the nation.

During the Middle Kingdom, Uast or Waset (Thebes, present-day Luxor and Karnak) first gained prominence. Uast ("Dominion") became the nation's capital during the 12th Dynasty. Uast was home to the most significant and wealthiest religious centers until the Late Period; it reached its pinnacle as the capital of Egypt during the New Kingdom, particularly during the 18th Dynasty when it served as the religious heart of Egypt. However, external forces (primarily from the east) resulted in the fragmentation of the state, bringing down the era of the Middle Kingdom.

The 2nd Intermediate Period began with the collapse of the Middle Kingdom during the 13th Dynasty (c. 1775 BC). These turbulent times lasted over two centuries; disorganization and brief reigns by weak foreign rulers were typical. During the 14th Dynasty, the Asiatic Hyksos, known as "Foreign Kings" or "Shepherd Kings," took over as rulers of Egypt. The Hyksos, who traveled across the desert and settled near the eastern border of Egypt, established trading centers throughout the Delta, expanding control over most of this region. Their origins are unclear, but most scholars agree that the Hyksos likely came from Palestine or Syria. These "vile Asiatics," as the Egyptians called them, had frizzy hair and curly beards as illustrated in pictures from this era. The new capital was established at Per-Ramessu ("House of Ramses"), otherwise known as the town of Avaris.

When King Ahmose finally expelled the Hyksos, thus re-unifying Egypt, the New Kingdom was ushered in. The New Kingdom began with the 18th Dynasty (c. 1550 BC); this era is also known as the Greatest Era and Golden Age. During this time, the population has been estimated at close to 3 million, quite a high figure for the times.

It was during the New Kingdom that the most remarkable figures ruled the land of Egypt. Pharaohs such as Tuthmose I to IV, Hatshepsut, Amenhotep I to III, Akhenaten (Amenhotep IV), Tutankhamen, and Seti I and II reigned during this prosperous time. The Ramessid Era also occurred during the New Kingdom, during the reigns of Ramses I through XI. During the New Kingdom, Egypt reached new heights of power and greatness. The worship of Amen, "the Creator," was restored and the capital was relocated to Uast.

However, during the highly controversial reign of Akhenaten, the capital was moved to Akhetaten (Amarna). Political and religious differences between the priesthood, the military and government officials, along with increasing foreign pressure from the Hyksos and Kushites (Nubians), brought on the decentralization of the state and served as catalysts to bring this era to a close. The 3rd Intermediate Period began with the 21st Dynasty (c. 1087 BC). At this time, the Egyptian empire crumbled and was overtaken by the Kushites, and later, by the mighty Assyrians.

The Late Period began with the 25th Dynasty (c. 712 BC), when Egypt was under Kushite power — and twice, later, under Persian rule. This was a troubled era. In 332 BC, the Greeks came to power and established the 31st Dynasty, ushered in by Alexander the Great and continuing as the Ptolemaic Dynasty. The capital was moved to a settlement called Raqote, which was re-named Alexandria by the Greeks in honor of the founder of the dynasty and the city.

The empire, however, crumbled under the formidable weight of the Roman invasion in 30 BC, which brought the end of ancient Egyptian civilization, culture and history. Egypt became a province of Rome. Pharaohs no longer ruled their land.

PART I
DAILY LIFE

1. THE PEOPLE

Who were they?

The ancient Egyptians were an intelligent, social, active, and peaceful people. Despite the many hardships that challenged their remarkable civilization, they maintained their pride, optimism and love of life. Their priorities were centered on their gods, their families and their work.

It has often been written that no other ancient people cherished life as dearly as the Egyptians and that no other, at any time in history, devoted so much attention to planning for death. Life was so precious to them that they sought to extend and preserve their lives throughout all eternity. Preparation for the next life began as soon as one was well-established in the present. The afterlife was regarded as a continuation of their temporary existence on earth.

Life in ancient Egypt was not easy; the lifespan of the average citizen was about 35 years. Life expectancy was higher for the upper classes, who were spared a life of strenuous physical labor and were healthier, as they enjoyed a better diet. Ramses the Great is believed to have lived to the ripe age of 96, while Pepy II, a 6th-dynasty pharaoh, lived to be 100 years old. The work of a pharaoh often went on throughout his lifetime and was taken over by an heir, in turn.

The gods, or *neteru*, and Egyptians of every class lived by the laws of Ma'at. A concept and a deity personifying truth, order and justice,

Ma'at was, in mythology, the daughter of the sun god Ra. She was recognized by the single white ostrich feather she wore upon her head. Ma'at was the embodiment of the harmony that prevailed in this life and the next. Life without Ma'at was inconceivable; actions contrary to the concept were punishable by law. No other civilization experienced less change in its culture and no other did so much to uphold the laws of decency, honor and order throughout its history.

The citizens were divided into five social classes as determined by their profession. The royalty, of course, came first; they were followed by the Vizier or chancellor, High Priests and the nobility. The third class comprised government officials, scribes (or *Sesh*), priests, doctors and engineers. Artisans, craftsmen, soldiers, merchants, and skilled laborers constituted the fourth class. The poorest level of society and the largest class was comprised of unskilled laborers and fishermen, followed by servants (or *Hemu*), with slaves at the very bottom of the social scale.

Slaves were mainly brought in from foreign lands, Asia, or Nubia. Caucasians and people of color alike might be captured as prisoners of war, and then sold into slavery. Citizens could also sell themselves into slavery — and then buy themselves out of it. However, slaves and servants were treated well and compensated with food and lodging, in addition to receiving such provisions as linen and oils. Some even owned their own property. A member of the poorest class could rise to the position of the highest official with the proper education, training and determination. Such is the popular story handed down from the 9th Dynasty entitled *The Eloquent Peasant*.

The story revolves around a peasant who made his modest living by trading goods such as salt and herbs. From this, he was able to provide for his family. Each day, he and his heavily-laden donkeys would travel the same route to the local villages. One day, however, he crossed paths with a workman who had in mind feeding his family through less-honest labor. The workman blocked the path with a large piece of cloth, closing the route that the peasant was about to traverse. The peasant had no choice but to drive his donkeys off the road, trampling the margins of the workman's cornfield. The two men began to argue, and the workman beat the peasant and stole all his goods. Humiliated and distraught, and with no witnesses to come to his aid, the peasant took the matter before the High Steward and explained his misfortune.

The peasant related his tale in a most articulate and expressive manner; he was asked to return the following day, so that his words could be recorded by the royal scribes for the pharaoh to hear. The peasant presented himself the following day, and again for nine more days, hoping to see his goal of justice finally served. As the High Steward read the scribe's account of the peasant's tale, the pharaoh was most amused, and even touched. Meanwhile, without the peasant's knowledge, the pharaoh was having his family looked after, as a reward for his entertainment and in compensation for the unfortunate incident. On the tenth day, the peasant lost heart, believing that his words were falling on deaf ears. The High Steward realized it was time to reveal the pharaoh's true motives and intentions to the dispirited peasant. The workman was stripped of his belongings, which were given to the peasant in reward for his words of wisdom, honesty and fairness. The peasant, as the story goes, eventually became a trusted minister and chief overseer to the pharaoh.

The tale is emblematic in that it illustrates the feasibility of advancement for those who were educated and skillful. This was the equivalent of the modern-day college degree. In Egypt, thousands of years ago as well as today, talent was recognized. It has been estimated that in ancient Egypt the literate population was between 1% and 5% — quite a high number, in an age when writing was a fairly recent invention — and a large number of commoners were at least semi-literate. Proof remains in the form of graffiti inscribed at rock quarries where men worked and in the villages where they lived. From the 26th Dynasty on, literacy increased among the population. Boys were educated by priests in the temple schools. Students had to master about 700 hieroglyphs; by the end of the Pharaonic Era, nearly 5000 different symbols were in use.

Professional scribes enjoyed several privileges, including exemption from paying taxes and from performing manual labor, for life. Scribes were among the most respected members of society and were free from the fear of unemployment, as this qualification made them candidates for many jobs within the royal service, nobility, administration, army, temples, state and governmental offices. A scribe could rise to a position of authority in law, taxation, or diplomacy, as well as becoming a skilled architect or engineer. Scribes were better-compensated than sculptors, draftsmen and artists.

Among the many duties of the scribe were the recording of daily activities, contracts, and census figures, and drafting correspondence and memorial inscriptions. The scribe also kept records of food supplies, tax surveys, routine reports, animal and grain inventories, special events and the all-important annual level of the Nile.

One particular scribe and army chief named Horemheb, who lived during the New Kingdom under the reign of Tutankhamen, went from being a military leader to being pharaoh of Egypt. Having no heir, Horemheb appointed another military leader as his successor — Ramses I, who launched the 19th Dynasty.

Unlike any other ancient civilization, women were regarded as almost equal to men. They were highly respected in ancient Egypt; social status was determined by rank and not gender. Egyptian women enjoyed more freedom, rights and privileges even than those of Greece, and myriad goddesses were venerated throughout Egypt's history. Showing disrespect to a woman, under the laws of Ma'at, meant going against the basis of Egyptian beliefs and ultimate existence.

A woman could even be legal heir to the throne, although it was the man she chose as husband who became ruler and pharaoh. It was her duty to preserve and to pass on the royal bloodline.

Women enjoyed many legal rights. They participated in business transactions and owned, managed and sold land and private property. Women could arrange adoptions, liberate slaves, finalize legal settlements and execute testaments. They could testify in court and bring suit against other parties, and they could represent themselves in legal disputes, without the presence of a male relative or representative.

Many "professional" positions were open to women, such as mourner, weaver, baker, midwife and advisor to the pharaoh. They could also hold high positions in the temple, as dancers or high priestesses — a highly respected position.

It was neither unusual nor forbidden for the self-made woman to rise in status and position. One remarkable non-royal woman was Nebet. She was the wife of a *nomarch* who lived during the 6th Dynasty. Nebet held the most prestigious administrative title of Magistrate, Judge and Vizier to the Pharaoh.

Although much less frequently than their male counterparts, women did find work as scribes and as doctors. Records exist of female physicians, going as far back as the Old Kingdom. One such woman was Lady Pesheshet, who lived during the 5th Dynasty. She held the title of "Overseer of Physicians," according to the inscription on her stela (in an Old Kingdom tomb, discovered during the 20th century of our era). Lady Pesheshet is regarded by scholars as the first female physician in recorded history.

2. Family Life

Marriage was held in the utmost respect; it was an honorable partnership. Husband and wife were expected to live in equality and to demonstrate care and affection for each other. Couples generally married within their social class, although special rules applied among the upper class and particularly within the royalty where a man might take more than one wife, and where marriages between cousins and other close (or distant) relatives often occurred. Unions between siblings took place only within royal families — the pharaoh's firstborn daughter often married her brother or half-brother — in order to preserve their regal bloodline.

In ancient Egypt, couples affectionately referred to each other as "brother" or "sister." During the New Kingdom, the word "sister" was synonymous with "dear," or "wife." This, no doubt, has led to the modern misconception that brother/sister marriages often took place among ordinary, non-royal Egyptians.

A wife — and then some

A pharaoh might have a chief wife and several lesser daughter- or sister-wives, in addition to many concubines. Ramses II had seven great wives, several lesser wives, and a harem full of legal concubines. The existence of harems is believed to go back to the Early Dynastic Period. Foreign princesses often became part of the harem, as political wives who were sent by their fathers to cement diplomatic alliances between the two rulers. Among his many wives (or *hemetu*), Ramses II married a Hittite princess from Tarsus (Turkey) in order to settle longstanding differences between the two countries. During the 18th Dynasty, both Pharaohs Tuthmose IV and Amenhotep I married Mitannite princesses (from Syria). Amenhotep took several wives, including a sister of a Babylonian king.

Harems were not for entertainment and politics alone; they helped ensure a supply of male heirs. However, they might also breed trouble. Those associated with or belonging to the harem of Amenemhet were believed to have been responsible for his demise; and it was a secondary wife named Tiye who brought on (or, at least, was held responsible for) the death of Ramses III. During the Pharaoh's 31st year of reign, he was the target of what came to be known as the "Harem Conspiracy." Tiye, with the help of 32 other conspirators, plotted to assassinate the Pharaoh in order for her son Pentewere to inherit the throne. The deadly scheme was exposed just before it was to be implemented; however, during the trial that ensued, Ramses III died, and Tiye and her accomplices were blamed for his death. Among the accessories to the crime were several women from Ramses' harem, plus state officials, military men and even a priest. In punishment, these men and women suffered facial mutilation — and some were ordered by the royal court to take their own lives. Ramses IV assumed his rightful position as heir to the throne, as his father had intended.

Candidates for the harem also included dancing girls and other pretty females who had caught the pharaoh's attention. Their mutual offspring could be counted among the royalty, or not, according to the pharaoh's choice.

Girls were married early, between the ages of 13 and 15, and peasant girls often married as young as 12; by 30, they were already grand-mothers. Young men were expected to take a wife as soon as they had the financial means to support their life together and raise a family.

While marriage partners were occasionally chosen freely, most unions were arranged by the future husband and the father of the young bride. Consent was, however, required of both the man and woman. Marriage was sealed with a contract that could later be annulled or terminated, in a form of divorce. During the Late Period, pre-nuptial agreements were drawn up and became quite popular.

No evidence has been found to prove that marriage ceremonies existed in ancient Egypt. A great celebration did take place, where the newlyweds received gifts and participated in festivities with family and friends honoring the marriage. The bride moved into the home of the new husband, which often included his family as well. The new bride assumed her role as "Lady of the House" or *Nebet-Per.* One can't help but wonder about the dynamics in these new households, as the mother-in-law ceased to be recognized as the head of her household.

Until we part

Divorce was not common among the ancient Egyptians, but in the event, the ex-wife was entitled to keep what had been hers when she entered the marriage as well as a third of the couple's joint property and possessions acquired while married. Custody of the children went to the mother (or *mut*). The divorce itself was a simple and private matter, consisting of a statement to annul the contract and union, given before witnesses. Once this was accomplished, both partners were free to remarry.

If the wife had been unfaithful, she was not entitled to receive support; indeed, she was often sentenced to the painful and disfiguring punishment of losing her nose. Interestingly, affection was expressed by rubbing noses together, and the hieroglyph for the concept of joy, pleasure and a kiss, was a profiled nose. Since infidelity on the part of the wife would raise questions about the paternity of a child, women were liable to more severe punishment than men.

In the event of the husband's death, the wife was entitled to two-thirds of their communal property. The remainder was divided among the children, followed by the husband's siblings. Prior to his death, a man might adopt his wife as a daughter (or *sit*) in order for her to inherit a larger share — not only as a spouse but as an heir, as well.

Be fruitful

Providing a male heir was a wife's primary duty, and failure to do so constituted grounds for divorce. Couples were encouraged to have children as soon as they were married. Children were considered to be the greatest blessing; they said that the gods smiled upon those who raised large families. Some families could boast of having 10 to 15 children. A house without the sounds of children's laughter was frowned upon, and barren couples were expected to adopt, if necessary, to make up for the deficiency. How Ramses II must have been admired and respected — he is reckoned to have fathered at least 100 sons and 50 daughters!

If a couple already had many children and could not afford more, contraception was an option. A popular recipe consisted of plant fibers coated in a mixture of honey, sour milk, crocodile dung and natron. (Natron is found in the large deposits of sodium salts in the dried lake beds of Egypt, particularly at a site known as *Wadi Natron*, situated near modern Cairo. Natron was processed since Predynastic times.) Another recipe consisted of cotton soaked in a mixture of dates and acacia bark. The lactic acid acted as an effective spermicidal agent.

Conversely, if a couple had difficulty conceiving, they could resort to magic. Rituals consisting of having the hopeful mother squat over a steaming potion of oil, frankincense, dates and beer. If she vomited from the aromas generated by this mixture, she was thought to be able to conceive. If she did not, it was believed that the smell of the mixture had become trapped within the woman's body, preventing her from conceiving.

A childless couple would pray to the deities for divine assistance. Letters were written and placed upon the tombs of departed relatives, asking the deceased to use their celestial influence with the gods. If all else failed, adoption offered the last alternative. Records show that adoption was quite popular during the New Kingdom.

Children were of utmost importance; they supported their parents in old age, while ensuring their immortality by providing a proper burial. In the event of the couple having difficulty conceiving a male child who would look after them when they advanced in age, the husband, with the consent of his wife, was granted permission to bring forth a child with a secondary or lesser wife, or even a servant or slave. The child, if male, would then be adopted by the father and his barren wife. If the pharaoh had only daughters, succession to the throne passed to the man the firstborn daughter would marry, or to a son (or *sa*) by another wife. Such was the case of Akhenaten, who had six daughters and no sons by his chief wife, Nefertiti.

New brides often gave birth within the first year or two of marriage. An early pregnancy test consisted of passing water over reeds, to see if they germinated. If they did, then the woman was with child. Another diagnostic method was practiced to determine the gender of the unborn baby. The mother passed water over wheat and barley. If the wheat sprouted first, the baby would most likely be a girl; if the barley sprouted first, a boy could be expected. If neither the wheat nor barley sprouted, she was not pregnant. Unfortunately, no records have been found to indicate the success rate of these methods!

Although a birth was a most joyous event, it was also considered to be susceptible to many dangers, as pregnant women were thought to be vulnerable to evil spirits and demons; after all, the mortality rate both mother and child was high. One in three babies died at childbirth.

Before the highly anticipated moment arrived, the mother received the best of care and special treatment for about two weeks while being guarded by protective amulets and magical formulas.

Taueret was the guardian and goddess of expectant mothers. She had the body of a pregnant hippopotamus, the legs and paws of a lion, and a crocodile-tail headdress. Her image, in the form of a statue, was always visible during childbirth as she was prayed to and invoked for assistance and success in the delivery of the child. Bes, the merry dwarf god, also aided in keeping evil spirits away during childbirth. Heqet, the frog goddess of fertility and birth, was called upon during labor to facilitate the process. Heqet was also known as a spiritual midwife.

Most mothers brought their children into the world in a squatting position, inside a birth box, at home. These were rectangular mud-brick boxes, about the size of a bathtub, with an opening at the end to allow entry. They were inscribed with images of powerful and protective deities, as well as goddesses of childbirth, helping the mother to safely deliver the child. If the family was not wealthy enough to afford one, the expectant mother gave birth on the roof of the house; a modest version of the birth box consisted of two large bricks, set wide apart from each other, on a secure platform. In many temples, buildings called *mammisseums* were constructed on the sacred grounds where Auset (Isis), the "Great Mother," was portrayed on the temple walls giving birth to Heru (Horus.) At the mammiseum of the Temple of Denderah, images are inscribed with the divine union between Het-Heru and Heru, resulting in the birth of their son, Ihy.

The mother was assisted by two midwives, representing the protective guidance of Auset and her sister, Nebet-Het (Nephthys). Together, they performed a ritual of safety and healing while bringing forth the child. Clappers made of ivory, often carved in the shape of hands, were played to repel evil spirits. A protective circle with magical symbols was drawn around the mother, and later around the child, while sleeping.

Local women might also deliver inside a birth house called a *mammisi*. After the successful birth, the mother remained in seclusion at the mammisi for two weeks of recuperation and special care. Then a feast was prepared and a great celebration took place, where the new mother received many gifts.

During the first three years, the child was nursed by the mother or a wet nurse, who was highly respected and regarded as a member of the family. The infant mortality rate was high, and many did not survive past the age of three or four when the protective milk of the mother or wet nurse was replaced by solid food, exposing the child to higher risks of infection and disease. Numerous graves of children, of about three years of age, have been discovered. One cemetery, at Deir el-Medina, contains over 100 graves of young children.

When an heir was born to the pharaoh, the afterbirth was preserved; it was perceived as the life force energy of the newborn child.

Few twins are known to have survived. One set of twin brothers, named Khnemuhotep and Neankhkhnemu, lived during the 5th Dynasty. They were so close that they were buried together in a vast tomb at Saqqara. Touching scenes of the brothers embracing each other capture their closeness and mutual affection.

Children are the future

A child was not thought of as a person until a name was assigned, and so names were selected and given immediately after birth. Names were often based on those of deities, who were believed to protect the children whose names honored them. Examples include Meritaten ("Beloved of Aten"), Sitamen ("Daughter of Amen") and Rahotep ("Ra is Satisfied"). Often, names were chosen in order to bestow upon children certain qualities that the parents desired — for instance, Neferhotep ("Beautiful and Satisfied") and Seneb ("Healthy"). Affectionate pet names for children such as Miw Sheri ("Little Kitten") were also popular.

In the unfortunate event of a miscarriage, a child whose name already had been determined would have access to the afterlife. Without a name, the infant would not be identified nor remembered by the gods. This was the equivalent of dying a second, permanent death, a death feared more than the first.

Among the lower classes, the mothers raised the children; in the upper classes, servants provide the day-to-day care. Children assumed their adult responsibilities early in life. Boys and girls followed different paths. Young boys learned a trade or craft from their father (or *it*), or from another family member or a craftsman, artisan, carpenter or pottery-maker. A boy was expected to follow in his father's footsteps, and it was his sacred duty to give life to his father's name after he had passed on to the world beyond.

Young girls received their training at home, as they helped around the house and, when needed, pitched in as well in the fields. From their mothers, girls learned domestic tasks such as cooking, sewing, weaving and cleaning. They also learned the arts of healing, dancing, music, and singing. Girls were also taught the ways of nature, beauty and grace, as well as how to be an ideal wife and mother.

Upon the death of both parents, the son inherited the land while the daughter inherited jewelry, furniture and household items. She was entitled to the entire property if there were no sons in the family.

Only in the upper class could families afford to send their children to school. Children of the pharaoh were taught and trained in the royal palace classrooms. Often, specially selected children, usually the sons of officials and nobility, were permitted to study and learn with young royalty. These privileged children were taught by a personal tutor or a major scribe.

Other boys of upper class families were fortunate enough to be sent to temple schools, starting at around the age of eight. Whether trained in the royal palace or by the priests of the temple schools, young boys learned such virtues as good manners, honesty, humility, self-control and respect. Writing, reading and arithmetic were the three main scholastic subjects, followed by religion, history, literature and geography. However, the teachings of the temple schools were naturally geared towards a more religious rather than an academic orientation. Many young scholars studied to become draftsmen, bureaucrats, or artisans as well as the most respected position of all, the scribe. The student would practice his lessons on ostraca (potshards or limestone flakes) — many such homework artifacts have been found, with corrections still visible. Ostraca were more expendable than the costly papyrus that was laborious to produce. It was every father's dream to have his son escape the hardship of manual labor and become a scribe, as the possibilities were limitless and lucrative.

This chapter ends with a popular tale from ancient Egypt, relating the close relationship between a father and son and the life lessons they learned. The High Priest and 11th son of Ramses the Great, Setna Khaemwast, and his wife had longed for a son. For years they prayed to the deities, without their wishes being granted. One night, a god appeared to the wife in a dream and provided her with a spell to conceive a son. She did as she was instructed, and soon became pregnant.

Once again the god appeared, in a dream, but this time to Setna.

He was told that this would be no ordinary child; and he was to be named "Sa-Ausar," meaning "Son of Ausar." Five years later, Setna took Sa-Ausar (as he was instructed in the dream) to study with the wise men at the Temple of Ptah. Sa-Ausar's extraordinary abilities enabled him to master hieroglyphs, at this tender age, in only a few short months. The child became the most brilliant pupil the temple school had ever had the privilege of teaching.

One day, when the boy was seven, he and his father were startled by a commotion outside their home. They rushed to the window, and saw a magnificent funeral procession for a deceased nobleman. The gilded coffin was being carried by a solemn procession of military officials and temple priests, while professional mourners wailed alongside. A short distance behind, another funeral followed. This procession consisted of nothing but the body of a poor laborer, who was wrapped in simple straw mat and carried by his two sons, while his wife and daughter mourned by his side.

Setna turned to his son and said, "Even in death, how much happier is the soul of a rich man!" The boy immediately answered, "I only wish for you to share the fate of the poor man." These words shocked Setna and hurt him deeply.

The boy took his father's hand and led him out into the streets and onto a ferryboat. This boat took them across the Nile into the City of the Dead, in the western desert region. With words of power, chanted by the wise son, they entered the realm of the dead — as spectators. They looked on as the souls of the dead were being judged and they witnessed the torment of those who failed to pass the tests of Ma'at. A man dressed in the finest linen stood beside Ausar (Osiris), the Judge of the Dead, and the boy said, "Do you see that shining spirit? It belongs to the poor man, whom we saw in the most modest of funeral processions." The poor man had been judged by the laws of Ma'at, and his myriad good deeds earned him his rightful place alongside Ausar. As for the rich man, Sa-Ausar explained to his father that he had been a cruel man with many selfish deeds behind him; he was locked up in the treacherous Underworld. So wise was Sa-Ausar that he knew the fate of the two dead men and, in wishing the fate of the poor man upon his father, he had wished him only the best.

3. Homes and Furnishings

The sweltering desert was an uninhabitable, fearful place, and the fertile land was needed to grow crops; the best home-sites, then, were along the narrow strip of land they called Khemet — near the indispensable river, the sole water source and main thoroughfare — but not in the way of farming. Gradually, settlements emerged on land that was higher than the floodplain yet near the cultivated fields. Space being at a premium, homes were built upwards, often consisting of two or three stories, and were crowded together. Some dwellings opened to a narrow street, while others faced a walled garden.

The layout of a royal necropolis and ancient village at Deir el-Medina, founded during the 18th Dynasty of the New Kingdom, is still visible; the lower walls have been preserved. This village, situated on the west bank of Uast (Thebes) was home to the workers and craftsmen who built the royal tombs of the Valley of the Kings. Although the villages and towns have died out over the centuries, the outlines of seventy houses can still be detected. Sufficient traces also remain in the city of Akhetaten (Amarna) to provide valuable insight into the construction of homes and the layout of the ancient villages.

Mud from the Nile was mixed with chopped straw, sand and pebbles and then poured into rectangular wooden molds. When the mixture set, by being baked in the scorching heat of the sun for several days, the mold was removed. The sun-dried mud bricks, known as *dje-bat*, were used to build walls that were then covered with mud plaster and decorated in white or soft colors. The brick walls were well suited to Egypt's climate as they kept homes cool in the summer and warm in the winter. The craft of the brick-maker is well illustrated in the tomb of an 18th Dynasty vizier named Rekhmere.

Only mud bricks were used in the building of homes, from the peasant to the pharaoh. Most were built upon elevated platforms to prevent major damage from the annual inundation, but many still needed repairs after the flooding. The homes eventually deteriorated; new ones were constructed directly on top of the crumbled remains.

Stone was reserved for the construction of temples. Strong timber was scarce in Egypt, and had to be imported from other lands. Wood was in high demand as it was required in the production of many necessary items such as doors, window shutters, frames, furniture, statues, stools, spears and sarcophagi.

Timber was also used in the construction of roofs, for those who could afford it. The best roofs were made of palm logs and topped with large slabs of mud plaster. The poorer class lived in one-room huts under roofs made of reeds, straw and grass. Roofs also served as sleeping quarters on hot summer nights, and were accessed by stairs built on the outside of the house.

The poorer classes lived very much in the open air and in cramped conditions with little or no furniture. The middle-class home consisted of a two-story house adorned by a modest garden. The residence of a court official might contain as many as 30 rooms. Above the doors of these homes would be an inscription bearing the owner's name.

Windows were small squares, set high up in order to mitigate the stifling summer heat and prevent dust, glare and flies from entering the house. Windows were arranged opposite each other to allow a cross draft or breeze to filter through; vents in the roof also permitted air to circulate. Loosely woven matting was used as a window shade to stifle the heat and the glare of the sun.

Upper class residences displayed walls lavishly painted with murals or were decorated with picturesque woven hangings. Ceilings of richly adorned stucco murals were secured by lengths of reed matting, wood and sticks. Mud plaster layered with hard gypsum or brick tiles covered the floors, which were protected and decorated by straw mats or by opulent rugs woven by professional women weavers. The poorer folk walked on floors made of beaten earth. Trunks of palm trees, carved in the form of plants, lotus flowers and papyrus bundles, made columns to support the roofs. Tiles and walls were often painted with delightful wildlife and floral motifs.

By the New Kingdom, glass began to be produced on a large scale. Advances in glazing technologies led to the making of tiles, which elegantly covered the floors and walls of the more affluent homes.

A wealthy nobleman's house was quite spectacular and consisted of three to four stories with dozens of rooms, including guest suites and main bedrooms. These luxurious residences were situated in the countryside or on the outskirts of town, while the laborers lived near the tomb sites or farmlands where they worked.

Harems were found in all upper class homes. The ladies were selected both locally and from foreign lands. Although the word *harem* means "house of the secluded," the ladies were not confined to the harem nor were others restricted from entering their private quarters. Many activities, besides the obvious, were enjoyed in harems, including sewing, playing with children, and gossiping among the women.

High walls surrounded the homes of the wealthy and their lovely gardens full of flowers that were prized for their scents and myriad uses as well as for their visual beauty. Flowers were worn in the hair, decorated and perfumed the homes, and were customarily presented to guests at dinner banquets as a token of welcome. The lotus, in particular, was frequently offered to the gods and to relatives of the deceased. Intricately designed vases filled with multicolored blossoms enhanced every room in the well-to-do household. Some villas boasted gardens or parks arranged around a reflecting pool, complete with paths and fishponds surrounded by palm trees, orchards and vineyards.

Elegant wooden stands supported water jugs and wine jars throughout the home. Wicks made of twisted fibers of flax or cotton would be saturated in fat and placed inside a vessel containing castor, linseed or sesame oil. Pottery, alabaster, hollowed-out stones and baked clay saucers served as efficient lamps. An exquisite oil-burning lamp (with small traces of oil still remaining) was discovered among the many treasures in the tomb of Tutankhamen. This work of art is carved from a single slab of alabaster and shaped into the image of a lotus plant emerging from a pond accompanied by a smaller flower on each side.

In homes of the affluent, the main entrance led to a reception area where guests were greeted. The family living section, private domestic quarters, sleeping quarters and guestrooms were situated at the rear of the house. In the case of a house of more than one story, the first floor was reserved for business matters and entertainment functions, such as banquets and soirees, and the family quarters were located on the second floor, for privacy. In two- or three- story homes, the various levels were connected by ramps or staircases, usually on the outside of the house. The estate of a nobleman was constructed around stables, shrines and workshops.

Servants — maids, gardeners, cleaners, cooks, bakers, musicians, banquet hostesses or nannies — were essential to every upper class household. They lived in special quarters of the homes or in nearby huts, and in the out-buildings they baked bread, sifted grain, weaved cloth, brewed and bottled beer.

Women would walk to the Nile, in groups, to fetch the water needed for drinking, washing and cooking. Female servants (*baket*) made frequent trips, transporting heavy jars balanced on their heads.

As the smell of cooking produced heat and strong odors, the kitchen was usually located in a separate, smaller building or in a walled enclosure behind the main house. Most kitchens were well equipped, with a domed baked clay oven. In a large household, baking and brewing were combined.

The streets of ancient Egypt lacked a proper drainage system. Canals were used to draw away waste. The disposal of refuse was always a major concern. Household garbage was heaped into a dump outside the town and burned, or leveled, and houses would later be built on the site. Sewage was disposed of in the river as well as in the alleys.

Most people, particularly in the poorer class, bathed in the river; some were able to bathe at home in a water basin. Inside the homes of the wealthy, lavatories and bathing rooms were usually located beside the bedroom. The bathing facilities consisted of a small square room with a water basin and a slab of limestone, where the owner would sit while the servant poured water over him. The wastewater drained through an outlet, like a pipe, and emptied into the earth.

Many members of the upper class also owned retreats outside the village limits. The nobleman's villa was protected by high walls enclosing stables, granaries, wells, a caretaker's lodge and workshops. Homes also contained shrines and chapels, providing residents with easy and direct access to the deceased in the privacy of their homes. Offerings were presented to the statues of ancestors and to the gods.

Iron and bronze keys were required to enter the better homes. Keys measuring up to 5" in length have been found, dating to c. 1550 BC.

Magnificent furniture was being produced as early as the 1st Dynasty. Chairs belonging to the wealthy had seats made of leather straps and elaborately decorated wooden legs carved in the form of an animal's paw, such as that of a lion. An imitation of a folding chair complete made of ivory and ebony, with a colorful leopard-print seat, with the legs firmly attached, was discovered in Tutankhamen's tomb.

Household furnishings were sparse, by modern-day standards. Furniture was often adorned with animal figures representing specific deities. Low wooden stools and tables with three or four legs were the most common items, found in all but the poorest of homes. Tables might be square, round or rectangular and often were supported by a decorative figure. Wood was the most common material for the construction of tables, although some were made of stone or metal. Large dining room tables were not used in ancient Egypt; people ate at smaller three- four-legged tables.

A pharaoh might have furniture made of solid gold, inlaid with colored glass and semi-precious stones. Elaborate chests for storing clothes, bed linen, cosmetics and jewelry were carved from ebony, while the less affluent used weaved baskets to store whatever possessions they owned.

The funerary furniture of Queen Hetepheres is most remarkable in terms of exquisite craftsmanship. She was the mother of Khufu, the pharaoh responsible for building the first Great Pyramid at Giza during the 4th Dynasty. Her mortuary furniture is second only to that of King Tutankhamen's in terms of beauty. Discovered in AD 1925, it exemplifies the elegance and sophistication of the royal standard of living. Among the treasures found were a bed and a head support, a low royal chaise, a chest for storing linen and a portable canopy frame, all carved out of gilded wood.

The poorer class slept on woven mats, while the wealthiest slept on beds made of imported ebony. Leather straps with interlaced cords and folded sheets of coarse linen (less expensive than that which was used in the making of garments) formed the mattress. The wooden rectangular frame was covered by linen and animal skins. These beds were constructed on a slant, higher at the head. The feet of the bed were often carved in the shape of short animal legs, for instance a bull's.

When it was time to take a rest, the Egyptians used decorative crescent-shaped headrests (called *weres*), which were carved from wood or ivory, or cool alabaster for the most affluent (with a modest pottery version for the poor). As these were too uncomfortable to actually sleep on, pads of coarse, stuffed linen were probably used for a good night's sleep. The headrests are believed to have helped induce peaceful sleep by protecting the sleeper from insects crawling on the floor; and figures of protective deities were inscribed upon the headrests to help ward off evil spirits, which were believed to induce nightmares. Headrests were also used for embalming and funerary purposes — they were thought to protect the head of the deceased.

4. FOOD AND DRINK

The Egyptians ate mostly cereal crops, grown in the fields. They transformed emmer wheat and barley into bread and beer, the staples of their diet. Small sculptured replicas from the Old Kingdom show workers making bread and beer, while tombs at Saqqara depict scenes of cattle-herding, hunting and fishing. A relief carving from the 18th Dynasty tomb of a field scribe named Menna, at Uast, shows how they worked in the fields and treaded out the wheat, with cattle, sheep and donkeys.

The first leavened bread seems to have been created here, as well as the first clay ovens. By the time of the New Kingdom, forty different types of bread were in use, seasoned with figs, honey, herbs and spices such as sesame, coriander and aniseed. Cakes of bread were shaped into flat, conical, oval, square or round loaves, as illustrated on a relief dated back to the Old Kingdom. The middle and upper class used wheat, while the poorer made do with cakes of barley. During the grinding process, where stone slabs were used to pound the grain, sand and grit would find its way into the flour; this caused rapid deterioration of the people's teeth, as we can see by examining mummies.

Religious custom dictated that families leave food and drink in the tombs to nourish the deceased in the afterlife. Thanks to the arid climate, the remains of these offerings have been preserved, and scientists have analyzed residues from pottery vessels retrieved from the ruins of ancient villages.

Not by bread alone

The Egyptians had a varied diet, including rice as well as the grains noted above, and fruits and vegetables such as lettuce, cucumbers, spinach, radishes, carrots, turnips, onions, leeks, dates, grapes, melons, pumpkins, figs and pomegranates. They found protein in lentils, beans, chickpeas, and meat — ox, pork and mutton. The most popular meats came from pigeon, duck, goose and quail. The fowl was either boiled or roasted, and often, the internal organs were used in medicinal recipes. Fowling scenes are depicted on the tomb of a princess named Itet (4th Dynasty), who was the wife of a pharaoh's son and vizier named Neferma'at, at Meidum. In this illustration, two men kneel, tugging at ropes attached to a net holding several trapped birds. From the desert came antelope and gazelle, which were enjoyed at special occasions. Raw cabbage was often served as an appetizer before meals as it was believed to promote the desire for wine — as well as encouraging its consumption to excess!

In the average household, the woman of the house did the cooking, in a walled enclosure behind the home. Among the upper classes, servants prepared the meals, which were either stewed, fried, grilled, pickled, boiled, baked in clay ovens or roasted over an open fire. Most foods were heavily flavored with garlic and onions and were strongly seasoned with spices such as salt, coriander, marjoram, cumin and thyme. Garlic was popular, as it was believed (and has now been proven) to contain disease-fighting properties. Fat for cooking was obtained from animals and oils were extracted from the seeds of the moringa, castor-berry and sesame plant. Coconuts were considered a luxury and mandrake was regarded as the fruit of passion. Lettuce, because of its milky sap, was believed to be an aphrodisiac promoting fertility.

The floral gardens of the wealthy attracted bees, which provided honey. Honey was used to sweeten food, drinks and desserts. It also served as a symbol of resurrection, as honey represented the tears shed by the god Ra, from which man was born. A similar myth holds honey to be symbolic of Ra's tears as he wept over the glorious creation of mankind. Fruit juice and dates were the sweeteners used by the poorer classes. The date palm flourished throughout the region, producing plentiful fruit.

Few knew the privilege of tasting beef, as cattle were not only costly to feed, but also were heavily taxed. Often, cows were kept solely for milking, or as religious sacrifices for the gods. Many people regarded the cow as sacred and would never consume beef, in honor of the highly venerated bovine goddess of joy, music and celebration, Het-Heru (Hathor). However, scenes at the tomb of Ptahiruk, the 5th Dynasty Superintendent of the Slaughterhouse at Saqqara, show four men slaying an ox and, in the small tomb at Uast of an 18th Dynasty man named Deserkarasonb, we see a butcher decapitating an ox, while his assistant holds the animal's legs.

Like beef, veal, antelope, gazelle, fruit and honeyed-sweetmeats were reserved for the wealthy. Goose, roasted upon an open fire, was a favorite dish. Wild fowl was highly popular and fish, abundantly available, was consumed from the earliest of times. Fish were caught with dragnets and hooks. Some hooks have been found dating back to Predynastic times. At Uast, in the tomb of a 19th Dynasty sculptor named Ipy, two men are shown tugging on a dragnet presumably filled with fish.

Fish was popular with the lower class, while their "betters" considered it "unclean" and therefore forbidden. This is most likely because of the strong smell — unpleasant odors were associated with sin and impurities. Fish were also avoided by those who were most devoted to Ausar, for legend has it that a fish swallowed the unrecovered piece of his dismembered body, when Set and his men cast it into the Nile. Temple priests never ate fish nor presented it as an offering to the gods. In fact, in hieroglyphics, the determinative of the concept of abomination and the forbidden was. . . a fish. The pig was also considered "unclean" and was associated with the feared god Set, often depicted in the form of a black boar. Thus, pork was forbidden, especially within the priesthood. Mutton was also prohibited, except in Zawty, where it was eaten out of respect for the wolves worshipped in this region. (The Greeks called Zawty Lycopolis, which means "City of Wolves.")

Offerings were constantly made to the gods in order to maintain friendly relations and open communication. After the gods fed on its spiritual essence, the divine food was later consumed by the priests.

Meals were eaten on small tables, low to the ground (about six inches high). Hands were washed both before and after meals — cutlery was not used. However, elegantly adorned spoons of ivory, bone, bronze and wood have been found; they were most likely used to pour soup and other liquids. The Egyptians ate only with the thumb, index and middle finger. To eat with the other fingers was considered poor manners and a sign of low class. Plates might be made of bronze, silver or gold; the poor used common clay or glazed pottery. Pottery was highly valued for its many uses in cooking, serving and storing food; it was well-suited for use in clay ovens and on open fires. Cow dung and wood were converted into fuel for cooking needs.

Food and water were stored in large clay jars. Water, obtained from wells, was often carried in animal skins. Many wells have been discovered at Per Ramessu and dated to the New Kingdom. Water was raised from the Nile with a lifting device called a *shaduf*, a simple pole or a long beam with a rope and bucket at one end and a counterweight at the other. The shaduf is still used today in irrigation works.

Milk, called *irtet*, was highly prized and sacred to Auset, as it was believed to replenish the spirit.

Bottle of wine, fruit of the vine

The word for wine was, amusingly enough, *irp*. Wine was being consumed as far back as we can see, and was originally used almost exclusively for religious purposes in temple services. Only adults were allowed to consume wine.

Sweet, dark wines were held to be most sacred to Auset — they were thought to possess medicinal qualities. However, inebriation was strongly prohibited in her temple ceremonies. The gentle cat-headed goddess named Bast was associated with drink and intoxication. It has been estimated that during one of her festivals in the city of Per-Bast (Bubastis) more wine was consumed than in the rest of the entire year.

Ramses III (20th Dynasty) boasted of having offered Amen 20,078 jars of wine and supplying another 39,510 for religious ceremonies.

Wine production was time-consuming and costly, and therefore it was accessible only to the wealthy. Many upper class households had their own vineyards but they also imported wines and unfermented grape juice from the western desert oasis of Bahariya and the Faiyum (Crocodilopolis) region. However, choice grapes also came from the land of the Delta as well as from along the Mediterranean coast. Half a dozen types of wine were produced from the grapes of these fruitful areas. Wine jars dating back to the 1st Dynasty have been identified by their seals as they were labeled according to quality and vintage, as well as the geographical location from which the grapes came from.

In wine-making, grapes were pressed and squeezed by placing them in a bag and twisting it with two poles, opposite each other; the extracted juice then emptied into a vase, placed below. Grapes were also mashed by hand and by foot press. In the tomb of an 18th Dynasty officer named Nebamen, at Uast, two men are drawn shown gathering grapes for the production of wine. One man stands while the other kneels, as they toss the grapes into the baskets. Inside the burial chamber of a mayor named Sennefer, of the same dynasty, a highly skilled artist painted a collage of leaves and grape clusters connected through vines that seem to run from the ground up to the ceiling. At Uast, in the tomb of the official and royal scribe Userhet (18th Dynasty), a wine-pressing scene is illustrated. Six men are shown treading out the grapes while clinging to branches from the roof for support and balance. Another wine-pressing scene is carved on the walls of the tomb of a singer named Nefer, at Saqarra (5th Dynasty). Here we see a large sack being twisted by men holding wooden sticks, as the juice pours into a large vat.

Preferred wines were sweetened and spiced with honey or juice from dates or pomegranates. These wines were sipped from bronze or glass goblets. The three basic kinds of wines were produced, from either grape, date or palm juice. Red wines seem to have been most popular during the Old Kingdom; however, whites became the wine of choice from the Middle Kingdom onward. The Egyptians were also the first to mix red and white wines to form a rosé wine; and during the New Kingdom, several types of wines were being mixed together.

Another round of beer

The chief national beverage was beer, or *heneket*. The Greeks credited the Egyptians with having created beer. Legend has it that Ausar taught them how to make beer from emmer wheat and barley, sweetened by adding dates. Like bread and wine, several kinds of beer were brewed in different flavors and strengths. Dark beer seems to have been more common than the lighter styles. This beverage was so popular that children brought it to school in their lunches (no doubt a low-alcoholic version!).

One of the many remarkable legends that have been passed down through the millennia centers on the consumption of beer and its powers to ability to pacify, soothe and transform. It begins when the sun god, Ra, was aging as a mortal pharaoh, on earth. His people turned their backs on him — he was regarded as old, feeble; a weak ruler. Ra felt betrayed by mankind. How could they be so disrespectful? After all, the Egyptians were born from his tears. Hurt and angry, he sought counsel from the gods. He was instructed to turn his mighty eye against mankind as punishment in the form of his daughter, the fierce goddess Sekhmet.

When Ra sent his powerful gaze upon the people of Egypt, Sekhmet appeared. The vengeful goddess went on a rampage, slaughtering people, drinking their blood. This destruction went on for several nights, and the Nile flowed red. Ra began to take pity upon the people. Many had perished as a result of Sekhmet's rage, and Ra deeply regretted having created her. He pleaded with Sekhmet to stop her destruction, but her appetite only grew. Desperate, Ra took matters into his own hands. He sent his messengers to the town of Abu to bring back mandrake plants and red ochre, products for which the town was known. He commanded women to brew all the beer they could; 7000 jars were filled. The men were ordered to mix the beer with the mandrake and the red ochre. This potion was spilt all over the land where Sekhmet had wrought her destruction.

The day came when Sekhmet gazed across the area where she had inflicted so much harm, and came upon what she thought was a blood-soaked terrain. She fell in love with her scarlet reflection, and began drinking the red-tinted beer. Soon, she became quite intoxicated, and fell asleep. During this time, her violent and destructive tendencies waned, until they vanished completely. (Other legends tell that Ra took away her powers, just as he had bestowed them upon her.)

When Sekhmet awoke, her desire to kill was no more. Ra changed her name to Het-Heru, the cow-headed goddess. Other legends have Sekhmet becoming Bast, the cat-headed goddess. Both Het-Heru and Bast are gentle goddesses of love, pleasure and intoxication. Sekhmet remained the Goddess of Destruction throughout ancient Egyptian history and mythology. Her powers would be invoked to benefit mankind, by banishing evil and disease.

From that day on, the priestesses of Het-Heru drank beer tinted with red ochre, in her honor, during the annual intoxication festival that fell on the first month of the season of inundation. The people consumed that beer with a particular joy, since this brew had once saved mankind from the ferocity of Sekhmet, the most powerful of goddesses.

Fashion statements

Then as now, the upper class devoted much time and attention to their appearance, while the lower classes made do. The men prided themselves on being just as fashionable as the ladies, if not more so. Still, the rules of fashion remained fairly constant throughout Egypt's early history. Simple, lightweight linen skirts or kilts were the basic men's garments; among the peasants, a loin cloth or short skirt made from a rectangular piece of linen cloth was wrapped around the hips. Men generally went bare-chested. This kilt remained the fashion throughout Egyptian history for peasants, servants and scribes. In more affluent circles, the garment gradually lengthened to mid-calf. It evolved over time, and by the Middle Kingdom was down to the ankles with a second layer added to the skirt; the upper body was left bare. By the time of the New Kingdom, decorative small vertical pleats were added, with fringes sewn at the edges. Women wore long, narrow, tight-fitting gowns that tied behind the neck or shoulders and extended from under the arms.

During the hot summer months, slaves, reed gatherers, brick-makers, fishermen, boatmen and children wore little or no clothing at all. Nudity was not a problem, in those days.

Linen was the fabric of choice, because of its light, airy quality and ease in mobility. It was made from the fibers of the flax plant, which grew in abundance along the banks of the Nile — the stalks would be harvested while in full bloom. Women would meticulously prepare and spin linen thread, which was then woven into fabric at special work-shops for elegant garment-making. Embroidery was widely used to add delicate, fancy and fringed border trimmings to the garments, and for the royalty, yarn was twisted and woven with threads of gold.

In Predynastic times, knives were made of stone and needles were carved out of bone. During the Old Kingdom, both were made of cop-per; and by the Middle Kingdom, knives and needles were made of bronze.

The quality of the fabric varied among the different level of social classes. Peasants often used a thicker type material, a coarser and less expensive linen or wool. Wool cultivated from goats and sheep was considered unclean and therefore was rarely worn as human clothing. When it was used as such, it never touched the skin of an Egyptian — but on chilly evenings and during the cooler months, a woolen cloak was donned for warmth over the linen garb by both men and women.

The standard garment of the upper class consisted of robes made of the finest, whitest linen worn for its cooling effect in the hot climate. The royal apparel of a pharaoh consisted of a skirt adorned with the tail of a lion and, during festivals, panther skins were thrown over the shoulder of the pharaoh.

Although white was the preferred color, robes were occasionally tinted with dyes obtained from the safflower plant for a soft yellow or reddish hue. This was popular with garments comprised of two or more layers. Colored cloth seems to have been worn primarily by for-eigners and by Egyptian royalty.

Foreign influence is apparent in the fashion trend of the New Kingdom, when colored patterns began to appear and women's gowns were adorned with a layer of patterned beadwork. Small stones and shells were also sewn in at the hems. Also, by this time, the vertical loom replaced the horizontal loom, which made colored patterning eas-ier. Operating this loom required additional strength, so men began to replace women in the workshops.

The Egyptians went barefoot even when donning the fanciest of costumes; but sandals or *tjebet* became fashionable during the opulence of the New Kingdom. The commoner wore sandals made of papyrus or plaited palm leaves, while the poorest classes settled for sandals made from grass and reeds. On special occasions (but never in the presence of a pharaoh or the image of a deity) the wealthy wore sandals made of leather or rawhide, intricately embroidered, with straps between the first and second toe. Often, sandals belonging to victorious pharaohs were decorated with scenes of conquered enemies in order to achieve the effect of having total control by literally "walking on the enemy."

A magnificent pair of gilded funeral slippers belonging to a Syrian wife of Tuthmose III duplicates the common leather sandal decorated with a floral pattern on the inside heel. In the tomb of Tutankhamen, a pair of stunning golden sandals was discovered intact, with delicately ribbed insoles with images of bound captives, and another pair of gilded sandals was found buried among Pharaoh Sheshonq II's funerary provisions.

Jewelry

Jewelry was extremely popular throughout ancient Egypt and was worn by men, women and children of all classes. It served as personal adornment, and was used in funerary work, adding color to the plain, white linen garb and indicating rank. It was also worn for magical purposes in the form of protective symbolic amulets.

During Predynastic times, jewelry was fashioned out of shells obtained from the Red Sea. Stones, animal tusks, teeth and bones were also used to produce decorative and imaginative jewelry. Both the dead and the living wore protective amulets; specific evil influences and illnesses were believed to be warded off by wearing specific pieces of jewelry inscribed with protective spells. There were spells intended to promote or induce endurance, health, stability, youth and prosperity.

Rock crystal, jasper, turquoise and agate were not only attractive but were worn for the supernatural powers these stones were believed to possess. It was also thought that amulets contained healing properties, which were magnified when worn in certain combinations and colors. Children often wore special pendants in the form of a fish to provide protection against drowning.

Precious stones such as diamonds and rubies were unknown to the Egyptians. Lapis lazuli was one of the most popular and venerated stones, as its deep blue hue and gold speckles was considered to represent the starry sky. Amethyst, onyx, garnet and carnelian were frequently imported and were most highly prized.

The lower classes wore jewelry fashioned out of copper and faience — a substitute for lapis lazuli. Even the poorest of the peasants had something — they wore jewelry fashioned out of blue glass or even strands of wildflowers.

The wealthy often wore wide bracelets, anklets, armlets, necklaces and collar inlaid with semi-precious stones. Thirteen wide bracelets were placed on the forearms of King Tutankhamen, seven on his right arm and six on his left. Fabulous bracelets, such as those belonging to Ramses II, were crafted with movable pins and hinges enabling the wearer to slip them on or off the wrist with ease.

Especially during the New Kingdom, magnificent pectorals were worn suspended upon the chest of members of the royalty. Jeweled or beaded collars (called *wesekh*) and heavier collars (*menat*), also made of round or oval beads and balanced in the back by an ornamental counter-weight , were often donned by men and women of the nobility and royalty. Made of metal, glass, stone or faience, the *menat* was held most sacred to Het-Heru as symbolic of life, fertility and rebirth. The *menat* was often presented to Het-Heru during religious ceremonies demonstrating devotion to the goddess and all that she represented. It was carried in the left hand, when offered to the deity. The *menat* was also claimed to bring health, joy and strength to its wearer; it was often inscribed with spells and prayers. At banquets, the host would present the guest of honor with a *menat* collar as a token of welcome.

Crowns of the most exquisite and elegant craftsmanship have been discovered, dating back to the 12th Dynasty. The crown of Princess Khnumyt, found in her tomb at Dashur, is regarded as a masterpiece. It was crafted of gold and semi-precious stones (such as turquoise, lapis lazuli and carnelian); the gold has been molded into a thin wire forming a cloisonné of the stones in the petals of blue flowers. Another remarkable crown of the same time period belongs to Princess

Sit-Hathor-Iunyt. Hers consists of a gold band with fifteen rose-shaped ornaments embellished with lapis lazuli and carnelian. Two golden, upright plumes were attached to the back of the crown and three golden split ribbons hang loosely, decorating the hair or wig. At the front of the crown is the royal rearing Uraeus. Worn only by royalty, the sacred Uraeus cobra, when in its upright position, worn over the brow, symbolically protected the pharaoh and spat fire at approaching enemies.

The ancient Egyptians really had a penchant for rings, in various designs including shells, knots or snakes. As many as two or three rings would be worn — on *each* finger — but most were worn on the left hand and particularly on the ring finger. The thumb as well was often adorned by jewelry. Fifteen magnificent rings were found on the mummy of King Tutankhamen.

Gold (or *nub*) was believed to be the flesh of the sun god Ra; symbolizing the sun, it was highly valued by the Egyptians. Silver, called *hedj* or "white gold" was rarer still, and therefore more precious than gold. Silver was associated with the moon and was regarded as the bones of the lunar deities. Electrum, called *tjam* (a natural alloy composed of one part silver and three parts gold), was found in the mines of Nubia. Copper (or *hemt*) was obtained from the mines of Sinai. Bronze was not as popular but was often employed in the making of signet rings; many such rings were found containing the seal of a king's name. Even the less wealthy wore rings, though theirs were likely to be made of ivory or blue porcelain.

Earrings were especially popular, particularly among women and young princes. The most common style worn by women were large, round hoops of gold. Excavated mummies dated to c. 1400 BC have revealed pierced earlobes, and Tuthmose IV, Seti I and Ramses II all bear traces of pierced earlobes. A vivid portrait of Queen Nefertari, chief wife of Ramses II, shows her earlobes to be pierced by an earring in the shape of a serpent and other artistic representations of pharaohs also indicate pierced ears.

Jewelers were highly valued members of society and were well-compensated for their skills. In the earliest of times, dwarfs or midgets were trained and employed as goldsmiths, as their smaller hands were able to work intricately with the tiny, hollow spaces to be filled in with semi-precious stones. However, over time, foreign craftsmen gradually replaced them in the making of fine jewelry.

Tales from the papyrus

This chapter ends with a wonderful story from a papyrus written during the 18th Dynasty. It is a tale set in the Old Kingdom at the time of the building of the pyramids, and illustrates the Egyptians' fondness for jewelry.

King Sneferu, father of Khufu, the great builder of the first pyramid, found himself quite bored and disenchanted one hot and uneventful summer afternoon. Sneferu decided to summon his personal magician to offer ideas or provide some sort of entertainment. The magician suggested to the restless pharaoh that he should take to his royal boat and have himself rowed through the Nile by 20 of the loveliest singing ladies, clad only in fishing nets.

This proposition pleased the pharaoh greatly, and he went ahead with the plan. As the fair young maidens sang and rowed the boat, the pharaoh was delighted. However, shortly after the excursion began, one of the young ladies lost a piece of precious jewelry that she had fastened to her long and flowing hair. She immediately stopped singing and rowing, and so did her lovely companions. She boldly informed the pharaoh that she would not continue participating in the voyage unless her pendant was recovered. The pharaoh was at a loss and once again summoned his devoted magician, who appeared instantly and recited a powerful spell, parting the waters of the Nile. There, at the bottom of the river, lay the golden pendant. The magician took the jewel, returned it to the grateful maiden and proceeded to restore the waters as they were. The young maiden continued to sing with all her heart and rowed with all her strength, and so followed the other maidens. King Sneferu was once again amused and entertained. The magician was suitably rewarded for his ingeniousness and magical skills.

Bad hair day?

Wig-making was a flourishing trade in ancient Egypt, and many varieties were available. Men and women of all classes wore wigs, indoors and out; they were status symbols and also served as protection against insects and the heat of the sun. Wigs were a particularly important part of one's toilette at banquets, where they were adorned with beads, tasseled ribbons and floral garlands. There were some exceptions, of course. Priests shaved their entire heads and bodies, and never donned wigs — human or artificial hair was strictly forbidden among the priesthood, as it was believed to attract impurities. Commoners wore their hair short and servants fastened their hair at the back of the neck.

During the Old Kingdom, wigs were manufactured from animal hair; later, by the New Kingdom, the wealthy were wearing heavy black wigs made of human hair. Less costly alternatives, produced from plant fibers (such as palm fronds) and other sources such as sheep's wool, were worn with an inner padding of date palm fibers which emphasized the fullness of the wig.

The remains of a wig workshop has been discovered at Deir el-Bahri, and several wigs have been excavated. Also found was a model of a head, with original markings for the attachments used in storing or adjusting the wig. The residue of a cleaning agent remains, probably a form of shampoo.

Hairdressers and manicurists were in high demand among the ranks of nobility and royalty. Among the best remembered are the male twins Khnemuhotep and Neankhkhnemu, who held the prestigious titles of "Overseers of Manicurists of the Palace" as well as "Royal Confidants" (as inscribed in their tomb at Saqarra). Not only did they share titles, but they were buried together. Since the tomb's discovery in 1964, there has been much speculation as to these men's relationship. Rare scenes within the tomb show the pair embracing. Other illustrations, however, reveal that each had a wife and family; there are separate scenes of each one with their families, happily engaged in spearing fish, and fowling. Perhaps Khnemuhotep and Neankhkhnemu were best of friends and domestic partners, in addition to being twins; what is most important is their message of mutual fondness and devotion.

Women often wore chin-length or shoulder-length voluminous wigs that covered their ears; the hair would be parted down the middle, terminating in a blunt cut. Bangs on the forehead were very much the style and human hair extensions were also quite popular. Men wore their hair short or close-shaven, with their ears exposed. Black seems to have been the color of choice, for both. One funerary relief includes a lovely depiction of a female servant carefully adjusting the coiffure of Queen Kawit, wife of Pharaoh Montuhotep II (who ruled during the 11th Dynasty). The queen is shown seated, holding a mirror in one hand and in the other, a small bowl from which a pleasant aroma wafts upwards. Her tomb at Deir el-Bahri is noted for the elaborate and elegant scenes of her cosmetic rituals.

A beard was considered unattractive and unclean — the mark of a barbarian. Only in times of mourning did men allow their beards to grow into stubble length. However, a false beard of plaited hair attached around the ears was the mark of a great pharaoh, as it indicated his respected status, masculinity, and divinity. A rare exception of facial hair appears on the limestone sculpture of a late 3rd or early 4th Dynasty official named Rahotep. Rahotep was a son of Sneferu and a high priest of Iunu (Heliopolis), and he is depicted with a somewhat scant mustache. At his side is his wife, Princess Nofret, and her depiction is noteworthy as well — the sculptor portrayed her wearing a black wig with a floral headband; however, underneath the headband, traces of her natural brown hair are peeking out.

Wig styles were elaborate and involved plaiting and interweaving with jewels and beads. A setting lotion of beeswax or resin was often applied to keep the carefully styled strands in place. To strengthen the hair, an application was used that consisted of the tooth of a donkey crushed in a honey mixture. Grey hair was considered unattractive and was darkened by using a potion consisting of the blood of a black animal (such as a cat, bull or calf) boiled with oil, accompanied by the proper spell. To prevent greying, an unguent was created from boiling the black horn of a gazelle; and another lotion was used that required the fat of a black snake. It was believed that the blackness of the animal would transfer onto the part of the body where it was applied. To treat hair loss, the fat of a lion, hippopotamus, crocodile, cat, snake or ibis could be used.

Young boys wore their hair shaven, except for one lock that was usually left hanging, on the right side, and was often braided. This style was called the *Sere* or the "side lock of youth." It was believed to be the fashion in which the young god Heru (role model for all children) wore his hair. Young girls occasionally wore the side lock of youth but mostly kept their hair tied in a ponytail or in pigtails.

Frankincense and myrrh

On special occasions such as banquets, sweet-smelling unguents in the shape of a cone were placed on top of the wigs of upper class women. These cones began to appear in illustrations during the New Kingdom. They were composed of a perfumed or incense-laden fat, grease or wax which slowly melted, perfuming the body and garment with a sticky, sweet, aromatic fragrance. These cones also served other purposes, acting as air fresheners and insect repellents. Illustrations reveal that men wore perfume cones too, albeit not as frequently as the women.

Recently, certain scholars have suggested that these cones may have been merely symbolic of the fact that the individual was wearing a perfumed or scented wig. However, the tomb of two sculptors in Uast (Nebamen and Ipuky, of the 18th Dynasty), reveals much information on this subject. In this illustration, a young female servant holds a small tray with one hand, containing one such perfumed cone, and with the other hand she molds the salve in place on the head of the female guests, who are seated in pairs. Three other women, seated in front, are being offered perfume by another young servant girl; she pours the substance into a small bowl that one of the female guests is holding. These three women, being ahead of the other two, have already had their perfumed cones perfectly molded and set in place upon their wigs.

In the ancient Egyptian language, *nefer* means "beautiful" or "good," thus giving us the names of the queens Nefertiti and Nefertari. *Nefertem* is the lotus god of fragrance and is depicted with a crown of lotus flowers upon his head. The lotus flower was enjoyed for its natural aroma, and it was presented to guests at banquets. One illustration shows a priestess from the 5th Dynasty inhaling with pleasure the floral scent of the lotus.

Residues and remains found during archeological excavations have provided convincing evidence as to what ingredients were used at that time in the production of perfumes and oils. It is indisputable that these people devoted much time to their appearance and grooming. Cleansing rituals were most elaborate among the upper class. In lieu of soap, animal or vegetable oils mixed with powdered limestone or alkaline salts were used. Cleansing oils were also produced from the essence of the wild castor plant mixed with ash (for its abrasive quality); this mixture could also be worked into an effective lather. Natron, mixed with water, was most likely used as a mouthwash. Mint was available to the Egyptians since Predynastic times, and its leaves were chewed to freshen the breath. Auset, major deity and wife of Ausar, is believed to have had perfumed breath, more fragrant than the scent of flowers.

Perfume was not only an expensive luxury but a valuable export. Egypt eventually became renowned throughout the ancient world for its perfumes. Men and women wore perfume to mask body odor, which must have been quite considerable. Perfumes were concocted from oils derived from plants, animal organs and the fat of such animals as the ox, goose, cat, hippopotamus and crocodile, scented with various aromatic ingredients.

Popular fragrances were composed of yellow-hued saffron oil, henna leaves, cinnamon, bitter almonds, iris and lily flowers. The essence was extracted and soaked in oil of moringa to produce a liquid form. To make perfumed cream, the extracted essence was blended with wax or animal fat. Residues of creams made of oil and lime have been discovered; and vanilla was worn as both a perfume and an aphrodisiac. Other ingredients included almonds, castor oil, sandalwood, flowers, sweet-smelling wines, honey, frankincense, myrrh and cassia (which is similar to cinnamon).

These spicy fragrances were stored in elegantly carved alabaster jars of original and appealing design. One such container is in the shape of a dwarf carrying a jar over his shoulder; others have been found in the form of a swimming girl, or a fish. Vases or containers made of faience, onyx, colored glass, ivory and bone have been found decorated with shells or semi-precious stones. A spectacular jar belonging to Merenra (who ruled during the 6th Dynasty) is in the shape of a seated female monkey. What is so remarkable about this transparent alabaster jar is that, within her torso, one can see the monkey holding a baby tenderly against her body as if it were still inside her womb.

In ancient Egypt, oil was regarded as a symbol of joy and a necessity of everyday life. Oils were of vital importance against the drying heat of the sun, arid winds and hot air of the Nile Valley. When perfumed, it was transformed into a luxury item. So important was body oil to the ancient Egyptians that it was one of the most common supplies issued to workers as wages. Oils were also presented as offerings to the deities and statues were anointed with aromatic scents. In funerary work, a ceremonial assortment known as the "Seven Sacred Oils" was applied to the mummy during the process of embalming. On the back panel of King Tutankhamen's golden throne is an illustration of his wife, Ankhesenamen, tenderly anointing her seated husband from a chalice she holds.

The more aromatic oils, such as myrrh, frankincense and lily, were the most highly prized and often were blended with scents of flowers, fruits and herbs. Honey was used for its scent and to keep wrinkles at bay; mudpacks made from powdered alum, dried crocodile dung and oil of the aromatic fenugreek plant were also important in helping to maintain youthful-looking skin. It has been written that Cleopatra VII bathed in asses' milk, as it was believed to prevent wrinkles and retain suppleness of skin.

Putting a good face on it

Men, women and children of all classes were applying cosmetics 2000 years before the pyramids were constructed. Cosmetics were also meant to be used in the afterlife. Many items of this nature have been found in tombs and are depicted in funerary works of art. Palettes for grinding cosmetics, crafted from slate, have been found dating back to c. 3300 BC.

Cosmetics served as adornment, of course, but were also worn for religious purposes as well as for protection against the sun's glare. Cosmetics were also thought to contain magical and healing properties, and special formulas were developed to treat poor eyesight and cure infections of the eye.

The eye was the main focus in the application of make-up or *Mesdmet,* and it was applied in such a way as to imitate or recall the shape of Ra's and Heru's eyes. Eye makeup included green or black powders — the colors of resurrection and joy, respectively. A common style consisted of applying eye cosmetic consisted of a heavy line of dark grey or black on the upper lid and green as a liner on the lower eyelid. It was drawn in a fashion that gave the eye an attractive almond-shaped look as it extended towards the hairline.

Green eye paint was obtained from malachite, the green ore of copper found in the Sinai and Eastern desert; kohl, or black eye paint, was formulated from galena, the dark grey ore of lead. White lead, cinnabar, antimony, powdered lead, soot, frankincense, almonds and coal were also used in eye make-up. These ingredients were ground and then mixed with fat, oil, water and gum to form a paste. These compounds were mixed and stored in small, ornamental pots, bottles and jars made of alabaster or faience. One type of small tubular container made of reeds was used for storing kohl, and another — in the shape of a tubular container being held by a monkey — were discovered in a New Kingdom tomb; the products are labeled "genuine" and "most excellent." While the makeup was being applied, a cosmetic dish or palette in the shape of an animal (such as a ram or a fish) was used. The mixture was applied with a small wooden, stick, brush or simply with the fingertips. Spoons made of stone, ivory, bone or metal were also popular. Typically, these cosmetic spoons were crafted into spectacular shapes and varieties. Spoons discovered from New Kingdom excavations included one made of alabaster in the shape of a young girl swimming with her arms extended, holding a container carved in the form of an animal. Another spoon from the same time period was made of wood and carved into the shape of a female dancer playing her square tambourine in between two tall lotus flowers.

Red ochre, a powdered hematite, was ground and mixed with water to add a blush to the cheeks and color to the lips. Red was also obtained from the pigment of the leaves of the henna plant (or *henu*), which was grown in the fields. The fashion-conscious women of ancient Egypt also used henna to tint their fingernails, toenails, hair and even the palms of their hands and soles of their feet. Feminine beauty was also enhanced by tattoos. The earliest evidence of this has been discovered on paintings and statues dating back to Predynastic times. Often, the tattoos consisted of small dots, or the image of a deity such as Bes. Of course, it is possible that, unlike the perfumed cones, the tattoos were merely artistic representations.

Tools of the trade

Highly polished mirrors (called *ankh*) crafted of bronze, copper or silver were used when applying cosmetics. Mirrors have also been found placed under the head of mummies or in front of their faces, such as that of an 11th Dynasty official buried at Uast. Metal smiths produced elegant handles in exquisite shapes such as that of young girls, flowers, animals, or the symbol of everlasting life — also known as *Ankh* — and many other intricate designs. The image of Het-Heru, goddess of love, pleasure and beauty, often adorned both sides of mirrors, the handles of which were often shaped into a papyrus stem.

Wide-toothed combs and hairpins were made of bronze, silver, bone, wood or ivory. Combs have been found dating to Predynastic times; some have handles embellished in the shape of a gazelle. Fashionable ladies used bronze tweezers to shape their eyebrows into narrow arcs. Pumice stones as well as bronze or gold razors served to remove unwanted hair. Such razors were found in the tomb of Queen Hetepheres and Princess Sit-Hathor-Iunyt. During the 3rd millennium BC, razors were made of sharpened stones fastened to a wooden handle.

Boxes carved out of rare materials such as ebony and ivory, inlaid with semi-precious stones and painted in the most vivid of colors, held the cosmetics jars. The cosmetic chest of Sit-Hathor-Iunyt was carved in the shape of a shrine and fashioned out of gold, silver, ivory, ebony, carnelian and faience. These boxes also contained combs, mirrors, make-up applicators and stone palettes. Women attending banquets often brought their own cosmetic boxes or chests along with them for the inevitable touch up; they kept them close by, under their chairs, just as they do with handbags today.

7. RECREATION

Eat, drink and be merry

Egyptians were highly sociable and knew how to enjoy their leisure time, a welcome break from the drudgeries of everyday life.

Banquets and extravagant dinner parties were often given by wealthy. The guests, arriving around midday, were welcomed by having their heads anointed with a sweet scent mixture. It was customary to offer one's guests flowers from a lovely bouquet. A servant of the house would remove the guest's sandals and present him or her with a lotus flower to sniff, or perhaps to attach to the headband. Garlands and floral necklaces were given, as well as lotus buds, which might be woven into the tresses of the wigs. Servant boys and girls would walk around offering aromatic ointments, floral wreaths, exotic perfumes and bowls of sweet wine to the guests. A lovely portrait of four seated ladies attending a banquet is found in the tomb of a royal cook (who lived during the 18th Dynasty) named Neferonpet. In this scene, one lady smells the lotus flower while another holds it up to her friend to enjoy.

Ladies were offered wine from a small vase, poured into lovely drinking cups, while the men drank from goblets or larger vessels.

Music and dance were an integral part in ancient Egyptian banquets. As the elaborate dinner was being prepared, a band of hired musicians entertained the visitors, while female acrobats and dancers kept the guests amused. The orchestras consisted of both men and women;

or a single dancer might be accompanied by three or four female singers. Depictions of female figures in dancing poses have been found that date back to Predynastic times. In the tomb of Nebamen at Uast dated to the 18th Dynasty, two young dancing clapping girls are illustrated performing at a banquet. Back-up singers stood or sat directly behind the dancer. The beat was marked by rhythmic hand-clapping, much as in the flamenco music of Spain where it is considered an art in itself. Dancers, customarily, were trained female servants, slave girls, ladies from the harem, or professional dancers hired for special occasions. During the 4th Dynasty, some dancers were presented with gold necklaces as payment.

After the dinner, it was customary to bring out a one-and-a-half to three feet-high wooden image of Ausar, the god of resurrection. This replica was meant to serve as a reminder of how precious this life was, even though they spent their whole earthly existence preparing for death. It also helped to humble the ancient Egyptians, by recognizing that their time here was limited and that their actions in this world influenced and determined the conditions of the next.

Music and dance were enjoyed by all social classes as an integral part of festivals, celebrations and ceremonies. Chanting was done during temple rituals and funeral ceremonies. Love songs were popular and were passed down through the generations. And the Egyptians sang songs when working in the fields as well as during banquets, celebrations and festivals. Ihy, a son of Het-Heru, was the ancient Egyptian god of music and dancing. He is usually depicted as a young child playing the sistrum or sacred rattle. Het-Heru and Bast were goddesses of music, dance and joy. Unfortunately, no musical notations nor written records of musical pieces have been discovered.

Instruments

Clappers, a simple percussion instrument, were among the earliest musical instruments recorded in Egypt. It is believed that the shape of the clapper was inspired by that of the throw stick. Clappers were not only used at banquets; constructed out of wood, bone or ivory, they were also played by men while laborers pressed grapes or worked in the fields. This served as a means to boost the spirit of the hard-working peasants, as they worked to the "up-beat" rhythm of songs. Clappers were also buried with other funerary belongings in order to frighten away evil spirits. A pair of elegantly carved clappers made of ivory and hippopotamus tooth were found in the tomb of Tutank-hamen, carved into the shape of hands, with the image of the goddess Het-Heru. Clappers were also shaken and played during childbirth, in honor of Het-Heru, to facilitate in the delivery.

The castanets or *castañuelas* of Spain, made of chestnut (castaña in Spanish) and wood, developed from Egypt's cymbals (which were actu-ally made from silver, metal or brass). Metal finger cymbals of nearly 4" in diameter were found in a tomb at Uast, dated late in ancient Egyp-tian history to c. 200 BC.

Harps and lyres were popular instruments and were often deco-rated in bright colors; they might be carved in the shape of various fig-ures and painted with such symbols as flowers. Great standing lyres (of up to five feet tall) were played by musicians standing up, smaller ones were strummed while kneeling or sitting cross-legged. Harps, the fa-vorite instrument of the time, might be simple or elaborate in design and craftsmanship; they could have from four to twenty-two cords, and often were supported on a flat base. This instrument was played by a seated or standing musician, depending on size. The tranquil and hyp-notic sound of the harp was thought to please the gods and so it was often played as a solo instrument; it was also used to accompany a singer, or as part of an elaborate orchestra. Large floor harps were popular during the Old Kingdom. Painted wooden statues of young la-dies playing the harp have been found dated to the 19th Dynasty.

Drums played with hands have been found dating as far back as the Middle Kingdom. Pipes and flutes were often played by men, while the small double pipe and tambourine were mostly played by women. Tambourines came in round, rectangular or square shapes. The tam-bourine accompanied the music played at festivals, military processions and — like the harp and the lyre, at religious rituals. The lute, similar to the mandolin, was also greatly enjoyed and, like the lyre and oboe, is believed to have been introduced to Egypt by the Hyksos during the New Kingdom.

In the tomb of a scribe and temple star-watcher named Nakht, a blind seated harpist is illustrated. A blind singer, clapping his hands, appears on the mural of the tomb of Horemheb at Uast. A picture of a female trio of musicians, dressed in tight white linen gowns, adorns the walls of the Vizier Rekhmere's tomb. Here, a kneeling woman strums a harp while another plays a lute; the third woman plays a rectangular tambourine.

A wonderful legend tells how the lyre first appeared. After the Nile had flowed over the land one year and returned to the confines of its banks, it left behind a bed of dead sea creatures. Among these creatures was a tortoise, whose flesh had been dried up by the heat of the blazing sun. Nothing remained inside the shell but hardened sinews and nerves. Having been contracted by the heat, they became resonant. One day, as Tehuti (Thoth), the god of communication and learning, was walking down by the riverside, he came upon this shell and kicked it, by accident. The sound the shell emitted pleased him immensely. He took this idea as a model and expanded it, constructing a musical instrument in the shape of a tortoise and stringing it with the ligaments of dead animals.

The trumpet (called *Sheneb*) and was mostly played during religious and military processions and events. A trumpet made of copper or bronze overlaid in gold was discovered, with its wooden stopper, among King Tutankhamen's treasures, as well as another one made of silver. Interestingly, the trumpet was never played in the cities of Zawty and Djedu (Busiris). Why not? — the sound was too similar to the braying of an ass, the animal associated with the feared and relatively unpopular god Set, who was depicted as a human with the head of an ass.

Dancing was a favorite indoor and outdoor pastime, but men and women danced separately, rarely together as a couple, and while peasants might have danced in the streets, it was considered inappropriate for a well-born Egyptian to dance in public. Egyptian dancing is believed to have originated with the women in the harems, as a way of entertaining themselves, and professional street dancers often amused crowds who gathered to watch. The dance itself was highly acrobatic and quite complex, choreographed with cartwheels, somersaults, leaps, handstands, backbends, twirls, splits and pirouettes. The dancer's in-struments were the tambourine and finger cymbals. She performed barefoot, with jewelry and hip belts. The dress of the dancer left little to the imagination, as it was usually transparent or light colored, made of the finest textures, and was draped loose and flowing. Often, a nar-row beaded or ornamented hip belt was worn.

Wonderful dancing scenes of men and women are depicted in tombs at Uast, including that of a Vizier named Antefoker who lived during the 12th Dynasty under the reign of Senwosret I. Another scene consists of a painted limestone relief on the walls of the tomb of Ny-Kheft-Ka at Saqqara, dated to the 5th Dynasty. It shows singers, harp-ists, dancers and women clapping and singing. Dancing was a most im-portant element in agricultural and religious festivals and was very much an essential part of the ancient Egyptian culture.

In general, the children preferred outdoor games. They played with spinning tops made of clay, stone or wood, as well as stuffed leather balls. A set of three ivory dancing dwarfs was discovered and dated to the 12th Dynasty; a string-and-pulley assembly enabled the figures to move. Animal figures carved of wood or ivory were common; crocodiles, cats and even a horse on wheels have been excavated. Some, including a lion, have moveable jaws operated by a piece of string. Many items have been found that could be pulled along by a string; one is a frog, made of stone, with a moveable jaw; others represent figures hunching over to wash clothes or kneading dough.

Girls enjoyed dancing, and they played with clay and wooden dolls complete with movable arms and legs. Boys enjoyed competitive sports such as wrestling, darts, stick-fighting and tug of war and upper class boys practiced archery and horsemanship. In the rock tombs of Beni Hasan, children are symmetrically illustrated playing a piggyback ball game with each other. Leapfrog was also popular.

Among the men, archery tournaments were held and wrestling competitions were popular. Men wrestling with each other (whether for sport or combat training) are illustrated on the funerary walls of the sage Ptahotep's tomb (5th Dynasty). Here, the men are shown fighting in pairs. Bull fighting — where two bulls fought each other — was even more fun. Prizes were awarded to the owner of the winning bull. Bird catching was also a common sport; the bird was stunned with a throw stick or lured with bait and trapped in a birdnet. Fowling was enjoyed by the entire family, and such outings are often depicted in funerary reliefs from temples at Uast. One such illustration shows Nakht holding a bird decoy to attract the feathered victims during a family outing. All classes participated in this sport. Professional sportsmen used nets and traps, while amateurs used wooden throw sticks.

The Nile provided many sources of diversion and relaxation. Swimming, boating, hunting crocodiles and fishing were popular. Fish were caught by spearing or net-fishing from small rafts constructed of papyrus; fish were also caught in baskets. The Nile perch was the largest and strongest fish, making it a popular sportsman's target. The hippopotamus was also speared, for sport, by with greater courage and larger harpoons.

A favorite pastime of the nobleman was desert hunting, accompanied by trained hunting dogs. The nobles hunted fox, jackal, wolf, ox, gazelle, hare, porcupine, baboon, goat, leopard, sheep, and hyena. Ostrich was a highly prized animal on account of its decorative plumes, which symbolized sacred truth. A hunting scene is depicted on the walls of the tomb of Userhet, where a large hare flees for its life. Dogs, particularly the greyhound, were often employed for their speed, loyalty and fearlessness as they accompanied their master. At first, men hunted on foot, of course, but by the New Kingdom horses and chariots were in use.

The royals were particularly fond of lion-hunting. No fewer than 100 lions were killed during a single outing by Amenhotep III. Due to their swiftness, fearlessness and ferocity, tamed lions also accompanied royalty during hunting expeditions. Ramses II often took along a tame lion.

Indoor games such as dice or draughts (a game similar to chess) were popular. Exquisite boards were crafted from wood, ivory, ebony, or other rare materials and knucklebones were a good material for dice. *Mehen,* played on a circular board, was a game enjoyed by the royalty, and perhaps others; mehen was played as far back as the Old Kingdom. The most popular board game, for all social classes — both living and dead — was called *senet.* The deceased were often buried with games of senet to enjoy in the afterlife. The earliest evidence of this game comes from a tomb painting dated to the 3rd Dynasty. Four such games were found among Tutankhamen's treasures, and a senet board fashioned out of blue-glazed ceramic belonged to Amenhotep III. In Queen Nefertari's funerary chamber she is portrayed, elegantly seated, holding a sekhmet scepter of power in her hand as she enjoys a game of senet.

Egyptians of all ages cherished storytelling, and they were as creative and original at that craft as they were in sculpture. They always had an ample supply of tales to improvise or recite from memory. One can easily imagine story-telling masters weaving magical tales in the village streets to a captivated audience.

Farming

Agriculture was the main occupation for the average Egyptian, with agricultural processing a close second. Barley was transformed into bread and beer while flax crops, grown in the winter, would be worked into linen (called *menkh*). Linen was very much in demand, not only for clothing but for bedding and for wrapping the deceased, where layers and layers of cloth were required. One of the most profitable industries was the production of linen clothing and textiles; another was the cultivation of papyrus, or *djet*, which came from the marshy lands of lower (northern) Egypt.

The *shaduf*, the lifting device used to raise water for irrigation, greatly facilitated agricultural work and vastly increased the production of the annual crops. A dwarf is shown working the *shaduf* in a scene from the tomb of Ipy. This indispensable tool is believed to have been introduced by the Hyksos during their invasion of the 2nd Intermediate Period. In rural areas of Egypt, the *shaduf* is still used today.

Autocratic by any standard

Everything in Egypt was owned by the pharaoh. The administration created a bureaucratic system to implement total supervision, making sure that crop surpluses would be passed on to the ruling class. The economy gradually became dependent, heavily dependent, on the taxes paid by the nobility; taxation reached a high peak during the Ptolemaic Era.

As mentioned earlier, taxes were levied according to the Nile inundation, since the flooding determined how much land would be fertilized. Royal officials visited the farms and set the grain portion, the amount of grain to be "paid" in taxes. The assessed amount was usually deposited in the temple granaries or the state granaries administered by government officials, and a large portion of farmland was directly owned by the temples; their harvest supported the priesthood. It has been estimated that the temple granaries often stored over two years' worth of grain.

Royal measures

Illustrations on a wall in the tomb of Menna show government officials stretching a cord across a field in order to estimate its area and therefore its probable yield, for state records; scribes are pictured below, duly noting the numbers. A royal cubit measured 20.6 inches; that was the standard unit of measure. (However, it should be noted that a second type of cubit also seems to have been used, measuring about 25 inches.) Land was measured by the *khet*, about 100 royal cubits. An area of land measuring 10,000 square cubits was called *setjat*; that would equal approximately 2/3 of an acre. For smaller items, the cubit was divided into units called *palms*, which in turn were divided into *fingers*. A *remen* was also determined from the royal cubit and measured 29.2 inches.

Labor relations

The week was made up of ten working days followed by a three-day weekend. Work ceased during the many important religious holidays. Farm produce was used to pay state officials and laborers alike. Wages were paid in the form of emmer wheat, barley, fish, vegetables, clothing and oils. Extras such as salt, beer, wine and other luxuries were occasionally distributed. Foremen and scribes were among the highest-paid professionals, with the officials of the royal necropolis at the very top, while unskilled laborers, as always, were at the bottom of the pay scale.

During the months of inundation, when there was a hiatus in agricultural work, the royalty and nobility called upon farmers to serve as laborers on public works such as building irrigation systems, repairing dams, quarrying minerals, constructing temples, and building tombs, as well as to serve in the army. There was always work for the able-bodied!

The first recorded strike in history took place in Egypt, in 1170 BC, during the sixth month of the 29th year of the reign of Ramses III. The government fell twenty days behind in distributing the wages of grain. The workers in the Valley of the Kings dropped their tools and walked off the job, after their pleas remained unanswered. The men gathered and marched off to the temple of Horemheb, next to the Ramesseum, and held a peaceful sit-in outside the temple walls. They refused to budge until the Royal Granaries were opened. The laborers were determined; they rebuffed the officials' pleas to return to work. The men were finally given half of what was owed to them, in the form of corn and rations of grain, with the promise that the balance would be paid "soon." It took several more walk-outs before the grievance was settled and the workers received their full wages.

The crafts

The temples and royalty kept many Egyptians employed as artists, architects, sculptors, scribes, teachers, bakers, butchers, accountants, butlers, musicians and carpenters. The craft of a carpenter is illustrated on the walls of the tombs of Nebamen and Ipuky. Carpentry, along with painting, stonemasonry and pottery-making are among the oldest crafts. Egyptian craftsmen operated their small shops in a community where they produced most of the manufactured goods. Carpenters were in high demand not only for home furnishings but tomb furnishings.

Women were predominantly involved in the textile and dress-making industries, and in spinning and weaving shops catering to the nobility and royalty. Women were occasionally employed as potters, and the best transformed clay into remarkably elegant pieces of ceramics. Pottery was widely used in making bowls, cups, goblets, pots, vases, jars and dishes. Often, pottery was glazed with minerals and used in fine jewelry and amulets. Potters fashioned terracotta vases decorated with stylized animals, aquatic motifs and human figures; many have been discovered dating to the late Prehistoric Era at the end of the 4th Millennium BC. A distinct type of pottery from the Predynastic Age (which began c. 5200 BC) was unearthed at the tombs at El-Badari in Upper Egypt; this was the "Badarian" phase of cultural development, and the pottery of the time might be described as having a rippled surface that has been polished.

Some of the most elegant pottery ever created was discovered in tombs of Upper Egypt, dating back to c.4000 BC, in village north of Uast, called Naqada. The artifacts discovered here led to the naming of another cultural phase, Naqada I, or Amratian. The pottery from this period is known as "black-topped ware." It is a distinct style of red pottery with a decorative smooth black rim, an effect achieved by firing the pots standing upside-down.

Prehistoric stone vases and finely crafted flint knives have been excavated, and the remains of a pottery workshop have been dated to the 6th Dynasty. Among the ruins are areas for clay preparation, firing, drying and finishing.

Leatherwork has also been found dating to the Prehistoric Era. Sandals, carrying cases, cushions and drinking skins were made of leather, which was also used to decorate furniture and in overlaying wooden musical instruments, such as lyres and harps.

Egypt underwent a burst of social, cultural and economic expansion during the phase known as Naqada II (or Gerzean), which began c. 3600 BC. The pottery and vessels created during this period were decorated with animals, boats, and scenes of wildlife. The use of such motifs seems to have been inspired by foreign influence stemming from trade with bordering lands. Late in this period, dwellings evolved from simple oval huts constructed from thick reeds and tree branches to rectangular homes made of sun-dried mud brick.

The Naqada III phase dates to late Predynastic times (c. 3300 BC), which led to the cultural unification of Upper and Lower Egypt two centuries later.

Stone and Metal

Egypt was rich in minerals and stone. Lebanon may have had timber, but Egypt had quarries producing large supplies of granite, limestone and sandstone that enabled them to construct the pyramids and other monuments; those projects employed thousands of men.

Semi-precious stones and metal were obtained mainly from the desert. Copper is believed to be the first metal worked by the ancient Egyptians. There is evidence that they had learned how to extract metal from copper ores in the Sinai and the Eastern Desert, and gold from Upper Egypt, as early as Predynastic times. Samples of lead, which was quite rare, also have been discovered in Predynastic tombs. Thousands of men worked in mines, establishing an important and profitable industry that grew into an organization run by high officials and princes. Metals became monopolies of the court as the management of the mines and quarries fell under the supervision of high state officials.

Hammerstones and copper chisels have been found dating back to the Old Kingdom. Artisans fashioned weapons, tools, toiletries, and jewelry out of lead, gold, silver and copper. Dwarfs were among those employed in metalworking, as shown in the illustration found on the *mastaba* of a 6th Dynasty Vizier named Mereruka. The most highly regarded artisan was the goldsmith, who transformed gold into sheets for gilding furniture, weapons, jewelry, face masks and sarcophagi. Silver, rarer than gold in this region, was imported from Ancient Near East and was used in tool-making, weaponry and dinnerware for the wealthy. A stunning silver vase in the shape of a pomegranate engraved with flowers and leaves was found in the tomb of King Tutankhamen.

This vase and a trumpet were the only objects made of silver found in his tomb. One of Tuthmose's Syrian wives, who died c. 1460 BC, was buried with exquisite silver cups and canisters engraved with hieroglyphs.

Gradually, metallurgical technology progressed and the Egyptians found a way to create bronze, and later iron, which were clearly superior materials for tools and weapons — if you could get them. Iron was called *ba-en-pet* (the metal from heaven or the sky), suggesting perhaps that it may first have been smelted from meteors. Iron was especially valued on account of its rarity as well as its strength. Iron swords and tools first began to be manufactured towards the end of the New Kingdom. During the 23rd Dynasty, iron became somewhat more common; however, not until the Greco-Roman period did the use of iron become widespread. Records show a Hittite king sending an iron sword to Ramses II (c. 1300 BC) with a promise of similar gifts, of the same metal, to come.

The people of ancient Egypt were the first to develop a science of extracting and transforming various metals. They used quicksilver to separate silver and gold from the native ore. From this process, a black residue resulted which was believed to contain immense powers; it was thought to contain the ingredient required in the transmutation of inferior metals into gold. The Arabs slightly altered the Egyptian word for this black powder ("black = "khem"; as mentioned earlier, the people of Egypt called their homeland *Khem*, "The Black Land" — a sort of homage to the rich and fertile black topsoil the Nile left behind) and added the prefix "al-," so that this art became known as *Al-Khemia*, or alchemy as we know it. In this sense, the roots of chemistry and alchemy trace back to ancient Egypt.

9. TRANSPORTATION

Going with the flow

The all-dominant Nile was the main artery for commercial traffic and all other travel; it was (and, of course, still is) Egypt's highway connecting all its important cities. By c. 3200 BC, Egyptians were constructing rafts from bundled papyrus reeds secured by ropes of twisted fibers. Two hundred years later, they had a growing need to import goods, defend their land and transport heavy materials, and this demanded the construction of larger and stronger vessels capable of navigating the open seas. Wooden planks were needed, and that meant importing timber.

Simple wood (or *heti*) and rope constructions enabled the Egyptians to travel, trade with foreign lands, transport government officials and laborers, to ship cargo including building stones and obelisks, and to move troops and fight in sea battles — Egyptian battleships were not the best of their era, but tremendous feats were accomplished in terms of trade expeditions and the sea battles achieved by Tuthmose III and Ramses III. Egypt's ingenuity in building and sailing boats was vital to the land's economic and political strength. Trade and communications between the pharaoh and foreign rulers established Egypt as a powerful unified nation in the ancient world, while contributing to the expansion of the realm. Good communication between Upper and

Lower Egypt, as well as between the pharaoh and his nomarchs, were vital. With the use of ferries, these connections were easily established and maintained as the ancient Egyptians traveled up and down the Nile. Smaller boats and rafts continued to be made from papyrus reeds; and small papyrus rafts were often used in fishing. They could lie in shallow waters, for net-fishing; in deeper waters, fishermen also caught fish with harpoons and spears.

By c. 3200 BC, the Egyptians had developed sailing boats and wind became a motor force, a welcome relief to the oarsmen! Since the wind was generally from the north, and the science of sailing into the wind would not be developed until much later, oars were best used in traveling downstream while sails made traveling upstream less strenuous. The sails were designed to be easily dismantled when not in use. The word for sailing downstream (*khed*) was represented by a determinative depicting a boat without a sail, while *khenti* referred to sailing upstream and was represented by a boat with a sail.

Most villages and temples were situated near the Nile and were accessible by boat (which the Egyptians called *depet*) — and that is just as well, since during the season of the annual inundation, roads were cut off and villages were isolated from each other. Boats were thus the most efficient year-round means of travel and transport, even after the Hyksos brought in the wheel, during the 2nd Intermediate Period.

By the 3rd Dynasty, Egyptian trading vessels bearing cargo ventured regularly into the Red Sea and eastern Mediterranean. Boats were not only used as cargo vessels in trading expeditions, but were used in transporting granite blocks from quarries to the selected construction sites of temple and pyramids. Heavily reinforced vessels transported huge columns of stone and obelisks — weighing over 300 tons — for the embellishment of royal palaces and sacred monuments. Boats were also used in ceremonial processions where the image of the deity in the form of a statue was carried during processional festivals. During the annual Opet Festival, dedicated to Amen (The Creator), his image was towed on a sacred barge from his home and temple at Karnak to his other temple at Luxor.

How to keep going, after you're gone

Boats and vessels were the main mode of transportation not only for the living but for the deceased as well. It was believed that at sun-rise, the sun sets out on its daily voyage over the skies on a solar barque, with Ra at the helm. The souls of those who had died that day would accompany Ra and the sun on the journey through the heavens. At sunset, the solar barque would take the recently departed through the realm of the Underworld to the Courts of Ausar, where each was judged according to his actions in life.

Small boat models were therefore left with the deceased in their tombs. A wooden model of Pharaoh Tutankhamen's solar barque was discovered among his many treasures, and seven model boats were also stacked among his possessions. One fine example is an ornamental ala-baster carving that was secured on top of a painted pedestal. The boat is finely sculpted in the shape of a two-headed ibix, complete with au-thentic horns. Two people are aboard, one dwarf poling the vessel for-ward and a young girl clasping a lotus blossom to her chest. Several model boats with men and women on board were also found in the tomb of an 11th Dynasty chancellor named Meketra, along with minia-ture versions of his pleasure boats as well as two model papyrus barques with 11 fishermen working, pulling on a net full of fish.

Not far from Khufu's great pyramid at Giza, a great rectangular pit over 100 feet in length was discovered in 1954 AD. The pit contained Khufu's dismantled ceremonial flat-bottomed solar boat. This is consid-ered to be the oldest ship ever found. The pit had been covered by more than forty cemented limestone blocks, it held huge planks of fine cedar from Byblos as well as twelve oars — over 1000 pieces were found, ar-ranged in 13 stacks. The principal timbers were marked, in order to be easily assembled. It took no less than 14 years to reassemble the boat, which measures 140 feet in length and is now displayed at the Boat Mu-seum at Giza. Perhaps this was the vessel on which Khufu made his final voyage to his tomb site. Or, perhaps the boat was never used at all, and was only intended to transport Khufu in the afterlife.

The Egyptians were not enthusiastic travelers, and when they had to leave their land, they did so with great trepidation. Dying in a foreign land would prevent a proper Egyptian burial from taking place, thus precluding any chance of achieving immortality.

In the dust

Traveling by land, commoners walked or, at best, traveled by donkey. Royalty, the wealthy and military chiefs rode on portable carrying chairs or thrones made of fine imported woods such as ebony. These thrones were supported by gold-plated wooden poles and were shielded from the sun by a parasol or canopy that was carried by a procession of attendants.

Although horses appear to have been adopted for many uses after the Hyksos introduced them (during their invasion, 2nd Intermediate Period), evidence of horses in Egypt begins some 200 years earlier, in the form of a carving of a horse dated c. 2000 BC. In addition, the skeletal remains of a horse have been discovered, dating from the Middle Kingdom. Once the Hyksos had brought in the wheel and the horse (c. 1600 BC), those with resources took to riding in horse-drawn chariots, made of metal; they were referred to as "ships that sail upon the desert." Horses were used to draw small private chariots for hunting as well as for transportation. Larger chariots were used during military expeditions and processional ceremonies. On special occasions, the horses were decorated with rich ornaments, including elaborately designed cloaks, long tassels and large feathers. Such display was exclusive to members of royalty, monarchy and military chiefs. Horses were a luxury — expensive to buy, and expensive to maintain.

The Egyptian military did not ride horses as a cavalry but exclusively within chariotry. Perhaps they regarded riding horseback to be degrading? It is believed that Ramses II owned rows of stables covering an area of nearly 2000 square meters.

Camels were known in ancient Egypt, however, they did not become a significant mode of transportation until they the Persians brought in larger numbers during their invasion (525 BC). The camel was able to survive longer than the donkey without food and water, and traveled faster. A camel grave, dated to the 1st and 2nd Dynasties, has been discovered, and at Djedu there are vases carved in the shape of this animal, dating from the Old Kingdom.

A tale of the times

An adventure set on the high seas, a popular tale entitled "The Shipwrecked Sailor," was inscribed on a papyrus dating to c. 1800 BC. It begins with a sailor relating his fabulous encounter on a lush island deep in the Mediterranean Sea to the Grand Vizier, with promises of gifts to the pharaoh.

The sailor and 500 of Egypt's most experienced and bravest men were traveling in a great ship, over 100 feet long and 30 feet wide, on an expedition to the mines. As they sailed, they ran into ferocious winds and a deadly storm. Mighty waves, 30 feet high, lashed against the vessel, and many men perished, falling into the sea; the ship itself eventually followed.

Our sailor, fighting for his life, flung himself overboard as the boat began to sink; he grabbed hold of a wooden plank and for three days and three nights he drifted along on the floating wood. On the fourth day, a giant waved cast him upon the shores of an exotic and mystical island, the Island of Ka. Gasping for breath, he crawled to shelter under a tree.

Having rested a bit, he soon decided to explore his new surroundings and look for other survivors. He was mesmerized by what he found. He saw legions of vines and bushes bearing grapes, figs and berries. Everywhere he looked was an abundance of life, with wheat, barley, cucumbers, leeks, and melons, fish and fowl; elephants, hippopotami, apes, greyhounds and giraffes all roamed the uninhabited island. After he filled his belly with fruits, he decided to dig a pit and kindle a fire therein. He proceeded to cook some meat and a fish for himself, and he made burnt offerings to the gods in gratitude for his safety and good fortune.

Soon the ground began to quake and the trees began to shiver. Suddenly, a giant golden-scaled serpent arose, rearing its head at the terrified sailor. The serpent opened its jaws and spoke in a thundering voice, demanding to know where the sailor came from — and he said that if the sailor's reply should be anything that the serpent had heard before, he would fill his belly with the sailor.

Trembling with terror, the sailor recounted the experience of the deadly storm and death of his fellow crew. So frightened was he that the serpent spoke and assured him that he was not in danger as he had come to the island by way of the sea and was the chosen and sole survivor of the disaster where many great men perished.

The serpent revealed that the he was one of 75 serpents living on the island with the recent addition of a young girl who came when the star fell. The serpent told the sailor that he had the gift of second sight and prophesied that a rescue ship would arrive in four months to take him back home.

Filled with gratitude, the sailor promised to return to the island with treasures and offerings — perfumes, incense and animals from Egypt — as gifts to the serpent.

The serpent laughed. His island was not in need of anything the sailor could possible give him. He added that the Island of Ka would perish into the sea where it came from after the sailor departed, only to reveal itself to the next chosen wanderer.

Four months passed by, and the ship did arrive. The serpent gave the sailor gifts of ivory tusks, kohl, precious perfumes, cassia, spices, woods, gold, silver, giraffes and monkeys to take back to Egypt. For two months he and his new shipmates traveled, and as he watched, the island grew smaller and smaller, until it vanished from sight — exactly as the serpent had said.

The Vizier was greatly impressed with this tale, and recounted it to the Pharaoh who, in turn, had his chief scribe Amen-Amena record it on papyrus. The sailor was awarded with the rank of royal official, in recompense for his ordeal and sense of adventure — or perhaps for his creativity in devising this story to explain how he came by such riches?

10. Early International Trade

In ancient times, Egyptians plied the seas in cargo ships; they traded with many lands. Trade routes were established, over time, to Nubia, Punt, Cyprus, Syria, Greece and Crete. Grain was a plentiful and profitable export commodity, as were natron, papyrus, beer, wine, perfume, jewelry, bricks and linen. Trade with Nubia and the Sinai contributed to the political and economic status of Egypt, and gold was helpful in securing political support from Asiatic rulers.

Timber!

Wood was imported in large quantities, as good workable timber was scarce, locally. The native trees — sycamore, acacia and tamarisk — do not produce wood of a quality suitable for construction. Wood was in high demand for building construction and for doors, window frames, sarcophagi, furniture, weapons, musical instruments, and ships — without cedar, the Egyptians could not have built the magnificent ships in which they fought battles. Ebony and other tropical hardwoods were imported from eastern Africa and would be often traded for timber such as cedar, pine and cypress from Byblos (Lebanon).

Byblos was one of Egypt's most important trading partners at the time, and it supplied iron and silver as well as timber. The cedar trade with Byblos goes as far back as the 1st Dynasty and it continued until about c. 100 BC. The Port of Byblos was strategically located, providing convenient access to the much sought-after trees. The Greeks referred to this city, and to papyrus, as "biblia." Later, this term came to stand for the word "book," and gave us the word "bible."

Treasures of all kinds

Turquoise was brought in from the Sinai Desert. Egypt's trade with Sinai goes back to the beginning of the 3rd Dynasty, when copper, semi-precious stones, oils and cedar were imported. Tin is believed to have been imported from Persia and Syria. Spices and rare animal pelts were shipped from areas throughout the Middle East. Horses began to be imported during the New Kingdom and soon became the only domesticated animal to be traded in large numbers with other lands.

Egyptian gold mines were reasonably productive, but they also imported much gold from Nubia (Sudan). *Nub* is the ancient Egyptian word for "gold" and Nubia became known as the "Land of Gold." From Nubia came exotic spices, ivory and copper, ebony, ivory, resin, and timber, granite, and amethyst; these were traded for other minerals and for Egypt's papyrus scrolls, and for wheat and barley. Nubia also supplied ostrich feathers and leopard skins, rings of gold, and slaves, and animals such as monkey, giraffes, dogs and cattle in exchange for Egyptian processed goods including copper tools, salted fish, jewelry, leather goods and linen, as well as grain.

From the "Land of Incense," known as Punt (believed to be Somalia, although this has not been confirmed) scented shrubs were imported for making perfume, oils and incense (known as *senetjer*). Trade between Egypt and Punt goes as far back as the 5th Dynasty. During the 18th Dynasty, the female Pharaoh Hatshepsut headed a five-vessel trading expedition to the land of Punt, which is well documented on her temple walls at Deir el-Bahri. In this expedition, which took place during the 9th year of her reign, Hatshepsut and her crew brought back large quantities of precious incense and exotic animals to Egypt. These elaborate scenes have revealed much about trading voyages to Punt.

Another famous expedition took place under the reign of the child-king Pepy I, who ruled during the 6th Dynasty. This expedition was led by an official named Harkhuf, who sent word to the Pharaoh that he had come across a delightful, dancing pygmy. The Pharaoh, still a child, was highly amused and waited anxiously for them to arrive home. Harkhuf and the pygmy arrived safely; according to funerary reliefs illustrated in his tomb, he returned to Egypt with 300 donkeys carrying cargo of incense, oil, grain, panther skins, ebony and elephant tusks. Harkhuf was handsomely rewarded and was promoted to governor of his region.

The Egyptians were the first to use the process of glass-blowing, creating masterpieces in the form of jars, ornaments and figures. As early as the Old Kingdom, amulets and animal figurines were made of glass; remains of glass works have been found dating back to the 18th Dynasty. Glass-blowing was conducted on a large scale, as evidenced in funerary reliefs illustrating the process. This art gained in popularity during the New Kingdom, when glass vessels began to be mass-marketed, and artificial pearls manufactured of glass were an export item.

Faience, or more accurately, frit (which they called *tjehent*), was manufactured by heating powdered quartz. Faience glaze became the fashion in adorning statues and vessels during the Middle and New Kingdom, as it was less expensive than the highly prized lapis lazuli stone that was imported from Afghanistan. Jewelry, amulets, vases and goblets were among the myriad items crafted from faience that soon became popular exports.

Weights

Standard weights were used for the measuring of goods and calculating their value. A *deben* was about the equivalent of 3.3 ounces. The *kite* (which was introduced after the 12th Dynasty) weighed 0.3 ounces. Gold and silver were measured by the *kite* while the *deben* was used to measure copper.

Currency is not believed to have been implemented until the Persian invasion of c. 525 BC. Prior to this, unstamped rings of gold, silver and copper were used as monetary values. Bartering items in-cluded gold, silver, copper and grain. Open air markets became com-mon, as commercial hubs where much bartering and trading went on.

Egypt became the world's first unified nation, or state, by joining the districts of Upper Egypt with Lower Egypt as one country under one pharaoh, in about 3100 BC, during the Early Dynastic period. This larger national entity required broad scale planning and coordinated action, with new administrative systems and a central government to manage it.

The pharaoh was the most powerful person in Egypt; he was perceived as half-man and half-god, the incarnation of a deity. As king and ruler, he served as an intermediary between the populace of Egypt and their deities. Believed to have been chosen by the gods themselves, the pharaoh was said to possess the secrets of the heavens and the earth. This perceived omnipotence gave the pharaoh total power, and conferred upon him many responsibilities to his people and the gods. His most important duty was to serve the gods by maintaining peace and harmony under the laws of Ma'at. The pharaoh controlled the government, the army, and the entire economy. He set regulations, managed trading and mining expeditions, controlled irrigation works and ran the legal administration; he served as High Priest, Commander in Chief, and Chief Justice.

As these obligations were more than one man could handle directly, the pharaoh assigned officials and priests to carry out governmental tasks and to fulfill religious obligations. The government was sectioned into branches, principally the civil, religious and military. The vizier, appointed by the pharaoh and recruited from within royal families, was the highest official and was referred to as "the man to whom all was reported." The vizier or Chief Overseer, which the Egyptians called *tjaty*, answered to no one but the pharaoh, whose orders and decisions he carried out. The vizier was in close contact with the pharaoh on a daily basis and also with the high priests and the army, and tended to matters of business and legal administration throughout the land, traveling in the name of the pharaoh and as his spokesman. Records exist of viziers in Egypt as far back to the 3rd Dynasty. Initially, one vizier was appointed; by the 18th Dynasty, the pharaoh appointed two — one governed Upper Egypt, from Uast and the other governed Lower Egypt, from Mennefer.

The vizier's responsibilities included the supervision of matters of justice, agriculture, irrigation, building projects and public works. The vizier was also in charge of finances, revenue, tax collection and civil order. He supervised and monitored granaries, farms, mines and quarries. In turn, as one may well imagine, the vizier was rewarded with considerable wealth and privilege.

During the 2nd Dynasty, Upper and Lower Egypt were divided into administrative districts; the Egyptians called them *sepat*, but the reader may be more familiar with the Greek term, "nome." Upper Egypt was divided into 22 nomes and Lower Egypt consisted of 20 nomes. Boundaries often shifted, but the number remained constant at 42. Each nome had its own treasury, administrative center or capital, a hall of justice, an army, and temples dedicated to specific gods honored in that particular region. The pharaoh appointed a "nomarch" who acted as a governor of his nome. He carried out his specific duties and maintained order within his nome, while contributing to the successful running of the country. Each nomarch or governor served within the main central government and administered his nome in the name of and under the sole authority of the pharaoh. On a daily basis, the nomarchs answered to the vizier(s). The vizier had his own staff comprised of other government officials or overseers, who answered to his commands. It was these officials who served as the interface with the peasants and farmers. Below these overseers were the scribes, who maintained records of all transactions and recorded all necessary information requested by the pharaoh.

Egypt was a theocratic state, partly controlled by the clergy. Many priests served as advisors and ministers for the pharaoh, as only they were deemed worthy to fulfill these duties. During the 5th Dynasty, the priesthood escalated in power and began to rival the pharaoh. To maintain amicable relations between the two powers and in the interest of mutual support, the pharaoh exempted the priests from paying taxes. This maneuver, however, only strengthened the religious power and somewhat debilitated the economy of the state, thus contributing to the decline of the Old Kingdom.

The nomarchs themselves gained considerable power by the 6th Dynasty as they too became entitled to many privileges and immunities. When this position became a hereditary post, the nomarchs began to rise in power and independence and became less accountable to the pharaoh; this too contributed to the downfall of the Old Kingdom.

By the Middle Kingdom and onwards, the pharaohs and viziers began to organize the administration in a different manner. Now, any qualified male with education and training could be admitted into civil service. This factor created a dutiful and hard-working class of Egyptians who stood to reap significant rewards for their work. "Professional" employment opportunities expanded; new positions needed to be filled. Schools began to open to train men as scribes and officials; all of this contributed greatly to the boosting the country's economy.

The most accomplished and well known vizier of all was the great Imhotep, whose name translates into "Come in Peace." He was Vizier to the Pharaoh Djoser of the 3rd Dynasty. Imhotep began his life as a commoner but rose through the ranks of government and temples, becoming a High Priest of Ptah and a trusted advisor to the pharaoh. He was not only a vizier but an accomplished physician and scribe. He is best known for his architectural genius as he designed the first monument in history built entirely out of stone, the Step Pyramid of Saqqara. Imhotep was regarded as a sage and, by the New Kingdom, the "patron of scribes," the son of the great deities Ptah and Sekhmet. Two millennia later, Imhotep became fully deified as the god of wisdom, medicine, architecture, and astronomy. Imhotep was the only non-royal to be deified and honored in Egypt. Throughout the country, temples were built and dedicated in his honor. Bronze statues depicting Imhotep as a god have been discovered. The Greeks identified Imhotep with Asclepius, their god of medicine.

Law and order

Ma'at was the basic law of all social classes. Justice, respect and morality were virtues all ancient Egyptians lived by; absolutely no one was above that law. In general, the citizens of ancient Egypt were law-abiding, as they feared punishment in this life and the next. Court cases were held under local jurisdiction with the exception of crimes involving capital punishment, which were carried out by the pharaoh as Chief Magistrate. In each nome, courts were instituted known as a *kenbet*. A high court was located in every nome capital. The best-known court case from ancient Egypt revolved around the Harem Conspiracy against Ramses III. Forty people were tried, including a minor wife, a high official named Hui who oversaw the royal cattle, a troop commander, the Overseer of the Treasury, several scribes, butlers and six women from the harem. The trial consisted of 14 judges who sentenced the criminals to facial mutilation or to take their own lives.

Perjury, bribing, robbery, damaging or looting tombs, fencing stolen goods and resisting state officials were criminal offences, but it was tomb robbery that was considered worst. One particular stonemason named Amenpnefer was charged with tomb-robbing during the reign of Rames IX; his detailed confession was beaten out of him with sticks. The crime of not honoring a debt was considered very grave, and offenders were often ordered to pay back the amount due with an extraordinary high rate of interest. Sentences could take the form of enforced restitution, fines, imprisonment, forced labor, exile into Nubia, property confiscation and the most severe — death. Common criminals were beaten, lashed, disfigured and mutilated. Grievances could be filed by citizens and investigations would be opened, leading to interrogation and inquiries into the suspects' background and history.

Often, religious authorities weighed in on minor cases, as oracles were called upon to settle disputes or to help catch criminals. One such case, recorded on papyrus, took place during the New Kingdom, when the statue of Amen is believed to have solved a crime involving a workman named Petjau-em-di-Amen, during the Festival of Opet, at Uast. Five articles of clothing were stolen from a storehouse while the guard was asleep. After being read the names of the various suspects, the statue of Amen, as an oracle, nodded when the workman's name was mentioned. Petjau-em-di Amen insisted that he was innocent, and requested (or more likely begged for) a chance with another oracle. This oracle confirmed the verdict of the first. The verdict was then confirmed once again by a third oracle, and after 100 beatings with a palm branch, Petjau-em-di Amen confessed to the crime and agreed to return the stolen clothes. He was ordered to swear that he would never go back on his word, on penalty of being thrown to the crocodiles.

Army officials often became law enforcers. During the Middle Kingdom or the beginning of the 2nd Intermediate Period, members of the Desert Corps were often recruited from Nubia; they were known as the *medjay*. During the 17th Dynasty, Medjay forces were described as excellent warriors of great strength and cleverness. By the New Kindgom, these rugged men who lived in the desert became synonymous with the word "police." During the 18th Dynasty, Menna accused the chief officer of the Medjay, Mentmose, of not honoring a debt owed to him. Menna brought the case to court; it lasted for 18 years. Eventually, an exchange of goods was settled upon.

The 20th and 21st Dynasties were plagued by corruption and robbery. It is said that during this era respect for the dead was nonexistent; their possessions were looted, stolen from the tombs by organized gangs of criminals. During the reign of Ramses IX (20th Dynasty), one particular trial concerning a tomb robbery was conducted. This trial illustrates the decline of the government, of royal authority and of the law in those days. Paser, a Vizier of the High Priest of Amen, demanded an investigation regarding tomb robberies by a prince and official named Pawero in conspiracy with other officials. Paser encountered many threats and much abuse from Pawero, who also happened to be the mayor of western Uast and head of the necropolis police at that time. Several high-ranking officials were found guilty; however, the fate of Pawero is unknown. The events of the trial are inscribed upon the Abbott and Amherst Papyri.

The Treasure Thief

We conclude this chapter with a popular Egyptian tale entitled "The Treasure Thief," believed to have taken place during the reign of Ramses III.

Egypt grew prosperous during the reign of Ramses III, who successfully fended off invasions from enemy lands, expanded state building projects and launched numerous trading expeditions. The pharaoh accumulated such wealth that he required a special treasury to store these riches. He summoned his Vizier and chief builder, Horemheb, and instructed him to build a vast treasury of solid rock with the thickest of walls, permitting no illicit entry whatsoever into this structure.

Horemheb, delighted with his new and most honorable duty, began plans for its construction. Under Horemheb's order, the best stone-masons of Egypt were recruited to work day and night on this paramount project (which is still standing today and is known as the mortuary complex of Medinet-Habu). Once this vast, spectacular vault was completed, the riches of Ramses III were deposited inside. The doors, made of stone, iron and bronze, were bolted with the heaviest locks imaginable and sealed with the royal insignia of the pharaoh.

Yet, unbeknowst to Ramses III (and everyone else), Horemheb had had a cleverly concealed passage built. His intention was to add a slight bonus to his remuneration from the Pharaoh, once the job was completed. However, shortly after the project was completed, Horemheb fell ill. Summoning his two sons to his deathbed, he revealed the location of the secret passage; they followed his example and made a few quick trips, dipping into the king's coffers. Meanwhile, the Pharaoh came to find out that, in some mysterious way, his treasury had been diminishing slightly, and frequently. The royal seals were never broken and the Pharaoh was completely bewildered; how could his riches be slowly melting away? In desperation, he set several traps inside his treasury.

On what was intended to be the day of the brothers' last foray, the younger of the two stumbled and fell into a trap set by the Pharaoh. There was no way to get him out — a huge boulder had fallen and crushed his legs, leaving him in agonizing pain. The rock was far too heavy for his brother to shift it even slightly. He was hopelessly pinned. Begging to be put out of his misery, the younger brother insisted that he be killed, for he could bear the pain no longer. The elder brother hesitated, but the younger urged him to hurry, adding that it would be better for at least one of them to benefit from the riches, for if they were discovered they would surely be put to death for this crime. Accepting that logic, the elder fellow drew his sword and cut off his brother's head. A decapitated corpse could not be identified and the family would be free from suspicion. He then departed, as discreetly as possible, brother's head in hands.

The next day, the Pharaoh came once again to admire and count his treasures. He was appalled to come across the headless body lying smashed within his trap. Still, the Pharaoh was confounded, as the seals remained intact. He ordered his men to hang the corpse in the village with the other prisoners. The Pharaoh hoped the deceased's family would try to get the body back so that they could give their relative a decent burial — and thus, of course, they would expose the identity of the thief. Soldiers were stationed nearby, but out of sight, ready to apprehend the family of the thief. When Horemheb's wife heard what had happened, she did indeed beseech her surviving son to take down his brother's body in order to bury him properly. He promised to fulfill his mother's wish, as there was no other way to ensure his brother a chance at peace and eternal life.

He disguised himself as a merchant and loaded two mules with goatskins filled with wine. On his way to the village center where his brother's body hung in public disgrace, he staged an accident so that his wine skins tumbled and spilled the liquid all over the ground. Such a commotion he made at this that the soldiers hiding nearby were distracted, and came to help. Playing the distraught victim, he struck up conversations with the soldiers, who were highly amused by the incident. Being careful to remain sober himself, he plied the guards with more and more wine, saying that it would have been lost anyway. It was not long before the guards blacked out.

When night fell and the town center was as dim as the guards' eyes, the thief cut the ropes and his dead brother fell to the ground. He wrapped the body in a clean linen sheet and draped it over one of his mules, and took it home. The burial was successfully completed by the time the sun ventured its first rays over the horizon.

The Pharaoh's rage was mighty when he learnt that the corpse had been stolen. One by one, the soldiers were beaten for their mindlessness. The Pharaoh would not rest until he found out the thief's identity. He devised another clever scheme, with the help and participation of one of his daughters. Her hand in marriage would be granted to the one who would reveal his cleverest and evilest deed to the princess. The Pharaoh thus hoped to trap the thief; however, Horemheb's son was no fool, and he suspected the trickery that lay behind this bizarre request.

Determined to outwit the Pharaoh, the thief cut an arm off one of the executed prisoners hanging in the village center, and hid it under his cloak. He then went to the palace and requested permission to visit the Princess, and he recounted to her the story of his illicit endeavors. Hearing his tale, the princess cried out for the soldiers who were hiding nearby to apprehend the thief. She clutched his arm to prevent his escape — but she was left holding the severed arm of a dead man, as the thief fled into the darkness of the night.

When Ramses III heard of the incident, he was impressed at the audacity and cleverness of the thief who dared to outsmart the Pharaoh. The Pharaoh realized that, at least, he had stumbled upon one of the most cunning men in Egypt; the crafty man's wit was too valuable to be exterminated. He ordered a public pardon and spread the word that that the clever thief was to be acquitted, and would be rewarded if he chose to serve the Pharaoh truly and loyally, for Egypt was known for it men of wisdom and this man's cleverness would benefit the realm.

The Treasure Thief then revealed his identity; and, indeed, he married the Princess and was rewarded with a position as a loyal servant to Ramses III.

PART II
BELIEFS

12. MUMMIFICATION

In Predynastic times, the deceased were laid to rest in shallow pits. The corpse was set on its left side, in a crouched position, with a few helpful belongings such as pottery jars filled with food and drink. The head was turned to face west toward the land of the dead and the setting sun; this was thought to be conducive to resurrection and rebirth. Often, the body was wrapped in a blanket of reed matting or animal skins, and later by life-sized baskets. Those with adequate means were buried in wooden coffins and provided with all the possessions they would require in the next world.

During the 1st Dynasty, the deceased were deposited in dwelling houses for the souls, or funerary compartments, called *mastabas*. This word translates into "bench," in modern Arabic, and the compartments resembled the low benches that are found outside modern Egyptian homes. Mastabas were low and rectangular in shape, topped with a white painted or mud brick structure that protected the body and the possessions for use in the afterlife. Mastabas were the basis for the pyramids of the 3rd and 4th Dynasties.

During Predynastic times, bodies were buried in sand; it was discovered that the body could be naturally preserved as a result of the exceptionally arid conditions. Building on that idea, mummification became customary during the 2nd Dynasty (although evidence exists of earlier mummification). Several corpses with their heads, arms and hands bandaged in linen wrappings have been found buried under reed matting dated c. 3500 BC. The ancient Egyptians believed that as long as the body remained intact, the soul could live eternally; thus it was imperative that the body be preserved and free from damage and decay.

With all due respect

Three options were at the disposal of the deceased's family, depending on their financial means. The economy plan required only a day or two to complete. The moderate plan took 30 days — the process of mummifying a relative and the cost of the funerary mask set the average Egyptian back about four months' wages. The luxury plan was completed within 70 days. Much more than mummification was performed during this period. The sarcophagus, carved out of stone during the Middle Kingdom, and the tomb, had to elaborately prepared to receive the body. The word "sarcophagus" stems from the Greek words "sark" (flesh) and "phagus" (eating). Sarcophagi — which contained the bodies of the deceased — were perceived by the Greeks as "flesh-eating" boxes. Preparing funerary items were an important occupation for artisans, craftsmen, and woodworkers as well as tomb builders. In addition, priests and scribes were kept busy preparing the funerary texts to be placed with the deceased.

The 70-day process, accessible only to those at the top of the financial scale, began with the cleansing of the body. The brain matter was first softened with a corrosive liquid injected into the brain cavity. Then the brain was removed, with a hooked instrument inserted through a nostril. There is evidence that the brain was sometimes removed through a hole made at the base of the skull. This organ was considered insignificant waste matter, conducive to moisture and decay, and therefore it was discarded; then the brain cavity was filled with resins. Next, the internal organs, likewise subject to rapid decay, were removed. A 3 ½" abdominal incision was carved into the left side of the body with a sharp knife of flint or Ethiopian obsidian.

The liver, stomach, lungs and intestines were removed and placed individually in what the Greeks called Canopic Jars. One theory holds that this name is derived from the village of Canopus (Abu-Qir), situated at the Nile Delta near Alexandria. In this town, human-headed jars were worshipped during the Late Period as the personification of Ausar. Greek legend has it that the jars were named after Canopus, fleet commander of Spartan King Menelaus of Alexandria, who started the Trojan War. Canopus died in Egypt and a city was named after him. Canopus subsequently came to be worshipped in the Delta region, during the late Period, in a form resembling a human-headed jar. The Canopic Jars were made of clay, wood, alabaster, limestone or faience, and were inscribed with spells believed to magically re-unite the body with its organs in the afterlife.

Among Tutankhamen's treasures, a miniature shrine serving as a Canopic chest containing four cylindrical compartments, carved out of a single block of alabaster, was found. The four protective goddesses, Auset, Nebet-Het, Selket and Nit, are carved into each corner to guard the king's mummifed viscera.

Each Canopic jar was designed with a lid or stopper in the form of the head of one of the four *mesu heru*, or the "four sons of Heru." Imset, represented with a human head, held the liver. Hapy, in his ape-head form, protected the lungs. The falcon-head Qebehsenuf guarded the intestines and Duamutef, the jackal-headed god, preserved the stomach. In turn, the sons of Heru were guarded by the four protective goddesses.

By the 22nd Dynasty, the jars became purely symbolic as the organs were removed, wrapped in linen and placed back inside the body cavity. The heart, or "seed of intelligence" or "source of life," as it was called, was usually left in the body, as it was the heart that spoke on behalf of the deceased at the Judgment Hall.

The next step was to remove all moisture from the body. Linen-wrapped packets of natron were placed inside the body cavities and more packets and natron in its loose form surrounded the body. This "divine salt," as it was called, acted as highly effective drying agent. Natron also doubled as an antiseptic, being a natural purifier. After forty days in this natron bath, the body became a hard shell, no longer susceptible to moisture and decay. Natron is a carbonate of sodium that occurs naturally in salt lakes and other deposits.

When the corpse had dried out, the natron packs were removed and the body was washed with palm wine or the healing, sacred waters of the Nile. Next, it was treated with special oils and scented resins such as myrrh and cassia. These resins were also stuffed into the body cavities, along with sawdust and wads of linen soaked in resins and oils, in order to preserve the shape of the body.

Once the body was sewn up again, the wrapping process began. Hundreds of yards of linen were used, and as the body was being wrapped, priests recited spells and prayers. The wrapping process took about 14 days; each finger and toe was individually wrapped in layers of fine white linen coated in *mummiya*, (the Persian-Arabic term meaning bitumen or tar) before the entire hand or foot was wrapped. The word "mummy" comes from *mummiya*, a black adhesive resin used in wrapping the mummy. Mummiya was found in the Near East and was thought to possess special healing powers.

The mummies of pharaohs were positioned with the hands crossed over the chest, as sign of kingship. Amulets such as the eye of Heru, the girdle of Auset or the scarab, the sacred beetle, were inserted in between the bandages in specific designated positions. The scarab, a powerful amulet, was placed over the heart of the mummy with a spell inscribed upon it to prevent the heart form symbolically incriminating or betraying its owner. Prayers and spells were sometimes inscribed on the linen itself, as well. Often, the heart was replaced entirely with a large scarab amulet to facilitate rebirth. The heart scarab amulet was made out of lapis lazuli, carnelian or other semi-precious stone. Over 140 amulets were found within the bandages of King Tutankhamen's mummy, which was wrapped in 13 layers of the finest linen.

At this stage, the cosmetician painted the face, adding color to the lips, eyes, cheeks, nails, palms and soles. Artificial eyes were often inserted in the eye sockets, if the family could afford such extravagance. For those who could afford them, a funerary mask and wig were added to assist the soul in easily recognizing its physical body.

The shrouded mummy was then deposited in two nested coffins of cedar or other fine wood. The outer case protected the first coffin and the body. The coffins were decorated with scenes of the deceased's life and deeds, providing a pictorial biography. Finally, the body and the double casket were placed inside the sarcophagus, its place of eternal rest. Eyes were painted on the outside of the sarcophagus so that the deceased would be able to look out. When the entire process was completed, the priests, relatives, friends and mourners transported the coffin to its burial site.

Tomb walls were illustrated with scenes of the deceased person's family as well as the activities that he or she had been enjoyed during this life and looked forward to in the next. Inside the tomb, the physical body was preserved, protected and surrounded by articles provided for use in the afterlife — the same items needed while living on earth. Among the possessions one would take to his tomb were clothing, wigs, professional tools, weapons, writing material, games, jewelry and nourishment for the Ka or "double." Miniature models, such as that of a boat, were often used; they took up less space and were less costly to manufacture, while symbolically serving their purpose as well as the authentic item.

The dead were also provided with cosmetics, perfumes, oils, jars, chests, utensils, linen, furniture, pets, amulets, and servants in the form of Ushabti or Shawabti. The Egyptian word for "answer" was *useb*. Ushabtis, or "answerers," were little figures or model servants, male and female, carved out of stone, wood, metal or faience that first appeared during the New Kingdom. Ushabtis were intended to perform the work and chores assigned to the deceased by the gods; the dead would be buried with all the Ushabtis he was expected to need to perform the cosmic duties that the gods might request in return for protection and immortality. The standard number provided for a wealthy man was 365, one for each day of the year, plus 36 overseers (one for each decan, or group of ten). King Tutankhamen was buried with 413 Ushabtis made of wood, limestone and alabaster, and no fewer than 700 Ushabtis, inscribed with the VI Chapter of the Book of the Dead, were found in the tomb of Seti I. Ushabtis were often inscribed with a spell on the back of the figure; this was supposed to be read in order to activate the servant. Often, they were simply inscribed with the name of the deceased.

With no respect whatsoever

In the modern era, "mummy abuse" has been rampant. By the 11th century, Egyptian mummies were being ground into powder and sold as *Mummia Vera;* this was marketed as an aphrodisiac and a medicine. The great Persian physician Avicenna prescribed *Mummia* for just about every illness. By the 16th century, *Mummia Vera* had become highly sought after and was sold in apothecaries throughout Europe well into the 17th century.

From medicine to amusement — early in the 19th century, it became fashionable to hold dinner parties in Europe where guests were entertained by the unwrapping of an authentic Egyptian mummy. Later in the 19th century, Arabs were selling powdered mummy mixed with butter as a salve to heal bruises.

In perhaps the grossest abuse of all, during the American Civil War, a paper manufacturer named Isaac Augustus Stanwood had the ghastly idea of importing Egyptian mummies to mitigate the critical shortage of rags needed for making paper. He imported huge quantities of mummies, for their linen bandaging; they were unwrapped, and the bandages were reduced to pulp. Soon, U.S. citizens came to expect their meat to be wrapped in brown paper — as it still is, at many butcher shops today. This process cost Stanwood less than half the price of purchasing rags in America.

He was forced to cease this operation when cholera broke out, claiming the lives of many workers employed in his paper mill — a curse, for disturbing the Egyptian deities?

13. DEATH AND IMMORTALITY

It has been written that no other ancient civilization cherished life as much as the Egyptians and no other — during any period of history — devoted so much time to preparing for death. Life was regarded as a journey and a preparation for death and what lay beyond. Life was so precious that the Egyptians placed great emphasis on extending it throughout eternity. All ancient Egyptians regarded the afterlife as a continuation and idealized version of their temporary existence on earth.

Since Ausar (Osiris) died a mortal death and was resurrected as a god, it was believed that worshipping the sun might provide access to everlasting life. The rising and setting of the sun and stars were symbolic of resurrection and rebirth. Thus, the deceased were transported to the west bank of the Nile, where the sun set — or "died," where the cemeteries were situated, in the Kingdom of the Dead; the living resided in the east, where the sun rose. The western horizon was perceived as the border between the Underworld of the dead and the land of the living. The ancient Egyptians called cemeteries *khert-neter*, translating into "beneath the god," and dying was referred to as "going west."

By the New Kingdom, royalty was a laid to rest in regal tombs carved deep into the solid rock of the royal necropolis on the west bank of the Nile, at Uast, in the Valley of the Kings. The Valley of the Kings served as the royal burial grounds for more than 500 years. Nearby, more than 80 tombs have been discovered in the Valley of the Queens, including the spectacular resting place of Queen Nefertari, of the 19th Dynasty.

When a nobleman died, professional mourners were hired. Women of an inferior class, called "wailers," were hired to work the funerals, weeping and wailing through the villages, their faces smeared with dirt, beating at their chests with one hand while pulling their hair and clothes with the other. A funerary procession of the deceased's relatives, friends and servants, headed by priests, would travel to the tomb site on the west banks of the Nile. Some mourners brought flowers, food and oils while others carried clothing and furniture to leave inside the tomb.

A funeral procession is illustrated in the tomb of Horemheb, and another illustration shows female mourners traced in bright red, graceful, smooth and flowing outlines — this may be why some Egyptologists have associated this color with mourning. Another group of women and little girls mourning with their arms raised in adoration (or *Dua*) as well as in the traditional mourning pose (called *Iakbyt*) is seen in the tomb of Ramose, a vizier and governor of Uast who lived during the 18th Dynasty. A female mourner is illustrated in the tomb of Ipuky and Nebamen and several are shown in the tomb of Userhet. Twice daily, the mourners met in public to chant funerary songs in honor of the deceased.

"Muu" dancers were groups of professional men who waited at the gravesite to greet the funerary procession as it arrived. The men performed a high-stepping ritual dance, in pairs. The dance was intended to conjure the presence of the Bau (souls) of Pe, which were Heru, Hapi and Imset. The Muu dancers often wore headdresses of papyrus stalks or tall conical caps. Musicians accompanied the dancers and funerary songs were chanted.

Upon the death of a pharaoh, a 70-day mourning period took place while his body underwent the required treatments and rituals. Hymns were sung and dedicated to his memory, temples were shut down, and sacrifices, feasts and festivals were strictly prohibited during periods of mourning.

A loved one's passage into the next world was as much to be cele-brated as a marriage or any other significant mortal event. After the fu-neral, banquets were held in honor of the dear departed, usually at the tomb site after the procession and ceremonies were completed and the tomb sealed for eternity. Guests were encouraged to consume wine un-til they reached a state of intoxication that placed them in a euphoric state, in touch with the deceased. This was done with the utmost re-spect to the dead and was taken very seriously. Prayers and food offer-ings were left at the gravesite. Family members often cut locks of their hair as a symbol of mourning.

The ancient Egyptian's greatest fear was of dying outside his be-loved homeland, or *ta meri*. If the corpse could not be returned to Egypt and the body was not available for preservation, immortality could not be granted.

Trouble either way

One of the most popular stories from ancient Egypt is called "The Adventures of Sinuhe." The tale is set during the 12th Dynasty under the reign of Amenemhet I and reflects the Egyptian's fear of dying in a foreign land.

The pharaoh was in constant danger from those who wished to do away with him in order to claim the throne for themselves. Amenemhet I heard rumors of a conspiracy among his harem and a threat against his life. Fearing for the future of Egypt, he began preparations to have his son Senwosret designated as the true and rightful heir.

Sinuhe, an official and one of Senwosret's faithful companions, overheard the planning of a murder plot against the Pharaoh. Fearful for his life, from both sides — whether he attempted to warn the Phar-aoh, or became implicated in this deadly conspiracy — and not wanting to witness the deadly conspiracy unfolding, Sinuhe fled to the land of Retenu (Palestine). There he was welcomed by the king and made com-mander of the army by the king. He married the king's eldest daughter and lived on a luxurious estate.

Sinuhe defended Retenu against neighboring enemies and tribes and served the king well for many years, earning him his trust and compassion. As the king had no sons, the succession naturally passed to Sinuhe, and when the king "went west," Sinuhe became ruler of Retenu. But as time went by, Sinuhe longed for his homeland. He sent messages to Senwosret, begging for forgiveness for abandoning Egypt years ago and requesting a royal pardon which would grant him permission to return to Egypt. Senwosret replied immediately and welcomed him back to Egypt. As a reward for his loyal service to Senwosret's father Amenemhet I, long ago, Sinuhe was promised a rich and proper Egyptian burial at western Uast when his time came.

Sinuhe left the land of Retenu in the care of his eldest son and successor, and returned to Egypt. Sinuhe became an Overseer of the Courts of the Pharaohs for the few remaining years of his life. Before he died, Sinuhe had scribes record all the adventures he had experienced before returning to Egypt; these are believed to be the basis of the popular collection of tales of Sinbad.

I want to live forever…

From the poorest of peasants to the richest of kings, the ultimate goal was immortality. Originally, in the beginning of the Old Kingdom, this privilege was reserved for royalty; however, by the New Kingdom, all social classes had access to eternal life. The deceased was required to pass many tests and trials and to complete a perilous journey through the Underworld, known as the Kingdom of Duat, governed by Ausar. By the Ptolemaic Era, Duat was regarded as a domain for punishment for those not pure of sin.

For one to dwell with the gods after physical death, many demons, obstacles, tests and unpleasant surprises had to be encountered and overcome along the way. There were sacred texts intended to guide the deceased through Duat; the *Book of the Dead* contained all the necessary spells, prayers, rituals and knowledge required to meet these perils successfully. With sufficient funds for a funeral and burial, and with a copy of the mortuary texts at hand, all Egyptians had access to immortality. However, it was their conduct throughout this life that determined the conditions of the next.

Duat was believed to be situated below the earth, where many demons resided and were encountered; the sun was presumed to pass through the Duat on its daily journey back from west to east. As life on earth were worlds apart for a commoner and a king, so were their conditions in the next life. A deceased pharaoh, as a divine being, would arrive in the afterworld via a celestial trip on a solar boat (*wia*) represented by *Sah* (Orion), symbolizing Ausar (Osiris) in his constellation form and the Great Cycle of Rebirth. He traveled through Duat to join his celestial equal in *Amenti*, the Land of the Dead, also ruled by Ausar. (Amenti was imagined to exist on the western shore of the Nile.) All non-royals remained bound to earth and were subjected to onerous trials and a hazardous journey through Duat.

In the underworld, the deceased was asked questions, the correct answers to which must have been learned from these texts while alive. The texts could be purchased in advance from the scribal priests. Most petitioners must have had a pretty good idea what to say when they came before the Judgment Hall, as it was unlikely that they would have failed to study these all-important spells while they had a chance.

However, there was a lot of material to cover. During the Old Kingdom, the answers could be found in the Pyramid Texts, inscribed on the inner walls of the kings' burial chambers; the texts consisted of over 150 hymns, maps, magical spells and rituals of protection and guidance to (and through) the perilous areas of the Kingdom of Duat. The inner chamber of the pyramid belonging to the 5th Dynasty Pharaoh Iunas, at Saqqara, is the first to display the Pyramid Texts. By the Middle Kingdom, the texts were known as Coffin Texts, as they were recorded inside sarcophagi. By the time of the New Kingdom, these funerary instructions were written on scrolls of papyrus and placed inside the sarcophagi with the body. These sacred texts were called *Pert em hru* by the Egyptians (which has been translated as the "Book of Coming Forth By Day"). We know them by the Arabs' title, *The Book of the Dead*.

Passing the Twelve Gates of the Twelve Hours of the Night in Duat, the spirit of the deceased arrived at the Court of Ausar. Having entered the Hall of Ma'at, his heart (or *ab*, in its spiritual form) was weighed by Anpu (Anubis), Guardian of the Dead. The heart was symbolic of thinking and feeling, as the heartbeat quickened with heightened emotions. The heart was regarded as the source of life and of all pure and evil thoughts. It was placed on the scales of justice and weighed against the feather of Ma'at, embodying the concept of truth and righteousness. The scales of Ma'at are the origins of the balance used as a symbol of justice, and of the astrological sign, Libra.

The results were recorded by Tehuti, God of Widsom and Scribe of the Gods. If the heart was pure of sin and innocent of wrongdoing, it balanced with the feather. The deceased then joined Ausar in Amenti. If the heart was weighed down with guilt and tipped the scales, the "Devourer of Souls," called Amment (or Beby, by other accounts), was eagerly standing by, waiting for a chance to feast upon the heart. Once the heart was devoured, the deceased lost all chance of immortality; to be devoured by Amment was equivalent to dying the second and final death. This mythological beast with the ravenous appetite had the jaws of a crocodile, the forequarters of a lion and the hindquarters of a hippopotamus: three of the most feared animals.

If the individual passed the test, Tehuti pronounced the deceased *Ma'at Heru*, meaning "true of voice." Anpu (or the mortuary priest wearing his mask and acting on his behalf) performed the final and most important "Opening of the Mouth Ceremony" at the entrance of the tomb after the funerary procession was finished. This was done with a metal instrument called an *adze;* a light touch on the eyelids and lips with the adze restored the senses and breathed life into the deceased. This ritual was followed by another, using an instrument called the *pesh-en-kef*. This was used in the same manner and its purpose was to enable the deceased to receive nourishment after his senses had been restored. He was now spiritually able to dwell in Amenti among the souls of the departed and the gods in the sky.

The ancient Egyptians believed that, upon physical death, the deceased (known as the *Khat*, in his mummified form), took on several life forms — the seven spiritual or astral entities formed after physical death. The *Ka*, or "double," is the primary one; it was born at the same time as the body and immediately reunited with it, upon death, while continuing to live thereafter. To die was also referred to as "going to one's Ka." The hieroglyph for the Ka is two arms extended upward, embracing the heavens. In life, the Ka acted as advisor and conscience. In death it resided in the tomb of the deceased, or in his statue, surviving on the spiritual essence of the daily food offerings or *Aut* provided by priests and relatives. Offerings were left specifically to nourish the Ka so that it could leave and re-enter the tomb at will. If the offerings eventually ceased, the illustrations of food inside the tomb nourished the Ka spiritually. The Ka was the life force, astral double or spiritual twin and dwelled in the statue of the deceased's image. Without the physical body the Ka could not exist; this is the main reason why the corpse had to be preserved. And without the Opening of the Mouth Ceremony, the deceased would not have been able to taste nor consume the offerings. A statuette of the Ka of Tutankhmen was discovered among his royal treasures, in black skin, the color of death, wearing a gilded kilt, collar and headdress.

The *Ba* was the impersonal life force of the soul, the essence of one's individuality and unique characteristics. When the body died, the Ba was born. The Ba was able to leave the tomb during the hours of daylight, only to return to the tomb at night. The Ba was believed to be the personality, spirit or secondary soul. In the Underworld, it took the form of a human-headed falcon with arms or wings and is often seen gracefully hovering over the mummy in funerary reliefs.

The *Akh* was the concept of the Ka and Ba combined. It was the spirit of light and form able to communicate and interact with the living, while traveling among celestial dwellings. It is to the Akh that relatives addressed their letters when requesting advice, help, guidance or forgiveness from a deceased loved one. Often, letters were written to deceased relatives were inscribed inside a bowl. Starting from the upper rim, the text made its way around and down to the bottom of the bowl, which was placed at the tomb of the deceased. The Akh was the final state of transformation of the spirit of the mummy. It was the bright, shining form and shadow that the transfigured spirit takes on after death, as the Akh travels through the Kingdom of Duat and soars into the heavens to dwell throughout eternity in Amenti, the Land of the Dead.

The number seven constantly emerges throughout ancient Egyptian mythology and history, as will be analyzed in a later chapter. Thus four more spiritual selves, in addition to the *Ka* (spirit), the *Ba* (personality) and *Akh* (immortality), were added for a total of seven. The *Khu* is another aspect of the imperishable soul, the spirit of the intelligence of the deceased. The *Sahu* is an astral soul, with an advanced degree of knowledge and power. The *Khaibit* is a shadow body or aura that provided protection from harm.

What's in a name?

Children were given two names, one for everyday use and the other to be kept closely guarded, for fear that it might be used against the child. It was thought that knowing someone's true name conferred power and control over the individual; it was believed that the essence of a person, animal or god was embodied within its true name. The deceased's real name (or *Ren*, as it was known), was carved in stone and believed to contain its divine spirit. To remove the name where it appeared obliterated any chance of immortality; the divine spirit vanished with the name. And without a name, one could not exist, nor enter the realm of the gods. It was also believed that to speak of the dead was to make them live again, by keeping their memory and spirit alive. The Ren was always mentioned in the deceased's funerary texts and was inscribed on tomb walls and burial items.

The gods had five names. Ra had several names but his *Ren* was the key to his true power and essence. By knowing a god's true name, which was never uttered, one could render him powerless. The importance of one's secret name is illustrated in the following tale.

The story of Ra and Auset

As Ra, the creator of all, was aging in his mortal form, he walked upon the land that he had created by dribbling from his mouth as an old man. Auset (Isis), full of ambition and longing for power, concocted a plan to strip Ra of his power in order that it should pass on to herself.

Auset secretly gathered a few drops of Ra's spittle and mixed it with earth. From this mixture, she fashioned and gave life to Apep, the poisonous snake and eternal enemy of Ra. Auset carefully placed Apep on Ra's daily path and then ducked out of sight. As Ra approached, Apep rose from the ground and bit his ankle as he walked by. Then Apep disappeared and returned into the earth.

Ra screamed in pain, and wondered where this evil creature had come from — for he had not given life to this poisonous creature and therefore had no control over it. In despair, Ra summoned the gods for help. They came from the winds, the earth, the desert and the waters. Auset was among them, and she was the first to step forward and speak.

As the "mistress of magic," she promised to rid Ra of his torment if he revealed his true name to her. She tried to convince him that she would be able to incorporate this new knowledge and power into a spell that would relieve him of his pain, but Ra resisted. Still, the pain grew even stronger as the poison spread through his body, and he eventually revealed all his names . . . except for his Ren. Clever Auset was not easily deceived, and began to grow impatient. Ra's anguish took over and became so great that he gave in and whispered his Ren into Auset's ear.

Immediately, Ra's power was transferred to Auset, and the venom ceased flowing through Ra's body. Auset promised to use her newfound power for good causes and to help mankind.

She would have had a promising career as a politician.

14. Deities

The ancient Egyptians worshipped myriad gods and goddesses, or *Neteru*, born from the collective thoughts of the people. All that took place in nature — famine, floods, earthquakes, storms and all events affecting human life in general — was thought to be the result a specific deity's actions. Everything was protected (or threatened) under this great pantheon of deities, who often merged into one god such as Amen-Ra, Ptah-Seker and Ausar-Hap. The divine powers were depicted in human or animal form and especially, as both combined. This was not polytheism in the sense of many gods of equal stature; rather, they worshipped one central deity as the immortal Creator, the one source and supreme entity, from which the other deities emanated.

The multitude of gods varied in character and features. Local deities were established in nomes, each with its own characteristics and traditions. The cults of the great Ra of Iunu, Amen of Uast and Ptah of Mennefer all began as local deities who were eventually promoted and elevated to state gods. Cosmic deities were also worshipped as entities who had participated in the creation of mankind. Universal deities such as Ma'at and Nun (the dark, watery mass from which all gods arose), were venerated throughout ancient Egyptian history. Minor gods such as Taueret and Bes were venerated on a more personal level inside the homes, as household deities.

Some of the gods were also assimilated into triads, clusters of three related deities — usually a family of two adults and a child. Among the triads were those of Abu, Uast and Mennefer.

The powers that be

The following is an alphabetical list of some of the Neteru who were worshipped for over three millennia. The gods are referred to in their true original Egyptian names, with variations as applicable.

Aker (Akeru in plural). The two lion guardians of the rising and setting sun. The name translates into "The Bender." Originally an ancient earth god, Aker guarded the gates of dawn from which the sun rose daily. He is depicted as a double-headed lion, or two lions positioned back to back with the symbol of the horizon in between. Their names are Duau or Tuau, and Sef, translating respectively into "Today" and "Yesterday." Aker was worshipped at Nay-Ta-Hut (Leontopolis) and his image appears in the tomb of Nefertari of the 19th Dynasty.

Amen (Amun, Amon, Ammon, Ammoun), the Theban King of Gods, also known as the Lord of Creation and Protector of the Poor and Weak. His name means "The Hidden One." Amen is portrayed as a handsome man wearing a crown with two feathers. His sacred animals are the ram and the goose; they were pampered and bred in his temples. Amen self-created; he is husband to Mut, "The Great Mother." Together they are parents of the lunar deity Khonsu. When Uast became the state capital during the Middle Kingdom, Amen was elevated to a state god. Since Ra was worshipped as another Creator, Amen became associated with Ra and venerated as Amen-Ra, King of Gods, as a composite deity.

Anpu (Anubis, Inpu, Yinepu), the jackal-headed god of embalmers, mummification and Guardian of the Necropolis. Anpu is an old deity, worshipped since the Old Kingdom. He fashioned the first mummy from the body of Ausar. The skin of Anpu is depicted in black, symbolic of death and rebirth. His name translates into "Royal Child"; he was conceived by the adulterous union of Ausar and Nebet-Het. Some believe Anpu was the son of Set and his consort, Nebet-Het.

Anqet (Anukis, Anuket). A goddess of water, venerated at Abu where the First Cataract is located. Anqet's sacred animal is the gazelle and she wears a feathered or reed crown upon her head. Her name translates into "The Embracer," as she embraced the Nile. Anqet is wife of Khnemu, together with their daughter, Satet (some believe her to be sister of Anqet and wife of Khnemu) form the Triad of Abu.

Apep (Apophis), the feared snake god of the Underworld, enemy of Ra and his daughter Bast. Apep is the personification of the darkness of the night. "The Book of Overthrowing Apep" provides magical spells intended to help people successfully combat Apep; one enables the petitioner to know his true name. This text is believed to date back to the Ramessid Era.

The ancient Egyptians attributed the sunset each day to the swallowing of the sun by Apep. He is believed to dwell deep in the waters of Nun. Each day when Ra travels in his solar barque across the skies, Apep continues his never-ending battle to destroy him. During storms that darkened the sun, and at times of eclipse, the Egyptians believed that Apep was getting the upper hand. One can only imagine the fear of the deeply spiritual and superstitious Egyptians during a total solar eclipse.

Atem (Atum, Tem, Temu), the self-created solar god and father of Shu and Tefnut. His name translates into "The Complete One." Those belonging to the cult of Atem credited this deity with the creation of the universe. Khepera symbolizes the rising sun and Ra personifies the sun at noon, when it was most powerful; Atem is the personification of the setting sun. Like Amen, Atem is usually depicted as a man and also merged with Ra and became venerated as Atem-Ra or Ra-Atem.

Aten (Aton), the visible solar disk and the sun itself, worshipped from the Middle Kingdom on. The essence of this deity emanated from the warmth and light of the sun. Under the reign of Akhenaten of the New Kingdom, Aten replaced the entire pantheon of Egyptian gods and became the sole deity. Aten is often depicted with outstretched rays ending with ankhs, or hands that enveloped mankind. His cult center was situated in the city he founded, known as Akhetaten ("Horizon of Aten"), which is today known as Amarna.

Ausar (Osiris, Asar, Wsir). Originally a god of earth and vegetation, reborn as the God of the Dead and of Resurrection. Upon his death, with the help of his son Anpu and wife Auset, Ausar became the original mummy. Anpu taught Auset the art of mummification and with this skill and knowledge, Ausar was resurrected. Ausar is the personification of the cycle of rebirth. He is judge and ruler of the Underworld and Lord of Amenti, the land of the dead. Ausar is also depicted in human form, in different colors: black symbolizes his funerary associations; white is his mummified form and green depicts his regenerative power, rebirth, while reminding us of his original status as a god of abundance and vegetation. His name translates into "He Who Sees the Throne," and his cult center was located at Abedju (Abydos) and Djedu or Per Ausar (Busiris).

Auset (Isis, Aset, Ast). Wife and sister of Ausar, sibling to Nebet-Het and Set. Auset is Mistress of Magic and Protector of Children. She is recognized by her crown in the shape of a throne, or seat, which is the meaning of her name. It was she, with the help of Anpu, who gave Ausar eternal life. Auset is the most important goddess in ancient Egypt. She is also one of the four protective deities of the dead.

Bast (Bastet), the cat-headed Goddess of celebration, love, joy, divine intoxication, music and magic. Bast is the daughter of Ra and Auset and was worshipped as early as 3200 BC in the Delta city of Per-Bast (Bubastis, present day Tell-Basta), where a vast feline necropolis was built. Her name can be broken down to Ba-Ast, translating into "Soul of Auset." Bast protects cats and those who worship these highly venerated animals.

Bes, the merry, clown-headed god of childbirth, protector of children and guard against nightmares. Bes is also a god of music, dance, merriment, and of the nuptial bed, and was believed to bring good luck to newly married couples. Unlike others, Bes is usually portrayed in the full frontal view. An amulet in his image was often worn as a lucky charm. Bes can be described as a dwarf wearing a beard, a feathered headdress and the mask of a lion-type beast. Gentle and kind, Bes ruled over inebriation. This deity did not have a cult center or temple dedicated in his honor, but was very popular and was often worshipped privately at home.

Duamutef (Tuamutef). Protector of the deceased's stomach, and ruler of the East. Duamutef is one of the four sons of Heru; he, in turn, was protected by Nit. His name translates into "He Who Praises His Mother." Duamutef is depicted as a jackal-headed mummified man.

Geb (Seb). God of earth and creator of the mountains. Geb is husband and brother to Nut, the sky goddess, and son of Shu and Tefnut. He is often portrayed as white goose, or a goose-headed man; he can be shown in green skin, representing life, or in black, symbolic of the fertile land. In some versions, Geb is known as "The Great Cackler" who broke the silence of the universe by laying the first cosmic egg of creation.

Hap (Apis). A fertility god, the sacred bull of Mennefer. In Ptolemaic times, he was merged with Ausar and known as Ausar-Hap (Serapis). Hap is portrayed as a bull with the solar disk and the royal cobra, or Uraeus, upon his head. This is the only deity represented entirely and exclusively as an animal.

Hapi. An androgynous deity personifying the Nile. Hapi is husband to both Nekhebet and Wadjet, the Ladies of the Two Lands. His name translates into "The Runner." Hapi is recognized by the crown of lotus flowers or papyrus plants that he wears upon his head, representing both Upper and Lower Egypt. He is shown as a well-fed, pot-bellied man symbolizing the abundance and fertility of the Nile.

Hapy. One of Heru's sons, protector of the lungs of the deceased. Depicted as an ape-headed mummified man, Hapy is governor of the north and is protected by Nebet-Het.

Heka. God of magic and divine energy. Weret-Hekau is his female counterpart. Together they personify the ways of magic and are portrayed as cobras or cobra-headed humans.

Heqet (Heket), the frog-headed goddess of birth, fertility and resurrection. Heqet was wife of Khnemu and was often invoked to facilitate the birth process and protect the mother. As frogs appeared during the inundation of the land, signaling abundance, Heqet was worshipped in this animal form.

Heru (Horus). The falcon or hawk-headed solar god of the sky and horizon. His name translates into "He Who Is Above." The two eyes of Heru symbolize the sun and the moon. Heru is a god of the living and lord of the heavens. He is worshipped in many unique forms, including the posthumous son of Ausar and Auset known as Heru-Sa-Auset (translating into "Heru, Son of Auset"). He is also known as Hor-Pa-Krat (Harpocrates), and Heru-Ur, meaning "Heru the Great." He is the warrior son of Nut and Geb and brother of Ausar, Auset, Nebet-Het and Set. He is also known as Heru-Behdety, avenger of his father Ausar's murder.

Het-Heru (Het-Hrw, Hathor, Hathoor, Athyr). She is the cow-headed consort of Heru, also known as the "Celestial Cow." Het-Heru is the goddess of the sky, love, joy, music, dance, pleasure, fertility and child-birth. She is also a goddess of intoxication and, according to one version, she came to be when Sekhmet was pacified after being intoxicated with mandrake-tinted beer. Her name translates into "House of Heru." She is another daughter of Ra and is known as an aspect of Auset. Her temple and cult center were situated at Iunet (Denderah).

Imseti (Amset, Mestha, Mesti), one of the four sons of Heru, he guarded the liver of the deceased and presided over the south. Imseti is depicted as a mummified man and was protected by the goddess Auset. Imseti is believed to have assisted Anpu in the mummification of Ausar.

Khepera (Khepre, Khaphre, Khepri, Kheper), the scarab-headed, self-creating god of rebirth and existence. Khepera is the personification of the daily rising sun. His name translates into "Become," "Exist," or "Create." It is Khepera who is worshipped in the form of the scarab amulet that embodied his physical and cosmic attributes.

Khnemu (Khnum), the ram-headed god of fertility, the inundation of the Nile and the creation of the world. Together with his wife Anqet, the water goddess and Satet, the goddess of fertility and of the Nile's flooding, they formed the Triad of Abu.

A story carved into a rock tells of Khnemu's power and importance. The legend begins during the 18th year of Pharaoh Djoser's reign.
For seven years, Egypt had not seen the Nile rise high enough and famine spread throughout the land. The people went hungry and the Pharaoh became distraught at the state of the land. Djoser summoned his
governor and questioned him about the source of the Nile and the deity
who ruled it. The governor explained that the Nile rose from a cavern
called Querti, at Abu, which was ruled by Khnemu. Here, the governor
explained, was a temple dedicated to Khnemu and offerings should be
made to this deity, as he was the one who opened the floodgates of the
Nile.

Djoser proceeded to make many offerings to Khnemu, seeking to
please him. Khnemu appeared and promised to make the Nile rise each
year at the same time it had risen previously. However, he named one
condition. His temple at Abu was being neglected; it seemed practically
abandoned. Khnemu required that Djoser restore the temple, in return
for his restoring the needed inundation. The Pharaoh repaired the dete-
riorating temple to the best of his abilities and passed a law consigning
land on both sides of the river near Abu to the temple of the Khnemu,
and he assigned priests to care for the renovated shrine. This royal decree was to be carved upon a stela to be displayed as a final token of
gratitude to Khnemu for ending the drought by bringing forth the
Nile's annual flood.

The entire event is inscribed upon a rock known as the "Famine
Stela," situated at the First Cataract of the Nile, where Khnemu was
believed to dwell. The story is set during the 3rd Dynasty, but the carving is believed to have been done during the Ptolemaic Era.

Khonsu (Khensu). A gentle lunar god depicted as mummified child
wearing the side lock of youth, with the lunar crescent as a crown.
Khonsu is the second adopted son of Amen and Mut and forming, with
them, the Triad of Uast. His name translates into "The Traveler" or
"The Wanderer," as he is a deity of the transitional moon. He also pos-
sesses healing virtues, as recounted in the following story.

During the reign of Ramses the Great, there lived a dazzling maiden in the land of Bekhten who was the eldest daughter of the prince. Her beauty was so great that she was compared to the gods. The Pharaoh, a great conqueror and used to having his way, desired to make her his wife. And so, in due course, he did, and named her Ra-Neferu ("The Beauties of Ra"). She assumed the duties of the Pharaoh's wife and together, they lived happily. There came a day during the 15th year of the pharaoh's long reign when a messenger brought word from the King of Bekhten, saying that the queen's younger sister, Bint-Reshet, had become ill. He begged the Pharaoh to send a skilled physician to heal his youngest daughter. Ramses II summoned the finest healer in the land and sent him forth to the land of Bekhten. However, before long the physician realized that he had no power over whatever illness, curse or demon was afflicting the queen's sister. The King of Bekhten once again sent forth a messenger to the Pharaoh; but this time he requested the powerful healing virtues of a deity. At this word, Ramses II went to the temple of Khonsu and prayed that the maiden's affliction would be banished. Legend has it that a statue of Khonsu arrived at Bekhten 17 months later. When the demon afflicting the princess was confronted by Khonsu, they made peace, and princess recovered her health.

The demon humbled himself to Khonsu but requested one favor before departing; the King of Bekhten was to arrange a grand festival honoring Khonsu — and the demon, as well. When the feast was over, the demon kept his word and returned whence he had come. However, anxiety preyed upon the mind of the king, as he feared the demon would return if the statue of Khonsu was returned to its origin in Egypt. The king kept the statue of Khonsu in Bekhten for three years, four months and five days, until it was returned to Egypt as a result of an ominous dream that will be discussed later. This story is inscribed upon a stela dated to 300 BC.

Ma'at, the personification of, and goddess of truth, justice, and harmony. Ma'at is the embodiment of law and universal order. She is a daughter of Ra and can be recognized by the white ostrich feather of truth she wears upon her head.

Maftet (Mafdet, Mefdet, Maldet), the lynx goddess who assisted Ra in overthrowing Apep. According to legend, Maftet befriended the deceased and offered protection against snakebites. Her name appears in the Pyramid Texts, as she destroys snakes with the strike of her sharp claws.

Menu (Min), the god of rain, vegetation, sexual powers, and male virility. Menu is one of the oldest of the Egyptian deities. He was offered lettuce, for the aphrodisiac properties it was believed to contain. Menu was venerated by those wishing for induced virility and fertility. Menu was venerated at Qebtu (Coptos).

Mertseger, the cobra goddess and Mistress of the West. Mertseger is a desert goddess and protectress against the feared serpents of that region. She is also depicted with the head of a falcon. Mertseger guarded over the Necropolis of Uast. Her name translates into "Beloved of Silence."

Montu (Monthu, Mentu), the hawk-headed or bull-headed god of war. Montu is the first adopted son of Amen and Mut and was worshipped at Per Montu (Hermonthis). His name translates into "Nomad."

Mut, the vulture goddess of the sky and another daughter of Ra. Mut is wife of Amen and mother of Khonsu. Her name translates into "Mother;" she was venerated as the "Divine Mother of All" and "Great Theban Mother."

Nebet-Het (Nephthys), the daughter of Geb and Nut, sister to Ausar and Auset and consort of Set. Her name translates into "Lady of the House." It is she who is believed to have fashioned the linen bandages for the mummy of Ausar. Nebet-Het was one of the four protective goddesses of the dead. She was worshipped in Upper Egypt alongside Set. The design of her crown spells out her name in hieroglyphs.

Nefertem (Nefertum), the lotus god of fragrance. He is a son of Ptah and Sekhmet (together they formed the Triad of Mennefer). Nefertem is connected with Ra, the solar god as the lotus opens its petals with the rising sun. He is believed to have emerged from the primeval waters of Nun. Nefertem is portrayed as a handsome young man and is identified by the crown of lotus flowers he wears upon his head. He is occasionally depicted with a head of a lion, in reference to his mother Sekh-met, a leonine deity. His name translates into "Beauty of Atem."

Nekhebet, the vulture goddess and wife of Hapi. It was Nekhebet who protected the pharaohs of Upper Egypt. She is also a goddess of childbirth. Nekhebet and Wadjet, who watched over Lower Egypt roy-alty, were known as *Nebti*, or "The Two Ladies."

Nit (Neith), a goddess of warfare and hunting. As one of the four protective goddess, Nit is also patroness of weavers. Her cult center was situated at Sau (Sais) and she is often depicted as a woman wear-ing the red crown of Lower Egypt. She is mother to Sobek, the croco-dile-headed god.

Nun, the god of the primordial waters from which all life was be-lieved to originate. Nun translates into "Abyss."

Nut (Nuit), the sky goddess and consort of Geb. Nut is also daugh-ter of the leonine deity Shu, and Tefnut. Her body was credited with creating and forming the sky, and therefore is often depicted in blue stretching above the earth. She is represented as a woman wearing a tight-fitting blue dress speckled with stars, representing the night sky. Nut is mother of Ausar, Auset, Nebet-Het and Set.

Pakhet (Pakht, Pekhet), the feline and leonine deity who watched over all Egyptians, dead or alive. Pakhet was identified as Artemis by the Greeks. Her name translates into "She Who Scratches," and is often associated with Sekhmet; she was considered to be an aspect of the lat-ter. Pharaoh Hatshepsut, of the 18th Dynasty, dedicated a temple to Pakhet.

Ptah, god of crafts, builders and artisans. Ptah ("The Opener") is one of the oldest and most beloved gods venerated in ancient Egypt. Ptah is the creator god of Mennefer and husband to Sekhmet. Like Khonsu, he was portrayed in mummified form. Followers of Ptah at Mennefer maintained that it was he who created mankind and all living creatures. From his mouth, he simply uttered the name of every living creature and thereby brought it into existence. Another myth says he created pet (the heavens) and ta (the earth), by the order of Tehuti. His name may be the result of a combination of the two words "pet" and "ta."

Qebsenuef (Kebsenuef). One of the sons of Heru, he guarded the deceased's intestines. Qebensenuef was protected by the scorpion goddess, Serqet. He is depicted as a falcon-headed mummified man who rules over the west.

Ra (Re). The falcon-headed solar god of creation. Ra is the father of kings and one of the most important deities, particularly in his cult center at Iunu (Heliopolis, meaning "City of the Sun" in Greek). He is regarded as the creator and is associated with the sun. Ra's followers believed that humanity and all life sprung from the tears of Ra as he wept over the creation and beauty of mankind. Without Ra or the sun he personifies, Egypt would exist in total darkness. It was believed that Ra was reborn at each dawn and died at sunset. Ra was recognized as a child at sunrise, a strong man in his prime at noon, and an old man as sunset approached. He came to be identified with Heru and was worshipped as Ra-Horakhty, translating into "Ra who is Heru of the Horizons."

Renenutet (Renenet), the cobra-headed goddess of good fortune, fertility and the harvest. Harvest festivals were held in Renenutet's honor; she was also a guardian during childbirth.

Satet (Sati, Satis), a goddess of fertility and of the Nile's annual inundation. Satet, either daughter or consort of Khnemu, and her sister or mother, Anqet, formed the Triad of Abu.

Seker (Soker, Socharis). Falcon-headed god of light as well as protector of the spirits who travel through the Underworld and the afterlife.

Seker is a major patron of funerary crafts and of builders in the Necropolis at Uast. Later, Seker was merged with Ptah and Ausar and was venerated as Ptah-Seker-Ausar. During the Middle Kingdom, Ptah-Seker-Ausar was worshipped as the personification of the Creator (Ptah), Stability (Seker) and Death (Ausar).

Sekhmet, a lioness goddess of war and destruction. Sekhmet is daughter of Ra, born from the fire of his solar eye as she punished mankind for its disloyalty and lack of respect for the aging Ra. Sekhmet is the dark side of Het-Heru and Bast, yet is unique in her own right. Sekhmet destroys in order to make way for progress. Sekhmet is also a goddess of healing as she banishes the evil that diseases bring. Her name translates into "She Who is Powerful." Wife of Ptah and mother of Nefertem, with them she completes the Triad of Mennefer.

Serqet (Selket). She is one of the four protective goddesses guarding the mummies' viscera. Serqet assisted in the birth of gods and pharaohs. She is also a goddess of magic. Serqet is recognized by the Scorpion perched upon her head. Her name translates into "She Who Relieves the Windpipe" or "She Who Causes to Breathe" as she provides protection from the deadly sting of the scorpion. Serqet stung the wicked and saved those pure of sin who were attacked by a scorpion.

Seshat. She is the goddess of writing, mathematics, architecture, record-keeping and measurements. Seshat is recognized by the tight-fitting leopard skin garment she wears as well as the seven-pointed star or seven-petalled flower placed upon her head. She is consort of Tehuti and her name translates into "Lady Scribe." Legend has it that she recorded the names and deeds of the pharaohs on the Tree of Life in order to grant them immortality. Seshat also calculated the days of the pharaoh's mortal existence by marking a notch for every year of his life on the palm branch that she carried.

Set (Sutekh, Seth). Portrayed as a dog, boar or donkey-headed man, Set is one of the most misunderstood of the ancient Egyptian gods. Brother of Ausar and Auset and consort to Nebet-Het, he was originally feared as murderer of Ausar; he was deified as a Lower Egypt god of chaos, storms, desert and of foreigners. Set was popular at Djanet (Tanis) and Nubet (Ombos) as well as with the Hyksos — he became their supreme deity. Set is also known as the Red God, as he is often depicted with red hair (the color representing evil, mourning and the desert region of the Red Land).

Shu, the lion-headed god of the air and the winds. Shu has a twin sister, Tefnut. The twins were believed to be the first human creation of Ra and were assimilated with the stars of Gemini. Shu is often portrayed wearing a feather upon his head and supporting Nut, the sky goddess. His name translates into "Dry" or "Parched."

Sobek (Sebek), the crocodile-headed god of fertility and of the waters. In funerary texts, Sobek is responsible for restoring the sense of sight to the deceased. He is son of Nit; his cult center was situated at Per-Sobek ("House of Sobek") or Crocodilopolis, "City of the Crododile," to the Greeks.

Taueret (Taweret, Thoueris, the hippopotamus goddess of childbirth and domesticity. Her name is believed to translate into "the Great One;" however, breaking down her name to *Ta* (earth or land) *Ur* (great) and *Et* (feminine ending) would indicate that her name means "She of the Great Land."

Tefnut, the lion-headed goddess of moisture and rain. She is twin to her brother Shu (wind) and mother of Nut (sky) and Geb (mountains/ earth). Tefnut is another daughter of Ra.

Tehuti (Thoth, Djehuty), the ibis- or baboon-headed lunar deity of writing, wisdom and literature. He is also known as the messenger and scribe to the gods. His cult center was at Per-Tehuti (Hermopolis, City of Hermes). In Greek mythology, he is identified with Hermes; in Roman mythology, he is Mercury. Tehuti is often seen carrying a pen and scroll. He is Vizier to Ausar and creator of hieroglyphic writing and of the calendar. As Tehuti was a lunar deity, he created the first calendar based on lunar phases; it was his duty to record time.

Wadjet (Uadjet, Edjo, Buto) is the cobra goddess and wife of Hapi. Wadjet was protectress of the kings of Lower Egypt. She is the counterpart of Nekhebet, both known as *Nebti* (one of the "Two Ladies"). Wadjet's name means "Green Lady;" she held dominion over the marshlands of Lower Egypt. That region and the goddess were called *Buto,* by the Greeks.

15. CREATION MYTHS

The Egyptians had various stories to explain how the world began, each defining their place in the universe; all the tales begin with the watery mass of the motionless dark sea of Nun. The major creative deities are Amen-Ra, Atem-Ra, (Ra-Atem) Khnemu and Ptah.

According to one legend, Ptah — the god of crafts — created mankind with his words and thoughts. Alteratively, Khnemu was credited with fashioning man from clay, using his celestial potter's wheel. The first man to be born created the first egg, from which the sun came forth and all life flowed. Khnemu placed such a wheel, or egg, inside every woman so that he would no longer be responsible for populating the earth. Another interpretation holds that Khnemu fashioned the *Kas* of every human on his great potter's wheel.

Another account, mentioned in the Pyramid Texts, names the Ogdoad or "Group of Eight" as creators of mankind. They consisted of four pairs of male and female deities embodying the primeval forces of nature. Nu and Nut brought forth the skies and rain, while Hehu and Hehut created fire. Darkness was attributed to Kekui and Kekuit and night and chaos were formed by Kerh and Kerhet. Other sources list the Ogdoad as being comprised of the deity pairs of Amen and Amenet, Nun and Naunet, with Hehu and Hehut, and Kekui and Kekuit.

According to one legend, at some time Shu, the god of air, and Tef-nut, the goddess of moisture, became separated from Atem-Ra. He then removed his eye and sent it forth to find his children. When the twins found their way back and returned with his eye, Atem-Ra wept for joy and from these tears, or *remyt*, mankind or *remet* (meaning man) was born. Another version says that Geb, the Great Cackler, created the universe as he laid the cosmic egg from which all life sprung.

At Iunu, during the Early Dynastic Era, nine deities known as the *Pesdjet* (or *Ennead*, in Greek) were established. According to this theory, the Pesdjet created the world. Just which gods were part of that elite clique is a matter of debate. Whichever list is correct, these deities are part of the most popular and widely accepted of the creation myths:

> Ra-Atem (or Heru, depending on which list you consult)
> Shu and Tefnut
> Geb and Nut
> Auset and Ausar
> Set and Nebet-Het

The most widely-accepted creation myth envisioned life as ema-nating from a giant lotus flower. The lotus was symbolic of resurrec-tion, as it embodied the continual cycle of rebirth, opening and closing each day. This sacred flower grew from a mound rising from the pri-mordial, dark, still Sea of Nun, which embraced the essence of all crea-tion. This parallels the notion that Egypt was born from water, the wa-ters of the Nile. It was believed that, as traces of land appeared after the Nile waters began to recede, the world and life itself sprang from a pri-meval mound arising from Nun, or chaos. The sacred mound, known as Ben-Ben, was thought to have been the very spot where a ray of sun first touched the earth at the moment known as *tep zepi* — the first time, or moment of creation. From this mound, Atem was born. The Ben-Ben, primordial mound of creation and source of all life, is the inspiration for the design of the pyramids.

A different version has the sun god Ra originating from a lotus flower or cosmic egg, which emerged from the primeval mound. By the 5th Dynasty, Atem was identified with Ra and was worshipped in the composite form of Atem-Ra. Ra or Atem-Ra created Shu, the god of air, and the winds began to blow. He then created Tefnut, goddess of mois-ture, and rain fell upon mankind. Their union brought forth Nut and Geb, forming the sky, the mountains and the earth. So much in love were Nut and Geb that Ra had to place Shu (air) between them in or-der to allow mankind to grow and reproduce. Another interpretation has Shu holding up the body of Nut to prevent the sky from falling. It was believed that Nut swallowed the sun each day at dusk and gave birth to it each dawn. During the hours of darkness, the sun was thought to travel on Ra's Solar Barque.

Ra was most ingenious — after all, he created the universe. His clever instincts warned him that it would be dangerous to have chil-dren by Nut, as one of them would come to betray him and end his reign over Egypt. Ra therefore uttered a spell, whereupon Nut was not able to bear children on any day of the Egyptian calendar. Other sources state that Ra was extraordinarily jealous of the relations be-tween Nut and Geb, and in a moment of anger, placed this curse upon the goddess he was so enamored of.

In grief and despair, Nut summoned Tehuti for help. Wise Tehuti suggested playing a game of dice, or senet, with Khonsu. The lunar god Khonsu wagered a portion of his own light, and eventually lost. Tehuti claimed this light for himself; he gathered it and formed five extra days of the year; they were appended to the end of the calendar. These five sacred days are known as the "Epagomenal Days." On the first of these holy days, Nut gave birth to Ausar, followed by Heru-Ur on the second day, Set on the third, Auset on the fourth day and Nebet-Het on the fifth and last day. These five gods, with Shu, Tefnut, Geb and Nut, com-plete the Pesdjet or Great Gods of Iunu (Heliopolis). As Khonsu had lost a portion of his light, he was not able to shine throughout the en-tire month. His light now had to dim into total darkness before it could increase again to full brilliance, and that is how we came to see the phases of the moon.

Relations within that family of deities were far from trouble-free. So in love with Ausar was Nebet-Het that she disguised herself as Auset one evening and went to see him; some sources say she intoxi-cated Ausar with wine, until he was unable to differentiate between his sister-in-law, Nebet-Het, and his consort Auset. From this union was born Anpu, the "Royal Child." Auset taught the people of Egypt the value of wheat and barley and showed them how to make and use agricultural equipment. He showed the people how to plant seeds and grow crops, taking advantage of the Nile's annual inundation that left behind a rich fertile mud ideal for growing food. Ausar and Auset taught the people how to plant vines and produce grapes, and transform them into wine. Ausar gave them the ways of a civilized nation by establishing a code of laws, under Ma'at, to live by. And he showed them how to express their gratitude by worshipping the gods. The people were deeply content, and Egypt prospered.

The more Ausar was adored and exalted by his people, the more jealous and wrathful his brother Set grew. Perhaps Nebet-Het's affair with Ausar was discovered and triggered his untimely demise. During Ausar's 28th year of reign, he fell victim to a murder plot devised by Set and 72 conspirators. While Ausar was away showing other lands the way to a prosperous and fulfilling life, Auset took his place — something she was capable of doing both efficiently and successfully. However, the treacherous wheels of Set's plan were already in motion, and in anticipation of Ausar's return to Egypt, he planned a great banquet in his brother's honor. Discreetly, Set obtained the precise measurements of Ausar's body, and had the finest artisans construct the most magnificent sarcophagus ever seen — to the exact shape and size of Ausar's body. The casket was built from the finest cedar from Byblos and inlaid with precious ivory and ebony from the land of Punt. When Ausar returned and the banquet was held, the elaborate coffin was displayed — and offered as a gift to the guest whom it fit best. Given the cultural focus on fine funerary accessories, this would have been a rich gift indeed.

Ausar was entirely unaware of the malicious conspiracy, as nothing but goodness flowed through his veins. During the banquet, a few carefully selected men lay down inside the coffin. One was too tall, one was too short, one was too broad — and so it was suggested (as planned) that the Pharaoh himself take a turn inside the magnificent coffin. Ausar merrily agreed, and was quite pleased when he realized that the elaborate box fit him perfectly — until it was slammed shut, nailed tight, and sealed with molten lead by the 72 conspirators, who then cast it into the waters of the Nile.

Auset cut off a lock of her hair and donned her mourning apparel when she heard of her husband's fate. Her grief was all-consuming, and she set out in search of the treacherous chest containing the body of her husband; she knew that, without the body, he could not be given the proper burial guaranteeing immortality. To the ancient Egyptians, the tears Auset shed for her husband became symbolic of the annual inundation of the Nile. Frantically, she searched for her husband and questioned everyone she encountered along the way. Children who had been playing by the Nile revealed that they had seen a spectacular chest floating upon the waters of the *Wadj Wer*, meaning the "Great Green" or Mediterranean Sea. So grateful was Auset that she instantly blessed the children of Egypt with the gift of prophecy.

The mighty waves cast the sarcophagus into the branches of a tamarisk tree that lay upon the shores of Byblos. The tree sprouted enormous limbs, so immense that the chest they covered was soon hidden from view. However, this extraordinary tree caught the eye of King Malcander of Byblos, who ordered it to be cut down and carved into a pillar to adorn his great palace — blissfully ignorant of what lay inside it. Meanwhile, Auset desperately continued her quest throughout the lands. She eventually came into the knowledge that her husband's body was imprisoned in a towering pillar at King Malcander's palace. Nothing daunted, Auset devised a plan to earn the confidence of the King's maidens, and thereby gain entry into the royal palace: Auset walked to the seashore, and sat down to rest where the maidens of the palace went to bathe each day. When the young girls came out of the water, Auset appeared and taught them how to braid their hair and breathed upon them the sweetest perfume that emanated from her breath. The disguised Queen of Egypt and the young ladies spent a delightful afternoon together. When the girls returned to the palace, Queen Astarte smelled their fragrance and admired their lovely new hairstyles. The Queen demanded to know where these refinements had come from, and then insisted on meeting the mysterious woman of whom the young ladies spoke so highly. Auset was brought to the palace and quickly befriended Queen Astarte, who entrusted to her the position of nurse to her son, the young prince. The child was sickly and Auset nursed him back to health by suckling him with her finger.

One night, Auset took the form of a swallow, and decided to grant the child (of whom she had grown so fond) the gift of everlasting life. As she was about to cast the young prince into the fire (so as to do away with his mortal parts), she was stopped by Queen Astarte, who was secretly standing by. The Queen leaped forward and caught her son, just in time to break the magic of the ritual. Auset revealed her true form and showed her mighty anger to the Queen who had deprived the child of immortality. The Queen fell to her knees when she realized that the "nurse" was actually the great Queen of Egypt. As a peace offering, the royal couple of Byblos offered Auset the richest of treasures of their land. Auset replied that her only wish was to find the body of Ausar, and that she had been told that it would be found enveloped in one of the king's prized wooden pillars. Her wish was immediately granted and, identifying the likely candidate, Auset had a pillar cut open — and there was the precious chest. She threw herself upon it with such a tremendous wail of sorrow that another young prince, standing by, died of terror at the very sound. Auset transported the chest back to Egypt.

When Set got word of this success, he flew into a rage. He located the chest and cut Ausar's body into fourteen pieces, and threw them to the crocodiles of the Nile. However, the crocodiles attacked neither the body of Ausar nor the papyrus boat that transported Auset, as she renewed her search for her husband; and that is why the crocodile, feared as it was, was also venerated in ancient Egypt. (Another version has it that a crocodile carried the body of Ausar on its back safely to the shore.)

Thus, once again, Auset began her grief-stricken quest for her husband's remains. Although Nebet-Het was consort of Set, she remained loyal to Ausar and Auset — perhaps out of love, or guilt regarding her evening with Ausar that resulted in the birth of Anpu. With the assistance of Nebet-Het and Anpu, Auset, as Mistress of Magic and goddess of healing, gathered the pieces that had washed up along the riverbanks and re-assembled the body. Wherever a piece of Ausar's body was found, a shrine was built in his honor; and that is reason why there are so many shrines to Ausar throughout Egypt. Legend has it that his head was found in Abedju (Abydos), which came to be the Holy City of the Dead, dedicated to the worship of Ausar. Every piece of his body was recovered except for the reproductive organ, which was believed to have been swallowed by a fish of the Nile. For this reason, the Nile was considered especially fertile and life-giving, while fish was regarded by many as "unclean" and forbidden to eat.

Anpu, god of embalming and guardian of the necropolis, performed the mummification process and the ritual required for the resurrection of Ausar. Ausar became the first mummy, and was now able to travel through the *Duat* into *Amenti*, where as he became Lord of the Underworld. With the help of her sister Nebet-Het, Auset magically fashioned a replacement for the missing organ and conceived a child with Ausar. The child was named Heru-Sa-Auset and was secretly raised by his mother, without Set's knowledge.

The child grew in strength until he was capable of avenging his father's death; at this point, he became Heru. A series of battles ensued between Heru and Set, who took the form of a huge black pig; since then, the pig was also considered "unclean" and many considered it unfit for human consumption. During one of these combats, Heru became enraged with his mother when she accidentally harpooned her son instead of Set. Other versions states that, in one brief moment, Auset felt sorry for her brother who was about to be defeated by Heru. In a moment of rage, Heru cut off Auset's head; so she reached for the first head she could find, which was that of a cow. And so the cow-headed goddess Het-Heru was born, as an aspect of Auset. Sometimes this tale says it was the royal insignia on Auset's crown, not her head, that Heru ripped off in anger. Tehuti then replaced the insignia with a helmet made of an ox's head, and she became the gentle Het-Heru, consort of Heru. Whether Het-Heru was born from Heru's anger or from Sekhmet's appeasement is for the reader to consider and decide.

In the final battle, Set disguised himself as a huge red hippopotamus. Heru took the form a giant man, armed with a harpoon thirty feet long. Heru struck Set with this harpoon, finally ending his life. It is said that this, the last battle between good and evil, took place at Behdety (Edfu), where a great temple in Heru's honor was erected. Heru became the Great Avenger, protector of the gods and lord of the sky, daylight, and order. The defeated Set became god of storms, desert, foreigners, confusion, chaos and the night. Ausar was assigned the role of god of resurrection and Judge of the Dead, while Anpu remained the god of embalming and mummification, and lord of the necropolis.

16. Animal Worship

One of the most fascinating aspects of ancient Egyptian culture is the multitude of animals they revered and personified in the pantheon of gods. Almost every known animal was held sacred and was believed to possess the spirit of one's ancestors and the qualities of the particular deity it embodied; and nearly every deity was represented and embodied by a specific animal.

Like pharaohs, certain animals were perceived as intermediaries between man and gods. Animals, as incarnations of deities, were offered gifts in exchange for favors from the god in question. There were special cemeteries exclusively devoted to specific species, like the animal necropolis located at Saqqara. Sometimes animals, like humans, were mummified and "went west" when their time on earth had been completed. However, other animals' lives were cut short, as they were chosen as sacrificial offerings in funerary ceremonies.

Live sacred animals were maintained in luxurious condition in the temples, where they were pampered by the priesthood. Hap, the Apis Bull, was recognized by its coloring. When one such animal died, another of the same breed was identified. The bull had to be purely black, with a white diamond shape on its forehead. Other special markings

included the figure of an eagle on the animal's back, the shape of a beetle on its tongue, and a tail of double hairs. When the new bull was
selected, he was venerated as the new Hap, sacred bull of Mennefer,
and underwent a 40-day preparation ritual attended only by women.

Legend has it that Hap was conceived by a virgin cow during a
lightning storm. His birthday was celebrated grandly, with a seven-day
festival. As Hap grew past his prime (around the age of 25), the bull
was sacrificed, and drowned by the priests in the sacred waters of the
Nile. This was followed by a lavish burial and a 70-day mourning period. Hap was entitled to the same mummification process and rituals
as the pharaoh. Hap was also entombed with all the provisions required for the afterlife. When Hap died, he became associated with
Ausar, and during Ptolemaic times he was merged with the god of resurrection and worshipped as Ausar-Hap (or Serapis, as the Greeks
named him). There was a vast underground cemetery especially reserved for consecrated mummified bulls. This catacomb is known as
the Serapeum of Saqqara.

Twenty-four stone sarcophagi containing bulls from the 18th Dynasty have been unearthed in the Serapeum. Each sarcophagus was elegantly crafted from a single block of granite, weighing more than 80
tons. The mother of the Apis Bull was also venerated and buried in special chambers situated north of the Serapeum. At least since the 26th
Dynasty, the mother was also regarded as divine and worthy of the
most honorable life and death. Oxen without a single black hair or spot
were often sacrificed to Hap; other sacred bulls were Mer-Ur (Mnevis),
who was worshipped at Iunu, and Bakha (Bachis), venerated at Per-
Montu (Hermonthis).

Cows, because of their association with Het-Heru, were highly
exalted and were considered divine. Upon their natural death, these
sacred animals were cast into the holy waters of the Nile. Pigs and
boars were forbidden as food and were feared in certain districts of
Egypt. The pig was detested due to its association with the unpopular
god Set. In legend, Set took upon the form of a huge black hog and appeared thus to Ra and Heru. The hog shot a bolt of fire into the left
(lunar) eye of Heru, and blinded him. Tehuti was called upon to heal

his eye, and this action was symbolically immortalized each month by the waxing (healing and restoration of the eye) and waning (losing the eye) of the moon. Ra placed a curse on the pig, and therefore, one animal at least was not to be revered. Historians tell us that any Egyptian whose garment touched a pig was immediately cast into the Nile for purification. There is also some evidence that upon every full moon, a boar was sacrificed in the name of Heru.

Anpu, protector of the dead and guardian of the necropolis, was depicted in a jackal form. This particular animal roamed the graveyards and as a result became associated with death. Dogs held an affinity with jackals and were very popular as hunting companions, particularly the greyhound. Dogs were often kept as faithful pets and loyal watchdogs. When one died, the family members shaved their entire heads and bodies. Often, beloved pet dogs were buried alongside their master. In Kasa (Cynopolis, in Greek — "City of the Dogs"), they were held sacred. Dogs also had a special bond with Auset, who was cosmically associated with Sopdet (Sirius, or Sothis, the Dog Star), which cosmically personified her soul. Duamutef, one of the four sons of Heru, was depicted with the head of a dog or a jackal.

In ancient Egypt, they had even more reason than other societies to fear the wolf: it was a mortal enemy to the ram, sacred animal of Amen, King of Gods, and Khnemu, a creator god. However, in Zawty (Lycopolis, in Greek — "City of Wolves"), wolves were worshipped, and many of their mummies were buried in tombs in the mountains above this city.

The snake, too, was both feared and worshipped. This reptile served as a symbol of eternity, as it forms a circle biting its own tail, and it embodies the concept of survival, renewal and resurrection as it sheds its own skin. Several deities are depicted in snake-form. Mersteger and Wadjet are cobra-headed goddesses (sometimes represented by serpents), as well as Heka and Weret Hekau. Apep, the giant serpent god of the Underworld, symbolized darkness and the primeval forces of chaos. Apep was regarded as a most dangerous enemy of Bast and of Ra. Mehen was a snake god who protected Ra from Apep while traveling on his solar barque across the sky each night.

The hare symbolized acute sensitivity and heightened awareness. Wennefer, a form or aspect of Ausar, was depicted as a hare.

The giraffe, due to its height and ability to see high above, embodied higher knowledge and foresight. Giraffes were not native to Egypt but were imported from Nubia.

The crocodile was sacred to the deity Sobek, yet others hunted this animal for sport. In the town of Per Sobek (House of Sobek) also known as Shet (or Crocodilopolis) was the cult center of this aquatic reptile and many mummified crocodiles were discovered there. It has been documented that in Lake Maoeris and at Uast, crocodiles were pampered and were considered most sacred; the crocodile forbore to attack Auset on her boat of papyrus as she searched for the body of Ausar, and this was not forgotten by the people of Egypt. Still, others regarded the crocodile as the embodiment of evil, as an ally of Set.

The hippopotamus symbolized female fecundity. The goddesses Apet and Taueret, later known as Reret, were depicted in the form of hippopotami. Amment, the Devourer of Souls of the judgment scene, is one-third hippopotamus. However, there were some who believed this animal too was league with Set, and possessed some of his dark qualities, and hippos were also hunted for sport.

Frogs were sacred to the goddess Heqet, who was worshipped as fertility goddess of rebirth. The scorpion was venerated and personified in Serqet, the protective goddess of deceased royalty.

The Sting

One evening, Auset was traveling in disguise with her son Heru-Sa-Auset and his companions, the Seven Scorpions. Seeking shelter for the night, they came upon the home of a nobleman. The wife was frightened by the Seven Scorpions and hastily closed her door they approached her house. Auset, Heru-Sa-Auset and the Seven Scorpions were offended and the scorpions in particular were set on taking revenge.

Meanwhile, a humble peasant girl opened the doors to her sparse abode and welcomed Auset and her retinue. During the course of the night, one of the scorpions slipped out of the girl's home, made its way to the estate of the noblewoman, and crawled into the house where it stung her son and then proceeded to set the building on fire. The child's mother roamed the streets, begging for help and for a cure for her son. Auset heard the women's deafening cries and took pity on the woman and her innocent son, who should not have had to pay for his mother's rude behavior. Since knowing someone's name conferred power over him, Auset learnt the names of the Seven Scorpions. She took the child in her arms and named the Seven Scorpions, one by one, and the poison tormenting the youngster's body departed. The noblewoman was grateful, and embarrassed by her own lack of hospitality toward Auset and the scorpions. The peasant girl, however, was rewarded with fine gifts.

Birds and bees

Bees were symbolic of Lower Egypt, as they represented the tears of Ra. For this reason, honey was sanctified; and it was recognized as a potent and effective healing agent in medicinal magic.

Birds were consecrated and regarded as the souls of deity. The more superstitious considered the sparrow, and the sight of a dead bird, to be ill omens. The falcon (known as *bik*), or hawk, was highly sacred due to its relation to Heru. When the falcon spread its wings, its symbolized a holy act of prayer, guidance and protection. The Ba was depicted as a human-headed falcon hovering above the body of the mummy. The cult center of the hawk was situated at Nekhen (Hierakonpolis in Greek, meaning "City of the Hawk").

The vulture, due to its connection to Nekhebet, was highly re-garded, particularily in Upper Egypt. The goddesses Mut and Nit were also incarnations of the sacred vulture. As the Bennu Bird or Phoenix, it was worshipped as an aspect of the sun. To the ancient Egyptians, the self-created phoenix embodied resurrection.

The divine ibis was a symbol of wisdom and mental concentra-tion. This animal was likely chosen to represent the god of writing, Te-huti, as the bird's beak resembles a reed pen pointing downwards as if to write. The ibis was believed to be the incarnation of Tehuti. Thousands were bred to be embalmed and offered as sacrifice to him; mummified ibises were found at Tehuti's cult center at Per Khnemu (Hermopolis, City of Hermes — the Greek equivalent of Tehuti).

As a result of their curious nature, the baboon and ape became associated with Tehuti as well, and symbolized mental aptitude. Asten is a form of Tehuti depicted as a baboon. Hapy, another son of Heru, is portrayed with the head of a baboon as he protects the lungs of the deceased in the Canopic Jars. These animals were bred and maintained in temples in honor of Tehuti. Monkeys were often kept as pets; this animal was also trained to gather fruit from high treetops, as illustrations have revealed. Monkeys were also trained to serve as torch-bearers at banquets, and were lined up outside the home to light the way for the departing guests.

Feline companions

The lion was admired for its strength and its fearlessness. Lions seem to have been portrayed as guardians, as the great Sphinx, in its lion form, guards the Pyramids of Giza. The Egyptians often placed statues of lions at the doors of their homes, palaces and temples for protection against evil. Lions were not to be hunted, unless they were from a foreign land. Amenhotep III boasted of killing 102 lions in Syria with his bow and arrow within a ten-year span. Ramses II and III often took a tame lion by their sides, whether heading into battle or on a hunting expedition. A battle scene on the outer walls of the mortuary temple of Ramses III at Medinet Habu shows the Pharaoh charging ahead in his chariot, escorted by a brave lion. Lions also protect the light-giving sun, and in astrology, the sun rules over the sign of Leo, the lion.

Sekhmet, Shu, Tefnut, Aker, Nefertem, and Menhyt were leonine deities. Lions were sacred at Iunu (Heliopolis, Greek for "City of the Sun") for its solar association. Lions were also highly venerated in Nay-Ta-Hut (Leontopolis), situated a few miles south of the other major feline cult center, Per Bast (Bubastis, meaning "House of Bast" in Egyptian and "City of Bast," in Greek) which flourished c. 3200 BC.

The ancient Egyptians were fascinated by cats (or *miw*, as they were called). Cats were the most beloved animal of all, and it was here that, over 4000 years ago, the cat became domesticated. Cats were regarded as mystical creatures who came to be much more than just pets or companions. When the family cat died, everyone in the household shaved his (or her) eyebrows as a sign of mourning. The body was mummified and brought to the necropolis at Per Bast. The death penalty could be incurred by anyone who killed a cat, even if by accident. Cats often accompanied their masters on bird-hunting expeditions (as seen in funerary illustrations). Cats were held in high respect not only because of their agility and diligence in chasing away the mice that destroyed supplies of grain, but because they were fearless and clever enemies of Apep. Rechet was a cat goddess and legend has it that Mafdet, the lynx, climbed the Persea Tree of Iunu and slew Apep; this has been depicted in funerary illustrations. In the *Papyrus of Hunefer*, Mafdet is shown just about to behead a subdued Apep with a large knife. Cats were well rewarded with food, shelter and affection in return for their valuable company and services.

17. Symbolism

A rich symbolic imagery was used throughout the history of Egypt. Symbols were illustrated on papyri, funerary reliefs, sarcophagi, jewelry, amulets, obelisks, and temple and palace walls, where they served a decorative purpose as well, but their primary duty was spiritual, religious and magical in nature.

The most popular, oldest and most recognizable Egyptian symbol is the *Ankh*, representing eternal life, the goal of their whole existence. The circle represented the sun and the cross signified earth; combined, the Ankh symbolized the union between god and man, heaven and earth. The solar deity Aten was often portrayed as a glowing sun with outstretched rays terminating in the symbols of life, Ankhs. This particular depiction was symbolic of mankind's being enveloped by the life-giving solar rays of Aten. Worn by royalty, the Ankh empowered the pharaoh with protection and eternal life. Mirrors, also called "ankh," were most often crafted into the shape of the symbol they were named after. The early Christians of Egypt adopted the Ankh as their holy cross, later replaced by the various forms of the Christian cross as it is known today.

The symbol of the Left Eye, the sign of Heru, or *Wadjet*, often adorned tomb entrances and sarcophagi in order to enable the deceased to "look out." The Wadjet became a potent symbol of healing and supreme wholeness when worn as an amulet — by the deceased, as well as by the living.

The right eye is known as the Solar Eye of Ra. Legend has it that Ra sent his right eye into the darkness of the earth to search for Shu and Tefnut. Lighting up the darkness, his eye became the powerful Solar Eye of Ra. Often, the eye of Heru and of Ra are shown together, conveying the message of healing (through Heru's eye) and protection (from the goddess Sekhmet, who came forth from the Solar Eye of Ra).

The lotus blossom (or *seshen*, as it was known) represented rejuvenation and rebirth. This was the only flower held sacred; it emerges from underwater and open up its petals with the rising of the sun. Symbolically, the lotus was a solar symbol of creation; it was believed that Ra was born from a gigantic lotus flower. It was thought that Ra could not exist without breathing in the delicate fragrance of the lotus flower, and certain pharaohs seem to have been buried with petals of the blue lotus so that they might enjoy the fragrance eternally. Other accounts have Nefertem, the lotus god of fragrance, offering lotus flowers to Ra in order to soothe him and ease his suffering. Illustrations of lotus blossoms were used to decorate chalices, tiles, vases, jewelry, chests, funerary equipment and mirrors, and it is a highly visible in Egyptian architecture, where the symbol adorned temples, palaces and pillars.

The papyrus, the heraldic plant of Lower Egypt, symbolized the world rising from the primeval marshes. In legend, it was believed that towering pillars of papyrus sustained the sky. A majestic pillar decorated with the lotus emblem and another with the papyrus symbol was erected by Tuthmose II c. 1475 BC at Karnak. Colossal columns topped with the shape of a papyrus plant were often illustrated on murals as symbols of omnipotence and strength. When worn as an amulet, the lotus was believed to bestow eternal youth and everlasting joy upon the wearer. The lotus and papyrus intertwined were emblematic of the unification or embracing of the Two Lands, Upper and Lower Egypt. This insignia, known as *sma taui* or *tawi*, was often shown on temples, palaces, boats and thrones.

The third emblematic plant of ancient Egypt was the sedge (*swt*, or *nswt*). As far back as the 1st Dynasty, the sedge plant symbolized Upper Egypt and the royalty. Sometimes it was shown together with the symbol of a bee, or *bity*, representing Lower Egypt, and the two were incorporated into one of the pharaoh's titles, designating him as ruler of Upper and Lower Egypt.

The *Shen* symbolized infinity, eternity, as it has no beginning and no end. The word "shen" comes from *shenu*, "that which encircles." The shen is the origin of the cartouche, the protective oval frame enclosing the name of the pharaoh. (The word "cartouche" is French for cartridge; this name was given by Napoleon' s soldiers as the Shen resembled the rifle shells they used.) The perfect circle was elongated to fit the name, and enabled the spirit to live as long as the inscription remained undis turbed. During the New Kingdom, royal sarcophagi were constructed in the form of a cartouche in order to protect the body and ensure immortality. The sacred vulture is often shown clutching the Shen within its claws.

The *Sa* symbol represented protection during childbirth. The goddess Taueret is often depicted resting her paw on this symbol, as she is a guardian deity during births.

Akhet is the symbol of the horizon, with the sun shown rising or setting between the two mountain peaks. This symbol held major cosmic significance for the ancient Egyptians. The sun was perceived as "the guardian" who watched over the mountains that supported the heavens. The symbol and hieroglyph for "mountain" (or *djw*) is the Akhet glyph without the circle representing the Sun.

Nub doubles as the word and symbol for gold, the divine metal and flesh of the gods. It represented immortality and royalty as well as solar power.

As the concept of rebirth was at the core of Egyptian religion and beliefs, many symbols incorporated the idea of resurrection. One of the most popular symbols of rebirth, going back to the Old Kingdom, was the scarab beetle, which was worshipped as a self-created deity, Khepera. He is often depicted as a human with a head of the scarab beetle. Beetle eggs not having been discovered by ancient Egyptian entomologists, when the scarab emerged from the earth it seemed to be bringing itself into this world; it thus came to embody the notion of perpetual self-renewal. Its birth was also symbolic of the sun commencing its diurnal voyage across the sky; the beetle rolls balls of dung and mud for food, and this behavior became a metaphor for the "daily rolling of the sun across the sky." Till this day, Egyptian women who wish to give birth to large families will dry, pound and mix scarab beetles with water, and drink it as a potion to induce fertility.

Many styles of scarabs were produced as amulets. By the First Intermediate Period, the flat underside of the scarab amulet began to be decorated as well. Such scarabs were available to rich and poor alike, as they came to be mass-produced. Scarabs, like most amulets, were made from semi-precious stones, hard stones, glass, glazed pottery and limestone. Faience scarabs were in great demand during the New Kingdom, and they were incorporated into bracelets, pendants, rings and necklaces.

Winged scarabs were meant to guarantee a safe passage into the Underworld. Heart scarabs were intended to prevent any evil from surfacing while the deceased stood before the Courts of Ausar; often, spells were inscribed to help make the heart truthful when weighed against the feather of Ma'at. Placing an amulet of the scarab beetle over the heart of a mummy was believed to guarantee rebirth and eternal existence to the deceased.

Amenhotep III inscribed and communicated news and important events on the underside of the scarab, such as the slaying of over 100 lions during his first decade as pharaoh. Scarab amulets were inscribed not only with pharaonic victories but with marriage announcements and commemorations. In addition, magical scarabs were inscribed with wishes or spells on the flat underside. On the underside of one amulet is a scene of Tuthmose I defeating the Hyksos ruler, Ipepi, during the 18th Dynasty.

The Winged Solar Disk was often inscribed above temple entrances. Placed over the name of a pharaoh, it designated him as victorious. Legend has it that Tehuti transformed Heru into a solar disk with outstretched wings at its side when he conquered the Nubians, and Heru was instructed by Tehuti to place winged solar disks upon the entrance to every temple of Egypt to commemorate this event and provide protection from enemies.

The *Tet* or "Knot of Isis" resembles the shape of the Ankh, however its arms are bent downward. The Tet is also called the "Blood of Isis," or the "Girdle of Isis." Legend has it that Auset hid Heru from Set by tying her girdle around him, covering and protecting the child. The Tet came to embody protection, and was worn as an amulet made of red glass or stones such as garnet and carnelian.

The *Djed* represents the backbone of Ausar, symbolizing stability and strength. The four arms of the cross stand for each of the cardinal directions. As an amulet, it was often worn by the living and was also placed upon the neck of the deceased. The Tet was often portrayed with the Djed column symbolizing the divine couple and their combined power. The Djed was thought to contain protective and strengthening virtues. It was also symbolic of the sacred tamarisk tree that enveloped and guarded the chest containing the body of Ausar.

The tamarisk tree was held sacred in honor of Ausar, and others also carried symbolic significance and therefore were revered in ancient Egypt. The Persia Tree of Iunu, with its magical leaves, symbolized protection and the afterlife; it was sacred due to its association with Bast. According to myth, Bast resided in the Persea Tree, called *ished* in Egyptian, when she slew the giant serpent god Apep. It was believed that immortality was granted to the pharaoh whose name was inscribed by Tehuti or Sheshat upon a leaf of this sacred tree.

The sycamore tree was also highly venerated, for the souls of the departed dwelled and rested in this tree. The sycamore, called *nehet* in Egyptian, was symbolic of the home of Het-Heru, also known as "The Lady of the Sycamore." Another legend tells how Het-Heru hid within the sycamore tree and provided nourishment by pouring water out of a vase for the recently and confused departed as she helped them climb the ladder to heaven. In the *Papyrus of Ani*, Het-Heru is shown offering food and drink to the deceased Ani, from a sycamore tree by a stream. The sycamore tree was also sacred to the sky goddess Nut, whose Ka dwelled in this tree.

The palm tree was symbolic of fertility and associated with such deities as Ra, Nut and Het-Heru.

Royalty was surrounded and protected by myriad symbols. The Flail or whip was a tool for thrashing wheat, but when held in the left hand of a pharaoh, it represented the fertility and prosperity of the land. The Crook or shepherd's staff projected leadership, guidance and protection over the pharaoh's people. The Crook was called *Heka* and, when held in the right hand, embodied the idea of rulership. The Heka was not exclusive to pharaohs and deities but was also conferred upon high officials, magicians and priests. In magic, it was used to conjure the energy and power of the gods during ceremonies, rituals and festivals. The Crook and Flail worn crossed over the chest of a pharaoh displayed his kingship, power and guidance. Ausar is most often seen in this royal pose.

The *Waas* scepter symbolized pharaonic power and dominion over the people. The Waas staff is believed to represent Set, whom it resembles.

The most visual symbol of royalty and power was the crown of the pharaoh. At least 20 royal crowns have been identified, worn by men, women and deities. Different crowns were donned for special occasions. Crowns were elaborately gilded and decorated with carnelians as well as inlaid with semi-precious stones. The tall white cone-shaped crown (known as *Hedjet*, meaning "white") represents the dominion of Upper Egypt. The Red Crown (called *Deshret*, meaning "red," and "desert") represents Lower Egypt. Combining these two crowns into one elaborate crown is the *Pschent* or the "Double Crown." Wearing the Pschent signified the union of both Upper and Lower Egypt and dominion over both. Narmer was the first pharaoh depicted wearing the Pschent, as he was the first king to unify the Two Lands in 3100 BC.

The *Atef* crown is comprised of the Hedjet crown of Upper Egypt ending in a solar disk with a red feather on each side. It is most commonly seen worn by Ausar. The feathers represent the city Per Ausar, also known as Djedu (Busiris), where his cult center in the Delta was situated.

The *Khepresh* crown is also known as the "Blue Crown" and "War Crown." This crown was donned during military expeditions, campaigns, state occasions, and victorious processions. The blue Khepresh was made of electrum and most often seen protecting the head of Ramses the Great.

The *Nemes* was the royal headdress or kerchief, fashioned out of linen decorated with blue and gold stripes. It is most recognizable when seen on the head of the Sphinx and on the famous bust of King Tutankhamen. The Nemes was fastened with a gold band tucked behind the ears and was often adorned with the Uraeus symbol above the brow.

The sacred cobra or royal Uraeus, when shown in a rearing position and worn over the brow, signified protection against all evil. Legend has it that the Uraeus provided protection against, and destruction, of enemies by spitting fire. The cobra was emblematic of wisdom, power, royalty and divinity.

The Uraeus also represented the serpent head of the Wadjet, snake goddess of Lower Egypt. Often, the Uraeus was used together with the vulture, symbolic of Nekhebet, goddess of Upper Egypt; in tandem, they embodied the Two Ladies and offered protection to the wearer. The snake was as highly visible symbol of royalty and regeneration, as it sheds its own skin and renews itself.

In Greco/Roman mythology, the god Hermes, or Mercury (Tehuti), cast his majestic wand against two fighting serpents. They immediately ceased fighting and coiled themselves around the staff, symbolizing reconciliation. Hermes' Staff or the Wand of Mercury became the Caduceus, the symbol of the medical profession consisting of two serpents entwined around a staff and surmounted by two wings.

The false beard, worn only by pharaohs and deities, signified vitality, kingship, virility and cosmic attributes. The pharaonic beard indicated that he was not of this world; and the length of the beard varied according to the pharaoh's level of power. On King Tutankhamen's spectacular royal funerary mask, the blue and gold striped Nemes headdress, royal false beard, rearing Uraeus and protective vulture above the brow are all displayed.

Colors conveyed symbolic meaning too, providing further clues to help us interpret illustrations. Green represented vegetation, rebirth, growth, health and joy — Ausar is often depicted in green, as he was originally an earth god of vegetation, before he died and was resurrected as the Lord of the Dead. Black was the color of death and the Underworld. Ausar and Anpu are most often shown in black, due to their associations with funerary events. Red stood for victory, vitality, life, anger, fire and mourning. It was believed that Set had red hair and red eyes, and so red became a color associated with evil and the feared desert. White expressed sanctity, as it does today, and omnipotence and purity. Blue was symbolic of cosmic spirituality and a god depicted in blue was displaying his celestial qualities — priests were often drawn in blue. Gold was especially valued as it was the color of the eternal life-giving sun, and symbolized the flesh of Ra.

18. The Priesthood

The entire civilization of ancient Egypt was based upon religion, and the laws and beliefs deriving therefrom. Potential priests underwent heavy training and discipline to become "servants of the gods." The priests were recruited by the pharaoh at an early age, and exclusively from the best of families. In fact, most priests inherited their position from their fathers. It was the priest's duty to be completely knowledgeable in all matters of religion and to maintain the temple in good order. These sanctuaries of the gods were called *Per Ankh* ("house of life").

Egypt had three religious centers, located at Mennefer, Uast and Iunu. These were homes to the three creator deities, Ptah, Amen, and Ra. Each city housed a temple for the specific deity worshipped in that region. These temples were surrounded by high walls, for here was the home of the gods. Only a few privileged men could enter, so that openings were made in the walls to permit communication between the holy men and the common worshipper. On the outer walls of the temples there were specially reserved places where the commoner was able to whisper his prayer, wish or question into a depiction of an ear. This "ear" was symbolic of the enhanced ability of the deity who was listening. Alternatively, one might inscribe a prayer on papyrus and leave it for the gods. The priests would receive the note and bringing the matter to the deity's attention.

Commoners — except for the blind — were not permitted inside the temples; gods were not be seen by common folk. However, there were special "sleep temples," where customers could spend the night and hope for a cure for an illness or answer to a problem. Otherwise, the commoner could only approach the gods through shrines set up in their homes and during processions in religious festivals, from the limits of the holy courtyard. During these festivals, the sacred statues, in their shrines, were carried outside the temple grounds so that the gods could communicate with the people through their images.

The shrine (called a *Naos*) was kept in the innermost chamber of the temple. This was the home of the stone, wooden or golden statue of the deity, the receptacle of the god's Ka. The shrine was the holiest part of the temple, where only the priests who bore the title of highest rank were permitted to enter. The sealed chamber housing the stone or wooden statue of the pharaoh or deity was called a *Serdab*, meaning "cellar" in Arabic. Often, a window consisting of two small holes placed at eye level symbolically enabled the deceased to witness the rites being performed and the offerings being received.

The priesthood performed a series of ceremonies that focused upon drawing the essence of the divinity into the temple. There were three main daily rituals. The first took place at dawn, known as the Awakening Ceremony, when the High Priest drew back the bolts and broke the royal clay seal on the double doors to the sanctuary. The High Priest removed the statue from the shrine and cleansed, clothed, anointed, purified, fed and adorned the Ka of the deity — the same ritual the pharaoh underwent each morning. Once this had been accomplished, the High Priest departed, walking backwards so as not to turn his back to the gods, while sweeping the floor of any traces of dirt left by his footsteps when he entered. The next ritual was performed at midday, and the last was conducted during sunset. The statue remained in its Naos during these two ceremonies, however, incense was burned and prayers were recited. In the evening, the shrine was sealed once again. Throughout the day and night, prayers were chanted, hymns were sung, and incense was burned in honor of the gods.

The sweet scent of burning incense, known as the "perfume to the gods," was believed not only to please the gods but to help the worshipper attain a state of harmony with the higher powers, inducing spiritual exaltation. Incense, or *Senetjer*, was so much an integral part of religious rituals that resin trees were planted within the temple grounds. This provided easy access to the principal material required for making incense, as well as purifying the atmosphere. The finest aromatic essences (such as myrrh and frankincense) were derived from the gum resin of the trees imported from "Land of Incense," Punt. *Kapet* (Kyphi) was a common temple fragrance. On the walls of the Great Temple of Amen dated to the 19th Dynasty, Ramses II is shown burning incense as an offering to Amen's barque as it is carried by the priestly procession.

Offerings included fruits placed in baskets or trays, and drinks such as water, milk, beer and wine. Granaries were located on the temple premises, to supply their breweries and bakeries. It was the responsibility of the High Priest to control the temple riches and granaries. After the spiritual essence of the food was received by the gods, the priests and temple employees consumed what remained. This act was known as the "reversion of offerings."

Precious minerals, artwork, oils, plants and bouquets of flowers were among the items offered to the deities. Flowers were frequently placed upon the sacred altars as offerings or used to crown the heads of the statues. Jewelry, in many cases apparently booty taken from other lands, would be deposited with the priesthood to provide offerings to the deities.

Temples also served as workshops, archives and administrative centers, libraries, and training schools for government officials, doctors and scribes. The more important and larger temples were run by the state, and the priesthood received goods and supplies from the government. All that took place in the temples or that involved them was recorded by the temple scribes. Many individuals of various occupations were required to maintain and manage a successful temple. General employment within the centers included farmers, gardeners, stonemasons, painters, carpenters, cooks, butchers, weavers, artisans and craftsmen.

Pharaohs had shrines in their royal tombs, where their statues were placed in the shrine of the funerary compartment. Religious temples housed the statue of the deity worshipped in that city. In the tombs of the wealthy, the image of the deceased Egyptian would be "immortalized" in a statue.

Several levels existed among the priesthood. The priests themselves were known as *Hem Neteru*, "servants of the gods." It was not the duty of a priest in ancient Egypt to proselytize on behalf of the gods, nor to counsel or see to the moral welfare of the citizens. His duty was to care for the deity, as a servant of the gods. The *Shemsu* were "followers" of the Hem Neteru. This group was comprised of devout worshippers and initiates of the priesthood. The *Shemsu* would leave offerings for the priests to bring in to the temple on their behalf as they were not allowed to enter beyond the outer court of the temple. This was solely reserved for the priests who had undergone years of training.

The most common order within the priesthood was known as the *Uab* or *Wab* (meaning "pure") priests. These holy men worked in the smaller temples as opposed to the major temples such as those in Karnak, Abu Simbel and Denderah. The temples contained outer courtyards where the required offerings could be left and where a small pool was available for the purification ritual that was crucial to performing the sacred duties of the Uab priest. These men were responsible for purifying and cleansing the statues, the temple's possessions, and offerings. All that came before the deity's image, in the form of the statue, had to be thoroughly purified with natron, water and incense. A priest who was also well versed in the arts of magic was known as *Hery Seshta*, meaning "Knower of Things."

Another level within the priesthood was the *Sem* priests, who were dedicated to performing mortuary rituals. These held the honorable title of "First Prophet of God," and offered sacrifices and libations in the temples. The Sem priest was a wise older man, usually appointed by the pharaoh. In other cases, he may have worked his way up through the ranks to this respected position. The Sem priest was recognized by the panther or leopard skin draped over his spotless white linen robe.

Kher-Heb was the title bestowed upon the Lector Priest who read the ritual texts and sacred scrolls at religious ceremonies and at the head of the priestly processions. The *Sunu* were the priests who practiced protective magic. The priesthood included musicians, teachers, sculptors, embalmers, physicians and dream interpreters. Priests of Uast, in particular, were regarded as sages and were often consulted in matters of divination. Some priests specialized in astronomy, which was used to measure time and the movements of the planets and constellations. This duty was crucial in matters such as agriculture, architecture, medicine, setting the calendar, planning festivals and calculating the Nile's annual inundation.

Women from noble families served as priestesses (known as *Hemet-Neter*, meaning "Wife of God") and evidence exists that women were part of the Egyptian priesthood as far back as the Old Kingdom. Some Egyptologists have stated that by the 23rd Dynasty, priestesses were almost equal to their male counterparts in terms of number and status. However, this is unlikely as their role seems to have been restricted during the Middle Kingdom, to that of temple dancer, singer, and musician, as these women were often illustrated in funerary reliefs. A priestess who possessed the powers of a medium was known as *Rakhet*. Some priestesses were also dancers, singers and musicians, including *sistrum* players who performed for the gods. On special occasions, drums, cymbals, harps and flutes were played, as these musical instruments were believed to please the deities.

The *sistrum* or *sesheset* was a musical instrument played by women of high rank during religious ceremonies and temple rituals; it was sacred to goddesses Auset, Het-Heru and Bast, deities associated with dance, music, joy and celebration. It was considered a privilege to play the sistrum. It was made of a wooden or metal frame fitted with loose metal bars and disks; shaken with the right hand, it made a jingling, rattling sound. The sounds sistra emitted were considered soothing to the gods and were thought to ward off evil influences.

The Egyptians' gods were dancing gods, and it was a great honor and privilege to perform in temple during festivals and sacred rituals, dancing for the gods. The priests often expressed the harmony of the universe through a sacred dance that celebrated the stellar bodies. Religious dancers were trained at the temple schools by priests who also taught singing and music. Musicians had their own god, known as Ihi, "the Sistrum Player."

The priests often chanted hymns to the deities. One in particular consisted of the sounds of the seven sacred vowels. The sounds of the vowels were believed to possess the secrets of the universe and were therefore omitted from hieroglyphic inscriptions.

Priests generally wore a long, simple dress folded across the left arm. It was imperative that the garb of a priest be of the purest and whitest of linen as well as being fresh and immaculately clean. It was unthinkable for a priest to approach his god with hair or impurities on the body. For this reason, priests bathed several times a day in the purifying cold waters of the Nile or in sacred lakes and pools surrounding the temple premises. Every third day, the priests shaved their entire bodies. Wool and leather clothing was strictly forbidden among the priesthood, as no skin of an animal must touch the pure, divine skin of a priest. It could however, be worn as an upper or outer layer, such as the leopard skin draped over the shoulder of the Sem priest. At Uast, the cult center of Amen, whose sacred animal was the ram, wool was strictly prohibited. The elaborately decorated sarcophagus of an early 22nd Dynasty High Priest of Amen-Ra, named Bakenmut ("Servant of Mut") shows him wearing a perfumed cone upon his head and a leopard cloak hanging loosely over his white linen garment as he makes offerings of bread, beer, ox and fowl to Amen-Ra.

Priests fasted for 7 to 42 days, and often longer. When they ate, their food consisted of plain food of small portions. Excesses of any kind, particularly in either food or drink, were not permitted within the priesthood. Fish, mutton and pork were considered unclean and therefore banished from the diets of the priests.

With the exception of the High Priests, priests and priestesses were only required to serve about three months of the year. This was done on a rotating basis, and they lived inside the temple while performing their priestly duties. The remainder of the time they lived normal lives, working at their profession while raising and taking care of their families. Some servants of god were placed on a rotation schedule where they devoted a week out of every month to the temple. Even High Priests maintained families outside the temple.

It was imperative for religious workers to abstain from sexual activity and certain foods for several days before returning to the sacred precincts. The priests did enjoy certain advantages, such as being exempt from paying taxes and having their necessary expenses, such as food, lodging and clothing, provided for. Priests also were entitled to receiving a state allowance of grain, corn and other provisions.

The people of ancient Egypt relied heavily on the priesthood to maintain and preserve the laws of Ma'at, and accorded them a high degree of prestige and privilege. By the 18th Dynasty, the priests achieved a level almost equal to the pharaoh, as they became the strongest and wealthiest class in society.

An early Reformation

This led to the overthrow of the Priesthood of Amen and all other gods by Amenhotep IV (Akhenaten). Akhenaten imposed what he believed to be a new and better religion, under the worship of the solar deity, Aten. Until then, Aten had been a minor deity, venerated near the region of Iunu during the Middle Kingdom. Akhenaten's father, Amenhotep III, built temples to gods including Aten at Mennefer and Uast during his reign. It seems that the idea of worshipping Aten was passed down to his son and successor.

At first, Amenhotep IV worshipped Amen dutifully while revering Aten privately, but as time went on, Amen's name was removed from inscriptions and all other temples were shut down, and Aten became the national god of Egypt. Akhenaten's inclination toward a monotheistic religion was more spiritual and abstract than the foregoing system, in which the land and the people of Egypt were controlled by myriad gods and the priesthood. Aten could not be merged with any other god, as Amen was with Ra. Aten was the only god in the visionary and altruistic mind of Akhenaten.

Akhenaten built up a strong following as well as making many enemies. His god was universal, covering not only the Nile Valley but all mankind. However, the change was too drastic for the people, and when he died, his religion went with him. The old gods were restored in the name of the young Pharaoh, Tutankhamen. Akhenaten is regarded as both a heretic and a pacifist, and as the first known revolutionary in history.

19. FESTIVALS

The priests who managed the calendar for the Egyptians did a good job, scheduling festivals or *heb* throughout the year. It has been estimated that a third of the year was spent in celebration. No other people took greater delight in ceremonies and religious festivals.

There were festivals to celebrate the life and death of relatives, and festivals in honor of national deities. During the New Kingdom, ceremonies and festivals were often conducted to commemorate the triumphant return of a victorious army from abroad. Birthdays of the pharaohs were celebrated as holy days, when no business was conducted. All public offices were temporarily shut down in the name of the pharaoh; and at the end of the year, the Five Epagomenal Days were a time of great feasting and celebration when the birth dates of Ausar, Heru-Ur, Set, Auset and Nebet-Het were honored.

The resurrection of Ausar as the ancient god Seker was celebrated annually throughout the land as the *Henu* Festival. At sunrise, the Boat of Seker, called the *Henu* boat, was placed upon a platform and carried around the temple in a sacred procession, symbolically representing the solar revolution. The Henu Boat was constructed in the shape of the head of a gazelle-type animal.

The pharaoh's coronation day and anniversary were also spectacularly celebrated. When the pharaoh reached his 30th year of reign, he was required to participate in the *Heb-Sed*, a great festival where the pharaoh danced, jumped and ran to demonstrate his renewed power, physical stamina, rejuvenation, and endurance while representing the fertility of the land. One ritual performed during the Heb-Sed jubilee was called the "Raising of the Djed Pillar," which was accomplished with the much-needed assistance of ropes and vigorous young priests. Originally, it was mandatory for the pharaoh to perform this ritual every three years after his first Heb-Sed; the ritual was also conducted when honoring the deceased pharaoh. The pharaoh, acting as Heru, was supposed to raise the pillar in order for his father Ausar to be able to resurrect and become god of the Underworld. This ritual became traditional at many festivals. Originally, it was performed at Djedu. Since the Djed column characterized the element of stability, this ceremony assured the ongoing stability of reign as well as the strength and endurance of the pharaoh and the land.

A representation of the Heb-Sed is seen on a relief panel in the tomb of Djoser at Saqqara. A separate area in his pyramid court contains a model shrine for the purpose of enabling the pharaoh to continue participating in the Heb-Sed during the afterlife.

Festivals honoring the gods went on for days and nights. An abundance of exotic foods was served while singing, dancing and drinking were enjoyed to the maximum. It has been documented that during one festival in the 12th century BC, temples distributed 11,341 loaves of bread and 3875 jars of beer to the crowds of attendees. Not including children, 70,000 people are reported to have attended one Per-Bast festival honoring the goddess of celebration, drink, dance, joy, music and intoxication. Festivals honoring Nit were held at her cult center in Sau, while those celebrating the life-giving sun took place at Iunu.

Astronomical observations were of great importance in setting the appropriate dates for ceremonial festivities, which relied upon the ascension of the constellations and stars. At the temple, a star watcher kept a lunar calendar by which the cycle of the stars could be determined, as well as the agricultural phases.

Festivals celebrating the major deities such as Amen, Ausar and Auset, were conducted by the priesthood while the citizens themselves held festivals for the minor gods such as Bes. On the day honoring Bes, work ceased as crowds paraded up and down the streets wearing Bes masks. Children followed behind, clapping and accompanying the dancers, singers, tambourine and castanet players.

Months were established in the lunar calendar by the priesthood. Each was given a specific name corresponding to the festival or deity venerated on that particular month. These celebrations were held on days of the new moon and the full moon as well as during lunar eclipses. Special holidays were held during each month, and the 1st and 15th day of each lunar month was held in reverence as well.

Many festivals related to seasonal renewals were observed. The beginning of spring, the harvest and the Nile's flooding were celebrated with lavish ceremonial festivities. In honor of Hapi, the personification and god of the Nile, a great festival took place on the occasion of the annual rising of the Nile. During this ceremony, a statue of Hapi was paraded through the towns and village of ancient Egypt. When the river began to rise, anticipation led to a celebration of music and dance, and men and women came from all parts of the country to participate. The Egyptians observed that the annual flooding of the Nile manifested shortly after the rising of Sopdet (Sirius). This event, known as the Ascension of Sopdet, symbolized the rising of the soul of Auset. The rising of the Nile and of Sopdet marked the beginning of the Egyptian new year, called *Wepet Renpet*. This was the occasion for one of their greatest and most important festivals. When the Nile reached its highest level, another festival was observed. Auset was honored in June when the annual flooding was commemorated; the tears she had shed for Ausar accounted for the annual overflowing of the river. Auset was also honored during the winter, when her return from Byblos and her victory over Set were celebrated. And during harvest time, another festival was observed in her honor, when she was offered the first fruits of the earth, placed on an altar.

The ceremony honoring the death and rebirth of Ausar was observed at the autumn equinox. His murder and resurrection were dramatically recreated by the temple staff, and massive crowds made their way to Abedju to witness the great spectacle. At the beginning of spring, at the new moon, another festival was held in honor of Ausar, called "Entrance of Ausar into the Moon."

Heru was commemorated during the winter solstice. The celebration honoring Het-Heru was a time of great festivity and intoxication when red-stained beer was consumed in large quantities to commemorate her birth. In legend, Het-Heru was born when the destructive goddess Sekhmet fell asleep after drinking too much red beer she thought was the blood of mankind. When she awoke, Sekhmet was appeased and became the gentle Het-Heru, goddess of love, beauty and celebration.

Another festival was held during the close of the season of agricultural labor. This event celebrated the preparation of the land for its future crops. As commoners were not permitted near the holy vicinities of the deities, the crowds lined the streets to witness and admire the priestly processions during these holy festivals. The statues would be paraded through the streets, while the priests fanned them and sheltered them from the heat of the sun. It was the priest's duty to hold these celebrations (which were called "Going Forth") in honor of the important deities.

Other events took place at various times of the year. The image of one deity might be transported to another deity's temple, for instance, Het-Heru and Heru, in commemoration of their sacred marriage. Each year, the procession carrying the statue of Het-Heru began at her main cult center at Iunet (Denderah) and traveled 100 miles upstream to Behdety (Edfu) where the temple of Heru was located. Scenes of this festival are depicted on the walls of the court of the temple at Behdety. The two statues were placed side by side for a period of two weeks, before the statue of Het-Heru was returned to Iunet.

Hymns of praise were chanted while the Kher-Heb or Lector Priest read the sacred rolls aloud. Crowds prostrated themselves in adoration and kissed the ground. Many stops were selected at specially chosen sites along the way. At these stops, a short public rite was performed and offerings were made to the deity, while incense burned. Often, at these stops, the priests and priestesses would offer their services in divination to the general public. When the shrine reached its final destination, another festival took place.

Magic and religion inspired the earliest dances of Egypt and no festival was complete without its presence. Crowds chanted and dancers performed amazing stunts. Priests clapped and priestesses shook their *sistra* to the rhythm of the orchestra playing in honor of the gods. Dance was a crucial element of the festivals honoring Ausar, Auset and Hap, the Apis bull.

On the holidays of the gods, their shrines were taken out of their sacred temples. Often, they were carried on portable shrines placed on a gilded boat or barge and transported by the shaven priests who were led, in turn, by the Sem Priest. The barge would make a short journey along the Nile before returning home to its naos. People traveled great distances to attend these public celebrations that were meant to honor and entertain the gods.

During the season of the harvest, the Festival of Menu (*Min*) a fertility and vegetation deity, was celebrated. His image was honored at this time in order to bless the crops with abundance. Each year during the season of inundation, the Feast of Menu was held in honor of the life-giving Nile. It is believed that during the feast of Menu, the ruling pharaoh and his queen consummated the sacred marriage in honor of this deity of renewal, rebirth and sexuality.

At Uast, the first festival of the year was known as "The Feast of Opet." This was observed during the second month of the season of inundation, which coincided with Sopdet's Ascension. Amen's statue was taken out of its temple at Karnak and placed on a sacred gilded barge was carved from cedarwood imported from Byblos and decorated with heads of rams, Amen's sacred animal. The barge was tied to sailing ships towed by a crew of men. The floating temple traveled upstream about one mile to Amen's other temple, at Luxor, where it remained for about 30 days. When the statue was returned to Karnak, a similar procession and festival took place. In later times, a second barge was added which transported the statues of Amen's wife, Mut and their child, Khonsu. During the Ramessid Era, the Festival of Opet was celebrated for 27 days.

Another major festival was dedicated to the worship of Hap; it lasted seven days. Hap was worshipped as far back as Early Dynastic times, and it was believed that children who smelt the breath of this sacred bull, as he was carried by the priestly procession, would be gifted with second sight.

At festivals, various modes of divination were often practiced, and questions were asked of the gods — as long as they could be answered with a "yes" or "no." If the barque (in the hands of the priests) tipped towards the petitioner, the answer was taken as a "yes." If it tilted away, the reverse was interpreted as the word of the gods. After the festival, the sacred statue was returned to the temple, where it was ceremoniously cleansed by the priests to remove all dust and dirt. The water consecrated by being used in this process was distributed as medicine to the poor, as it was thought to contain the healing powers of the gods.

The ancient Egyptians were highly skilled in the ways of magic, which they referred to as *Heka*. Heka was conceived as a spiritual activity, a thread linking man to the gods — a way of dealing with the unknown, with what was not understood and was beyond mortal control. People turned to magic whenever there was an illness to be cured, a threat to be removed, love to be invoked.

Heka, as the deity personifying magic, helped steer the solar boat of Ra as it traveled through the perilous terrain of the Duat. This is illustrated on the tomb walls of Seti I in the Valley of the Kings. No temple has been discovered that was dedicated to Heka's honor, yet this deity was highly venerated by the priesthood. His female counterpart was Weret-Heka, whose name translates into "She Who is Great in Magic."

Shai was the personification of destiny and fate. *Renenet* embodied the concept of good fortune. One look from Renenet could confer an abundance of crops and livestock. Renenet's gaze was also capable of protecting children from harmful creatures. Together, Renenet and Shai appear in the Judgment Scene whenever the Weighing of the Heart ritual is performed.

Sorcerers performed magic by reciting names or other words of power in a certain manner and tone. By "proper speaking" they were believed to cast out evil, to heal the living, and to restore life to the deceased. Magic was most effective when spoken out loud; however, it could also be inscribed upon papyrus or stone. Spells were often recorded on the wrappings of the mummies, as well as on funerary documents, tomb walls and sarcophagi; sometimes they offered protection against eternal hunger and thirst.

The *Book of the Dead* contains over 200 magic spells that are believed to go as far back as the mid-15th century BC. The many incantations provide for smooth sailing on the celestial boat and successful passage through the Kingdom of Duat and the trial in the Hall of Judgment. Another important funerary spell would help one to remember one's own name, in order to be recognized by the gods and the Ka; the name was as much a part of one's being as his Ba or Ka.

Seven has always been a mystical, occult number symbolizing exalted knowledge, illumination and spirituality. In Egypt, the number seven constantly emerges in respect to legends, deities, pharaohs, spiritual entities and astronomy, as a few examples illustrate:

- The seven major deities of early Egypt are listed as Ra, Heru, Set, Ausar, Anpu, Sokar and Sobek.
- Seshat, the Lady Scribe, wears a crown of seven petals or stars on her head.
- The seven spiritual or astral entities are Khat, Ka, Ba, Khu, Sahu, Akh and Khaibit.
- The seven planets worshipped were the Sun, Moon, Mercury, Venus, Mars, Jupiter and Saturn.
- The Egyptians were the first alchemists. In their transmuting process, they worked with the Seven Metals: gold, silver, mercury, copper, iron, tin and lead, each ruled by the seven planets, respectively.
- In the *Book of the Dead*, reference is made to Ani, the scribe, transforming himself into a golden falcon seven cubits in length.

Many spells relied on the number seven; in the *London-Leiden Papyrus*, spells recommended for healing, inciting love, and banishing evil were to be recited seven times. Often, these words had to be uttered under the constellation of the Great Bear, or Ursa Major, which consisted of seven stars.

Deities are often alluded to in their "seven" forms, such as Khnemu (the deity who ended the seven-year famine) and Sekhmet, who required 7000 vessels of beer mixed with mandrake in order to calm her fury against mankind. Plagues, illnesses and misfortunes were thought to emanate from the "Seven Arrows of Sekhmet." Her creator, Ra, is said to possess seven souls. The "Seven Wise Ones" (who were the daughters of Meh-Urt) came forth from the Eye of Ra. Legend has it that they transformed themselves into seven falcons and flew into the skies to join Tehuti and help him plan the universe.

The Seven Hathors are forms of Het-Heru. They were represented as young women playing tambourines and wearing headdresses of a disk with a pair of horns (recalling Het-Heru, the cow-headed goddess). The Seven Hathors were regarded as a positive form of energy, predicting the fate of newborns — at the child's bedside, the Seven Hathors would announce its destiny; they knew the fate of every Egyptian. It is believed that they would replace royal children born under unfavorable stars with those born under beneficial stars, in order to protect the dynasty and the land.

The Seven Sisters were worshipped and represented by the Seven Stars of the Pleiades. In the Zodiac of Esna, a pair of Wadjet are enclosed in an oval form with seven stars believed to signify the Pleiades. As far back as the 5th Dynasty, the Seven Sacred Oils were used in the embalming process. Alabaster jars found in the tomb of Hetepheres are numbered from one to seven, with the contents duly inscribed upon them.

The Seven Scorpions who accompanied and protected Auset and Heru-Sa-Auset were named Tefen, Befen, Mestet, Mestetef, Petet, Thete and Maatet. Two walked behind her, one walked on each side and three led the way, clearing the mother and child's path of danger. Auset, as the Mistress of Magic, knew their names and so she was able to render them impotent if she so desired.

The Seven Vowels were chanted by temple priests, in the utmost secrecy. The vowels were considered to be the seven primary sounds from which all others evolved. They were also known as "spirits," or "breaths," and they were regarded as the divine component of words.

The birthday of Apis was celebrated with an extravagant seven-day festival. According to Plutarch, the festival was held near the winter solstice, when the sun was at its weakest. The ritual called for a sacred cow to be led in a procession seven times around the temple. This was known as the "Searching of Ausar."

In the *Book of the Dead*, this number constantly emerges: Anpu appointed Seven Spirits or Seven Shining Ones to preside over Ausar's body; these seven gods included the four sons of Heru. References are made to the Seven Glorious Ones dwelling in the Underworld. A seven-headed serpent is mentioned in funerary texts, as well as seven gods in the land of Duat who inspect the slaughter of those who were punished for misdeeds during life. Seven other deities are often encountered during the boat ride through the Duat, and there are Seven Seated Gods who tow the solar boat at another stage in the journey. There are Seven Halls or Chambers situated in one region of the Duat, each guarded by a doorkeeper, a watcher and a herald. It was imperative for the newly deceased, passing through these chambers during the twelve hours of the night, to be able to name the seven doorkeepers, seven watchers and seven heralds in order to be met by Ausar in the Underworld.

In esoteric astrology, rulership over Egypt belongs to the seventh sign of the zodiac, Libra. Attributes assigned to Libra are beauty and artistry, words synonymous with Egypt. The scales of Libra are the scales of Ma'at, and the astrological symbol for Libra closely resembles the hieroglyph for Akhet, the rising sun, symbolic of ancient Egyptian beliefs in resurrection, the basis of their religion.

Tales of Seven

The number seven figures in a story recorded in the *Westcar Papyrus*; it was related to King Khufu, builder of the Great Pyramid, and concerned an event that took place during the 3rd Dynasty. The tale begins with an unfaithful wife of a High Official who is exposed by her husband's steward. When her husband is told of her straying ways, he, being skilled in the arts of magic, calls for his precious chest of ebony and metal. From wax, he molds a crocodile, seven fingers in length. He then speaks the requisite words of magic, in their proper tone and sequence, and places a curse upon the crocodile. The High Official gives his faithful steward the crocodile to toss into the waters where his wife's lover is used to bathe. And a day comes when the discreet couple spends some time together. When the lover slips into the water to bathe, the steward tosses the waxen crocodile into the waters and it immediately comes to life, grows to a length of seven cubits and devours him. The unfaithful wife is put to death by royal command, and her ashes are cast into the river. This story was apparently recounted to an amused King Khufu by his son Khafre. One hopes there was no unpleasant hint intended.

Another tale of magic from the *Westcar Papyrus* involves a sage named Teta, who was 110 years old. Herutatef, another son of King Khufu of the 4th Dynasty, was conversing with his father one day on the subject of magic and sorcerers. Herutatef praised the works of Teta, as this magician was apparently able to restore the head to its decapitated body.

So curious was Khufu about this old man that he ordered the royal boat to be prepared and commanded Herutatef to bring Teta into his presence. Teta immediately agreed to visit Khufu and added that this Pharaoh would be one to prosper greatly. Teta requested one boat to transport his books and another to carry his family; thus he journeyed along the Nile and was brought before the Pharaoh. Teta was was asked if he could perform the incredible act of magic suggested by Herutatef. Teta confirmed that he was, and the Pharaoh summoned his men to bring forth a captive for Teta to prove his magic upon. Teta quickly begged the Pharaoh to spare the man's life and to bring an animal in its place. The first animal brought was a goose. Once it had been decapitated, the head was placed at one side and the body at the other. Teta rose and spoke words of magic; the headless body slowly approached its missing piece and joined together. Teta successfully performed the same miracle with a bird, and later with an ox.

A sinking feeling

In the Harem Conspiracy, magic was used to harm Ramses III. Hui, Overseer of the Royal Cattle, secretly acquired a copy of a magical text from the royal library. In this manual, he learnt how to mold wax figures and apply amulets in order to cast a deadly spell over the pharaoh. With the help of a royal official, the necessary equipment were smuggled into the palace. The spells and the magical items were used to bring an end to the reign and life of the Pharaoh in order to place another upon the throne.

The last of the native Egyptian pharaohs was King Nectanbeo II, who ruled during 360 BC. Highly skilled at deciphering omens and interpreting sky charts, he was a renowned magician and astrologer in his time. It is said that once, when Egypt was about to be invaded, Nectanebo II went to his magical laboratory and fashioned wax figures of the enemy. Placing them in a bowl of water, he recited the required words of power, causing strong winds to sink the miniature enemy ship, with the men inside. As the waxen figures of the men drowned, identical results were achieved in real life.

Unfortunately, his last attempt at this type of magic failed, as the spell worked against him and the soldiers of Egypt. He interpreted this defeat as a sign that the end of Egypt was approaching, and that he would be the last true Egyptian pharaoh to rule the land. It is said that Nectanebo II fled to Macedonia, disguised as a commoner, and became a prophet and a healer.

The first legendary book of spells

A tale of magic involving a court scribe named Setna, father of Sa-Ausar and son of Ramses II, tells of how well-versed he was in the mysteries of performing magic. Setna longed for a book that contained all the magical knowledge written by Tehuti, the great magician. This book was buried at Mennefer with an ancestor of Setna's named Nefer-Ka-Ptah, who had been a great scholar and skilled magician. Setna and his brother set out to find the book, and they found it in the tomb after searching for three days.

The book was clutched in the hands of Nefer-Ka-Ptah. By his side were the Kas of his beloved wife, Ahura, and their son, Merhu, who were buried at Qebtu (Coptos), where they had died. Setna set out to pry the book out of the dead man's grasp when suddenly the Ka of Ahura spoke, begging him not to do it. She explained that the book had brought nothing but sorrow and death to the entire family, and she warned Setna that Nefer-Ka-Ptah had also been obsessed with acquiring the knowledge contained in the *Book of Tehuti*. It was this obsession that had brought death to the family.

Nefer-Ka-Ptah had been informed by an old priest of the priceless contents of the book. He was told that the book lay at the bottom of the river and was protected by myriad snakes and other unpleasant creatures. The book was to be found inside an iron chest that held an iron box that held a bronze box that held a wooden box that held an ebony and ivory box that held a silver box inside of which a golden box would be found. Inside the gilded box lay the *Book of Tehuti*.

Legend has it that Nefer-Ka-Ptah slayed the serpent coiled around the box twice, as it refused to die. A third time he severed the snake, this time tossing sand in between the two pieces of its body so that it could not reunite and come back to life. With this victory, Nefer-Ka-Ptah brought the container to shore and opened all the boxes, one by one, and finally held the magic tome in his trembling hands. With his wife by his side, he copied the spells onto papyrus, sprinkled them with incense, dissolved them in water and drank the wisdom of Tehuti. Tehuti was outraged when he found out that they had taken what was not theirs. He decided that the family would not return to Mennefer; and while the three were making their way back home, they all drowned — first the boy and then the mother, at Qebtu, and finally Nefer-Ka-Ptah (with the *Book of Tehuti* in his hands) drowned just as he was approaching Mennefer.

Word of this tragedy did not deter Setna from his quest, however; he was determined to get hold of the sacred book of knowledge. The spirit of Nefer-Ka-Ptah now spoke, and challenged Setna to a game of *senet*. The winner was to take possession of the book. Setna won the game and retrieved his much sought-after prize. A few days later, Setna encountered a breathtakingly beautiful woman, and lost his head entirely. This woman was named Tabubua; she was conjured by the spirit of Nefer-Ka-ptah. She demanded that Setna leave his wife and sacrifice his child for her; he was so blinded by her beauty and his love for her that he granted her wishes. After he abandoned his wife, and had his child executed, he went to embrace Tabubua. In that instant she turned into a skeletal corpse.

Setna awoke, lying in the middle of the street, and realized it all had been a horrific nightmare. He went to his family and declared his profound love for them. Setna was a wise enough man to see this dream as an omen of ill luck, and he returned the book to Nefer-Ka-Ptah. So grateful was he to have this second chance with his family that Setna had the bodies of Nefer-Ka-Ptah's wife and son relocated from Qebtu to his grave at Mennefer. The family, united at last, was laid to rest together, and they no doubt continue to guard the *Book of Tehuti* today.

21. Dreams and Divination

In ancient Egypt, oracles were frequently consulted in daily matters, as their prophecies were believed to hold the truth. Special statues were kept for this purpose and temple priests carried them out to the public in portable shrines during festivals and religious ceremonies. The oracle was often consulted in writing; the question or wish could be inscribed on papyrus and placed in the mouth of the deity's statue. Over the course of time, the priests became the voice of the oracles, and special compartments situated inside the temple enabled them to communicate with petitioners outside, while remaining hidden. Texts were available from the priesthood, foretelling the mortal fate of those born on specific dates in the calendar; whoever so wished could consult this oracle.

Oracles were not exclusively reserved for commoners but were available to royalty as well. Pharaohs consulted oracles when divine approval or advice was required in a major decision, event or action.

The *Cairo Calendar* is recorded on a papyrus that has been dated to the 19th Dynasty. This document denotes special dates that were considered lucky or unlucky. Each day was divided into thirds, and each division was designated fortunate or malefic. Slightly over 50% of the days of the year were regarded as fortunate in their entirety; a few were neutral, and the remainder were listed as unfavorable days to attempt any action — being born, for instance. The Cairo Calendar would have been consulted often in order to determine the likely outcome of a project or question. Its use was not confined to a specific individual but applied to everyone who required consultation about a particular date.

The dates' benign or malign influence was based on mythological associations or significant events related to the day. Traces of major events, whether positive or negative, were believed to linger, influencing all matters undertaken on every anniversary. The first day of the first month of the first season, Akhet, was considered promising, because it was not only the ancient Egyptian New Year's day and the beginning of the rising of the Nile, but the anniversary of Ra's birth. An adverse day was the 14th day of the 1st month of the season of Peret, as this was the anniversary of the day when Auset and Nebet-Het wept over the memory of Ausar at Djedu (or Per Ausar). As Nebet-Het embodied the hidden forces, she was regarded as the "Mistress of Dreams," and her sister Auset, was the "Mistress of Magic."

The anniversary of the battle between Heru and Set, on the 15th day of the first month of Akhet, was also regarded as less than auspicious, whereas the 27th day of the third month of the season of Akhet is the anniversary of the day Heru and Set stopped fighting, and therefore is considered favorable. The ominous portents of the Ides of March (a day still considered unlucky by the superstitious) originated in 44 BC, when, on March 15, Julius Caesar was assassinated — despite warnings from a dream, from his wife and from an astrologer.

Hap was often consulted in divinatory matters during the festivals dedicated in his honor. Hap would be asked a question, after an offering was placed to the right of his statue. Once the question was posed, the petitioner covered his ears and left the temple. The first words he heard were interpreted as the divine word of Hap.

Another method of divination involving Hap was to lead him, in the person of the sacred bull, into a hall crowded with devotees. Here he was let loose and set free to choose between two doors. One door signified a negative answer, the other, a favorable reply. Whichever door Hap selected was interpreted as his divine word.

In another divination ritual involving Hap, the petitioner was required to offer the bull some food, by hand. If Hap accepted, it was taken as a good omen; if he refused, it was interpreted as an ill omen. Is it fair to ask whether the sacred animal (whom the priests maintained so well) was fed before being led out to the people, or did he skip breakfast on these occasions?

Dream on

Many temples served as oracle centers and provided a means divination, particularly dream interpretation. Diseases were thought to be curable, using elixirs and potions communicated, during sleep, by the gods and the world beyond; dreams were regarded as divine messages that only a high priest could interpret. For a fee, of course.

Bad dreams were inscribed in red ink, the color representing Set and evil. Good dreams were recorded in black. *The Book of Dreams* contains a particular ritual to be performed upon awakening from a nightmare; it would cast away all demons and dispel their evil influence. The dreamer was instructed to eat or to smear his face with a mixture of fresh bread, myrrh, green herbs, and beer upon awakening from a nightmare; a specific spell was to be recited and the evil demon causing the dream would be banished.

To frighten away nightmares, the ancient Egyptian made snakes out of clay and placed them at the doors of their homes. (Snakes were regarded as evil creatures of the night, and therefore as bringers of bad dreams.) This custom was also believed to be effective in repelling real, and deadly, snakes of the desert. Headrests were often engraved with the image of the dwarf-god Bes, the bad-dream-preventer. One such headrest was discovered among Kebherkhopshef's mortuary belongings. Lions, enemies of snakes, were also carved upon the beds to protect people while sleeping.

The art of dream deciphering was highly regarded; experts were sought after and well rewarded. By the Ptolemaic Era, dream interpretation had become a profitable business. Specialists might be paid to dream for their customers, as well as to interpret dreams that were reported to them.

One such practitioner was a priest named Hor, who lived during the reign of Ptolemy IV of 180-145 BC. Through Tehuti, the god of wisdom, intellect and language, he made his living by giving advice. Hor left behind over 60 texts, inscribed upon *ostraca*, that reveal much about this spiritual man. Hor had two dreams in one night that left him profoundly shaken and altered the course of his life. He dreamt that a spirit warned him that Tehuti was enraged that he had neglected to feed 60,000 ibis. In another dream, Hor moved back to his hometown, only to be rejected and persecuted by the local citizens. A foreman appeared and said, "I am not a foreman, I am a god. Do not worship anyone except me." Upon awakening, Hor moved from his home in the delta to Saqqara, where he became a loyal servant of the cult of the ibis god, Tehuti.

If one was searching for an answer to a troubling matter or a cure for an illness, a priest was employed to sleep inside a "sleep temple" or an oracle's center; or the petitioner could pay to spend a night at a "sleep temple" himself, in order to receive divine assistance in health matters. Books on dream interpretation were kept closely guarded and were consulted only by the priests, while others relied upon their intuition in deciphering dreams.

Only one such handbook, written during the 19th Dynasty, has survived; it belonged to a scribe named Kenherkhopshef. He had a passion for collecting texts on magic, poetry, medicine and dream interpretation. This manual consisted of over 200 dream interpretations that were construed as the word of the gods. Several examples predicted a long life ahead — if one dreamt of seeing himself dead! Good luck ensued for the person who dreamt of eating the flesh of a crocodile. To dream of seeing oneself alongside a dwarf meant that half the dreamer's life had passed. To dream of drinking warm beer (even in the days before refrigeration) was interpreted as suffering on the part of the dreamer. Many of these interpretations were partly based on verbal associations and word play, which the ancient Egyptians enjoyed very much; and actual experiences were most likely catalogued and used as references for later occurrences in dream interpretation.

One of the most well-known stories dating from the Egyptian era comes from the Old Testament. The Israelite Joseph is brought into

Egypt as a slave. Joseph is promoted to steward of the commander of the guard. After he rebuffs the advances of the commander's mistress, she has him thrown into prison, out of spite, but before long Joseph earns the respect of his fellow inmates for his talent as a dream interpreter. Word of his unique skills quickly spreads to the Pharaoh, who has been suffering from a disturbing dream in which seven thin cows eat seven fat ones, and seven lean ears of corn eat seven fat ones. Joseph interpreted this to mean that seven years of prosperity would be followed by seven years of famine. The king was satisfied, yet worried, by this answer. He appointed Joseph the job of saving a fifth of all the grain during the good years to be used for the years of the anticipated famine; and famine did come, to all the lands except Egypt, where the store of corn and bread was sufficient to bridge the shortfalls.

Another dream-related story concerns a pharaoh who ruled during the New Kingdom. The Pharaoh, believed to have been Seti I, was known for his lack of respect for his army; he even went as far as removing privileges that other Pharaoh had granted to the soldiers. When Assyria was about to invade Egypt, the soldiers of the Egyptian army refused to co-operate with the Pharaoh in defending the land. In desperation, the Pharaoh sought advice at the temple. He fell asleep while praying to the deities and dreamt that a god appeared. In his dream, the god assured him of Egypt's victory over Assyria. With renewed courage and confidence, the Pharaoh summoned his army once again and this time they responded. Not only did the soldiers rise to the occasion but artisans, merchants and commoners all came forth to defend Egypt.

On the eve of the attack, the Assyrians rested in the fields nearby. During the night, field mice and rats gnawed through their entire inventory of weapons and shields, rendering the Assyrians defenseless. Many Assyrians died and others fled, disarmed.

Another dream-related story involves Merneptah, the son and successor of Ramses II. According to legend, during Merneptah's fifth year of reign, he was troubled by a military crisis: an impending invasion by the Libyans and the Sea Peoples. Merneptah consulted the Oracle of Amen, who spoke to him through Ptah. He was told that Egypt would not be defeated. The story is inscribed upon a victory stela at

Karnak that asserts that Merneptah slew thousands of men and brought back many prisoners and rich booty.

And let's go further with the story about the moon god Khonsu, mentioned in the chapter on the Deities. Khonsu cured Bint-Reshet, the sister-in-law of Ramses II; but the people feared that the demon that had caused her illness would return to the land of Bekhten and so Khonsu's statue was kept on hand for three years, four months and five days. Why was it returned to Uast, at all? A disturbing dream came to the Prince of Bekhten one night. He had a vision of Khonsu taking the form of a golden hawk and flying away from his shrine at Bekhten to his home in Egypt. Upon awakening, the prince consulted a prophetic priest. He was informed that Khonsu had already departed from Bekhten. The prince realized that their time was up with Khonsu, and interpreted the dream as a warning. The deity's spectacular royal chariot was immediately loaded with the statue of Khonsu and precious gifts for his temple, and sent back safely to the city of Uast.

It was believed that Nectanebo II knew how to induce dreams in others; he is said to have sent a dream to Olympia of Macedonia, through a waxen image. Nectanebo concocted a potion using dream-inducing herbs; he fashioned a waxen image and inscribed Olympia's name upon it. He anointed the figure with the herbal concoction and conjured a certain dream for her. That night Olympia dreamt that Amen came to her bed and informed her that she would give birth to a great child. Nine months later, she brought forth a son, Alexander the Great.

During the Ptolemaic Period, Hap became identified with Ausar and was worshipped as the composite deity Ausar-Hap (whom the Greeks called Serapis). The two souls were now united and Ausar-Hap became one of the most important deities of the Greco-Egyptian era; important enough to serve as a reason for war. Ptolemy I Soter, founder of the Ptolemaic Dynasty (also known as "the Savior") dreamt that a colossal statue appeared before him, a statue that he had never seen before. This strange statue commanded him to remove it from the place where it was standing and relocate it to the Ptolemaic capital of Alexandria. Without knowing to whom this statue belonged nor where it was situated, he recounted the dream to a friend. This friend revealed that he had just seen such a statue in Sinope (northern Turkey). After three years and much resistance from the locals (one can imagine), it was taken to Egypt. The ancient Egyptians believed this statue embodied the essence of Ausar-Hap. Ptolemy I established the cult center of Serapis at Alexandria, where a great temple sheltering the statue was erected as the home of Ausar-Hap.

Some of the greatest figures in human history were kings of Egypt and many pharaohs deserve to be remembered for their outstanding contributions and achievements, even if their names are not well-known today. Here, we will present a few highlights of the "lesser of the greats" and go into a little more detail about particularly brilliant or well-known reigns such as those of Tuthmose III, Ramses II, Alexander the Great and Cleopatra VII. We will also mention a few of the great explorers (some might say grave robbers), who literally unearthed the evidence of these remarkable historical feats. A table at the beginning of the book lists a more complete dynastic chronology.

1st Dynasty (3100-2890 BC)

Narmer
King Narmer, ruler of Upper Egypt, conquered Lower Egypt (c. 3100 BC) and, having unified the two, he was the first to wear the Double Crown of Egypt. This union established him as the first Pharaoh of Egypt, thereby inaugurating the 1st Dynasty. Narmer established Men-nefer (Memphis) as the capital of the newly unified land. This site ideally represented the unification, as it was situated at the apex of the

Delta, the boundary between Upper and Lower Egypt.

A slate was found, intact, late in the 19th century of our era, bearing inscriptions that commemorate Narmer's victory. *Nar* is the word for a catfish, and *mer* means chisel; since these two items phonetically spell his name, they were inscribed in hieroglyphics at the top of both sides of the slate; the hieroglyphs were placed between two representations of the face of Het-Heru. On one side, Narmer is shown wearing the *Deshret*, or Red Crown of Lower Egypt, as he marches in procession toward two rows of decapitated prisoners. Below, a pair of lions is shown intertwining their serpentine necks — symbolizing the joining of the two lands. Below that, Narmer, as a raging bull, is shown trampling over the defeated enemy. On the other side of the slate, Narmer wears the *Hedjet*, or White Crown of Upper Egypt; standing before Heru, he is about to strike the enemy with his mace. His message is clear: he smote the enemy and conquered their land, and he alone joined them as one under his rulership. The Narmer Palette, which was discovered at Nekhen, is one of the oldest surviving records of Egyptian writing, since it dates back to the Predynastic era.

Many believe that Narmer and Menes were one and the same man — pharaohs had more than one name, after all. According to the ancient king lists and that of Manetho (the Egyptian priest who lived c. 3000 BC and divided history into dynasties), Menes was the first king to rule during the 1st Dynasty of unified Egypt, c. 3100 BC. Not much is known about Menes and some believe he may have been a mythical hero; others believe that Menes founded Mennefer. *Men*, meaning "established," would be a fitting name for such a king. Still, this tablet commemorates the unification by a ruler named Narmer, who interestingly enough does not appear on any king lists.

4th Dynasty (2613-2498 BC)

Sneferu

The 4th Dynasty began with a pharaoh who ruled for about 24 years. Sneferu was a well-regarded pharaoh and is best known for his military campaigns to Nubia and Libya. He established trade relations with Mediterranean lands and initiated many construction projects throughout Egypt. Three pyramids situated at Meidum and Dahshur are credited to Sneferu's ingenuity. His wife was Queen Hetepheres, whose dazzling gilded bedroom and toiletries were discovered in 1920. Together they had a son named Khufu (known as Cheops, in Greek.)

Khufu

Khufu is reputed to have been an ambitious and hard-driving man who passionately pursued his father's architectural projects. The biggest of the three Pyramids of Giza was constructed under his direction. A small sculpture of Khufu is displayed at the Cairo Museum; this is the only image of him known to date. Legend has it that Khufu sold his daughter to a brothel in order to help finance his mortuary complex. She, in turn, demanded one stone from every client she accepted; the stones were used to build her own (much smaller) pyramid, which stands in front of Khufu's. Like father, like son: his successor, Khafre (Chephren, in Greek), was also regarded as a tyrannical ruler.

Khafre

The second largest of the pyramids belongs to Khafre, and it is believed to be his image that was carved on the Great Sphinx. His son and successor, Menkaura, also ruled during this time period; his is the smallest of the three main pyramids at Giza. Menkaura (Mycerinus, in Greek) and Sneferu were less harsh on the people and therefore were more beloved and popular than Khufu and Khafre.

Middle Kingdom
11th Dynasty (2050-1991 BC)

Montuhotep II

After battling for several years, Montuhotep's mighty army captured the town of Henen Nesut (Herkleopolis), c. 2040 BC. Henen Nesut was the capital of the rival kings during the 9th and 10th Dynasties of the 1st Intermediate Period. Power began to decline at Henen Nesut while Uast initiated important trade relations with Nubia, resulting in increased wealth and extended power. Montuhotep II re-established the capital at Uast, and ushered in the 11th Dynasty, inaugurating the Middle Kingdom. Montuhotep II reinforced Egypt's borders as he battled the Asiatics in the Sinai and the Libyans in the Delta. His reign lasted half a century.

12th Dynasty (1991-1775 BC)

Senwosret III

Senswosret III's achievements included supporting the rise and growth of the middle class. This segment of the population was mainly comprised of merchants, tradesmen, farmers and artisans. The post of the Nomarch was abolished under his reign; eventually, they came to compete for power with the pharaohs and posed a threat to national unity. Senwosret III repaired the canal by the 2nd Cataract of the Nile, thus facilitating trade and the transportation of troops into Nubia. In Nubia, he was extremely active militarily and he expanded Egyptian borders within that territory. One of the most realistic and artistic representations discovered from ancient Egypt is a life-size granite statue of Senwosret III.

Amenemhet III

Amenemhet III was Senwosret III's successor; he was an outstanding pharaoh whose accomplishments went beyond military victories. Amenemhet III brought economic prosperity. During his 50-year reign, he improved the irrigation system in the Faiyum, which provided a far greater yield of annual crops. This vast project added about 27,000 acres of fertile farmland. Under the orders of Amenemhet III, dikes and basins were constructed as well as a canal from the lake of the Faiyum to the Nile, diverting the waters into Lake Moeris. Present-day Lake Qarun is part of this ancient lake. Trapping the waters of the Nile here (as there was no point of exit), this project caused the region to become inundated and it was transformed into one of the lushest areas in Egypt.

Amenemhet III also provided Egypt with natural resources by conducting many successful mining expeditions, particularly to extract copper from the Sinai. He is also credited with providing the mineworkers and their families with more generous accommodations. Amenemhet III erected two colossal statues in his own image, commemorating his feats. The temple or administrative center he built beside his pyramid is known as the Labyrinth, because of its complicated design of corridors, shafts, colonnades and a dozen separate courts. Although that edifice no longer stands, Amenemhet III is remembered as last great king of his dynasty.

New Kingdom (1550-1087 BC)
18th Dynasty (1550-1307)

Ahmose

Ahmose was the founder and first king of the New Kingdom. Ahmose took over as Pharaoh when his older brother Kamose died during the war against the Asiatic Hyksos; their father, Seqenenre Tao II, also lost his life in the battle with the Hyksos. Ahmose succeeded in defeating them finally eliminating a huge threat to Egypt's nationhood that had disrupted all normal activity for over two centuries. He also fought in military campaigns against the Nubians, who were trying to remain independent from Egypt. Ahmose restored the government, which had been in shambles during the turbulent 2nd Intermediate period and thus inaugurated a new era of hope — the New Kingdom. Ahmose encouraged trade, re-organized the tax system and made improvements to the irrigation projects. Upon his death, his son Amenhotep I assumed the throne.

Amenhotep I

Twice, Amenhotep I led an army that successfully defeated the invading Libyans, and against the Nubians he was victorious as well, and brought back many Nubian captives. Amenhotep I was well-liked by his people. His interest in the arts and architecture is evident in the restoration of several temples and his elaborate building project at the Temple of Karnak, in Uast. Amenhotep I died before the age of 50, leaving the throne to a non-royal military commander who came to be known as Tuthmose I. Tuthmose I married the daughter of Ahmose I, Princess Ahmose, who thus became Queen of Egypt.

Tuthmose I

During his reign, extensive work was performed on the temple of Karnak, as he added pylons, a cedar wood Hypostyle Hall, obelisks, courts, gilded doors and flagstaffs. It was during his reign that royalty began to be buried in the limestone cliffs of the Valley of the Kings.

Like his predecessors, Tuthmose I led military campaigns into Nubia and against the Hyksos. Tuthmose I is credited with renewing stability and confidence among the ancient Egyptians, whose faith had been considerably shaken by the Hykos and their alliance with the Nubians, who eventually came to rule Egypt during the 25th Dynasty.

Tuthmose I was succeeded by his daughter Hatshepsut, who ruled as Queen along with her half-brother Tuthmose II, until his death at the age of 30 when she became pharaoh in her own right.

Amenhotep II

Amenhotep II was a fearless warrior who excelled in archery and horsemanship. He came to the throne as successor to Tuthmose III. Prior to becoming pharaoh, he was in command of the naval base at Mennefer; returning home to Egypt, in triumph, he hung beheaded Hyksos captives from the prow of his ship.

Akhenaten

Born into this world as Amenhotep IV, Akhenaten was the first ruler in history to adopt the concept of a single abstract god. He established what had been a minor deity up to then, Aten (the Solar Disk) as Egypt's sole god and new state religion. His father, Amenhotep III, had planted the first seed of this new development when Akhenaten was a child, by encouraging the worship of Aten; he even built a temple dedicated to that deity. Evidence exists that Akhenaten's mother, Queen Tiy, also supported his religious ambitions and aspirations.

What makes this change all the more surprising is the fact that Amenhotep IV, whose name meant "Amen is Pleased," was born in the religious center and heart of the cult of Amen, at Uast, c. 1395 BC; yet 20 years later, as Pharaoh, he renounced the priesthood of Amen and the pantheon of the existing gods and replaced them with Aten. Some believe that the Hebrew concept of a single deity evolved from the cult of Aten.

During the fifth year of his reign, he changed his name from Amen-hotep IV to Akhenaten, which translates into "Spirit of the Light of the Sun." As a new capital had to be established, Akhenaten moved it from Uast to a desolated stretch of the Nile about halfway between Uast and Mennefer, known as Middle Egypt. The site was named Akhetaten, translating into "Horizon of Aten." The city, founded in c. 1350 BC, is located on the east bank of the river in what is now known as Amarna — which is also the name given by Egyptologists to his 17-year reign. The site of Akhetaten was originally an unoccupied stretch of land, and was chosen for its abundance of sunshine and lack of shade. The traditional dimly-lit temples were now open, without roofs, in order to receive the rays of the sun, the personification of Aten, as they touched this sacred capital.

Once Akhetaten was established, its population is thought to have grown from 20,000 to 50,000, making it a major city for the times. The city housed the royal palace and buildings of administration, temples to Aten, a workman's village and an upper-class section where the nobility lived.

However, evidence was found at Amarna (in the form of sculptures and amulets bearing their names and images) of a few of the old gods, specifically in the poorer quarters of the city. These people most likely still venerated the old deities in the privacy of their homes. What a culture shock it must have been for them to be forced to discard the gods they had worshipped for centuries in place of a new and little known manifestation of the deity as the solar disk, and to relinquish the cool shade of the old temples for the blazing sun. The old temples of Amen and other deities were shut down or destroyed and all traces of the old gods vanished. Even the plural term of "gods" was erased, along with all the ritual and mythological events of the past. The mighty priesthood of Amen was now powerless.

Inevitably, while Akhenaten devoted his attention to establishing a successful cult of Aten, the empire began to fall apart; various territories began asserting their independence. Akhenaten was not a warrior; he was a poet, a philosopher, a spiritualist and a peace-loving family man who raised six daughters with his wife, Queen Nefertiti. This is the first time a pharaoh was depicted as a gentle man as opposed to the warrior-like depiction in battle scenes favored by the previous rulers.

Akhenaten was an extraordinary man; he may even have introduced monogamy and the liberation of slaves. Known as a man of his people, Akhenaten would not permit his subjects to kneel before him, although that show of inferiority had been mandatory in the past. His concern for the people's welfare is shown by his advice that mothers limit their families to two children, since more than half the women died while giving birth to large families. Under his reign, criminals were entitled to appeal, and he extended protection and fair treatment to animals. The leopard skin mantles traditionally worn by the Sem Priests were prohibited; fish spearing and bird catching were recognized as cruel sports and were therefore banned, as was the slaughter of animals in ways that involved unnecessary suffering. Akhenaten instructed all healers to offer their services to the poor, free of charge. Unfair judges and tax assessors who collected more than the legal share were punished.

While these modernizations must have won him the praise of many, it is easy to see that simultaneously they would have fanned the hatred of others, since his beliefs and actions profoundly affected their lives — particularly those in high positions, i.e., the nobility and especially the priesthood of Amen.

In scenes recording Akhenaten's reign, his beloved wife Nefertiti vanishes from sight at around the 14th year. Her departure coincides with the appearance of a young man named Smenkhare. Smenkhare became co-regent with the Pharaoh and, when Akhenaten died, he ruled independently for two years. Smenkhare married Akhenaten's eldest daughter, Merytaten, thus legitimizing his claim to the throne.

Smenkhare's origins remain a mystery and several theories have been proposed. He was portrayed in reliefs as Akhenaten's companion and his image seems to have replaced that of Nefertiti. Smenkhare could have been Akhenaten's nephew (as a son of one of his many sisters); or he may have been Akhenaten's son-in-law, or a younger half-brother by Amenhotep III and a different mother. Smenkhare could also have been Tutankhamen's father (assuming that Tutankhamen was the child of Akhenaten's eldest daughter Merytaten). The most remarkable and questionable theory is that Smenkhare was actually Nefertiti herself, disguised and ruling as a man, as Hatshepsut had done earlier during the same dynasty.

The Aten empire crumbled after Akhenaten's death (during the 17th or 18th year of his reign.) His mummy was, more than likely, destroyed by non-Atenists, so that we are left with no trace of the cause of his death. Without the founder of the Aten cult, the new religion began to dwindle, paving the way for the return of the cult of Amen. After his death, it wasn't long before the priesthood of Amen, with all its Egyptian gods and goddesses, was reinstated. In about 1334 BC, Smenkhare had the capital moved back to Uast. Due to the absence of male heirs, succession to the throne passed to Akhenaten's son-in-law (or was he a son, by Kiya, a lesser wife?). Others believe the boy to have been Akhenaten's younger brother and a son of Amenhotep III. In any case, the boy was named Tutankhaten and at nine years old he became the Pharaoh of Egypt. All traces of the worship of Aten were obliterated, and he was relegated to his former status as a minor god, while Egypt returned to its traditional deities and values. However, Akhenaten did leave a profound mark upon history, as he is remembered as the world's first true pacifist and individualist.

Tutankhamen

Tutankhamen immediately had his name changed from Tutankhaten, meaning "Living Image of Aten," when he took the throne. He remained a minor pharaoh who did not accomplish much (that we know of) during his eight-year reign. However, it is in his memory that the former pantheon of gods and traditions were reinstalled. For this reason, he was given a most spectacular burial when he died prematurely at the age of 18.

Upon examination of his mummy, specialists have theorized that he may have died from a dark lesion on his left cheek and/or from a fatal blow to the back of his skull. It is also possible that the damage was done post-mortem. The mummy shows no sign of disease, so that in all probability his untimely death was caused by violence. His death seems to have been unexpected, as his modest-sized tomb bears evidence of having been hastily converted from one for a commoner to one for royalty. Many treasures found in the four rooms show traces of having been upgraded in order to be fit for a king. The tomb contained nearly 5000 priceless objects of gold, onyx, lapis-lazuli and alabaster, that were (by the time explorers officially opened it) all scattered about the chamber. If to invoke someone's name is to make him live again, Tutankhamen indeed is immortal as his image and name are the most well known of the Egyptian Pharaohs; yet Tutankhamen was a minor king. Given what was found in his tomb, one cannot help but marvel at the thought of what might lie in the undiscovered tombs of such great Pharaohs as Tuthmose III, Ramses II and Cleopatra VII.

Archeologists and the Legendary Curse

It took ten years for the entire spectacular collection to be cata-logued by Howard Carter, the man who found the young pharaoh's tomb in 1922. Carter was an artist and an archaeologist; his discovery in the Valley of the Kings was the most outstanding to date, and it unlocked much of the secret world of the pharaohs. All things Egyptian became very much in vogue after the discovery.

Carter was sponsored and financed by George Herbert, the 5th Earl of Carnarvon, who shared his passion for Egyptology. Carnarvon originally funded Carter for a five-year archaeological expedition, but as time ran out Carter's confidence, persistence and determination to find Tutankhamen's tomb convinced Carnarvon to back him for one more year — and that made all the difference.

Shortly after the opening of the royal tomb, the story began to cir-culate that a curse was plaguing those involved with the disturbance of the pharaoh's slumber. According to Howard Carter, a clay tablet was found in the antechamber with the inscription, "Death comes on wings to him who disturbs the sleep of kings." The tablet itself was never catalogued and in all likelihood existed only in Carter's imagination. Egyptologists and archaeologists report no evidence of the tablet nor of any such curse or inscription found in Tutankhamen's tomb — or in that of any other pharaoh. However, newspaper reports were quick to jump on the bandwagon, promoting the notion of an Egyptian mummy's curse!

The story began when Carter purchased a singing canary to

brighten up his home. Nearly three weeks before the actual tomb was found on November 4, 1922, the workmen discovered a step cut into the rock, with 15 more steps leading to a doorway. That same evening, a cobra entered Carter's house and devoured his canary. The cobra being a symbol of royalty, was taken as an omen of the pharaoh's curse. However, as a man of science, Carter dismissed it as rubbish. Cobras apparently are not unusual in Egypt during the winter.

Lord Carnarvon died suddenly in Cairo just five months after the opening of the tomb — he became the mummy's first human victim. He died from blood poisoning brought on as a result of an infected mosquito bite that he accidentally nicked while shaving. Rumors of the "curse of the mummy" escalated when it was discovered that the mosquito bite on his cheek was in the same position as that of Tutankhamen's facial scar. It has been said that when Lord Carnarvon died, the lights went out throughout Cairo for 20 minutes. However, that was not an uncommon occurrence. Meanwhile, back in England, Carnarvon's pet dog was reported to have howled and fallen dead at the same time his master died.

Howard Carter lived for 17 years after his milestone discovery, and in 1939, at the age of 66, he died peacefully of natural causes in England. Lord Carnarvon's young daughter, who was present with her father and Carter at the opening in 1922, lived past 70.

Nevertheless, by 1929, eleven people involved with the discovery were reported to have died of unnatural causes in one manner or another, among them scholars, scientists and archaeologists, including an American who had assisted Carter — he fell into a deep coma after suffering heat exhaustion, and died in the same hotel as Lord Carnarvon. Another man, the son of the financier, visited the tomb and died the next day of a high fever; a railroad tycoon who was granted access to the tomb also died the next day of fever. A British industrialist who visited the tomb died of a high fever on board the ship that was taking him back home to England, and a radiologist who worked on Tutankhamen's mummy also died after returning to England. The list goes on, with two professors, four archaeologists and Carnarvon's wife — who also died of an infected mosquito bite, in 1929. His secretary died in his sleep the same year. Three months later, the secretary's father heard the news and took his own life by jumping out of a seven-story window; he left a suicide note blaming the death of his son and himself on the curse. On the way to his funeral, the hearse transporting his body fatally stuck a young boy, and at that exact moment, an employee of the British Museum, specializing in the department of Egyptology, also died. Within a space of two decades, Tutankhamen's curse was blamed for the deaths of 21 people.

In the 1970's, Egypt gave in to public demands and brought Tutankhamen's treasures to the world. Egypt's Director of Antiquities dreamt that he would die if the treasures left Egypt. He was killed in an auto accident three months after the first traveling exhibition was mounted, and the curse claimed its 25th victim.

More recently, scientists have suggested that the "curse" may have actually been the mold spores found in mummies by microbiologists. These spores can survive thousands of years in a dark and dry place; most are harmless, yet some can be toxic. These spores would have been released into the air when the tombs were first opened, and they would have entered the archeologists' bodies through the nose, mouth or eyes. The damage these spores can inflict may lead to organ failure and death, particularly in those with weak immune systems. Carter himself is reported to have noted a brown fungus covering the interior walls of Tutankhamen's tomb.

There are two theories as to who could have been responsible for Tutankhamen's death. General Horemheb stood to gain from his death; he rose through the ranks and became pharaoh in turn, and ruled for 27 years. During this time, he completely obliterated all traces of Akhenaten and Aten. Horemheb ordered the destruction of his predecessor's temples in order to construct a massive pylon at Karnak. Horemheb also ordered the removal of Tutankhamen's name, wherever it appeared, thus attempting to subject him to a second and permanent death. He also had it erased from the royal king lists, along with the names of Akhenaten and Aye (Aye was Tutankhamen's vizier and another strong suspect in the death of the young Pharaoh).

How did Horemheb get to the top, in the first place? Tutankhamen married his half-sister Ankhesenamen, who was previously known as Ankhesenpa'aten. Both were about the same age; they did not have any children. Two mummified fetuses were discovered among the treasures, suggesting that Akhesenamen may have miscarried. Illustrations show the young couple as being quite fond of each other.

After his death, the young Queen sent a desperate message to the Hittite King, pleading with him to send forth a son for marriage. This was a bold move, as it was inconceivable for an Egyptian queen to take a foreign husband and destroy her pure lineage. It is reported that Akhesenamen was very much afraid and had refused to marry "a mere servant." Many believe this servant to have been Horemheb or Aye.

The Hittite King agreed and sent one of his sons, but the boy never made it; he was murdered along the way. He is believed to have been killed at the order of Horemheb. Ankhesenamen then married Aye, who became her co-regent. When Aye died without male heirs, the succession passed to his military leader, Horemheb. When Horemheb also died without male heirs, the succession again passed to an army officer. This military commander was Ramses I, the first pharaoh of the 19th Dynasty; he ruled for about two years.

19th Dynasty (1307-1196 BC)

Seti I

Like his father Ramses I, Seti began as a military commander. He signed a peace treaty with the Hittites, thus stabilizing the frontier. He continued a decree set by Horemheb and sentenced criminals to forced labor in mines, quarries, the desert and oases. His military skills led to triumphs that are illustrated on the walls of the Temple of Karnak as well a stela commemorating his victory over Kadesh. Seti I undertook many building projects during his reign including adding a Hypostyle Hall to the Temple of Karnak.

Ramses II

In AD 1881, one of the most spectacular pharaonic discoveries uncovered the mummified bodies of Ramses II, Seti I and Tuthmose III buried deep in the Valley of the Kings. Ramses II was the son of Seti I and grandson of Ramses I (who left little mark in historical records).

Ramses II ("Born of Ra") was dubbed Ramses the Great by Egyptologists in the 19th century; he came to the throne at the age of 25, upon his father's death, and is believed to have lived to the age of 92. Ramses II was a fearless warrior who fought to regain control over territories that Egypt had held in Africa as well as in western Asia (Iran, Iraq, and Syria) where the Assyrians conquered. He also built many fine temples and erected many massive statues and obelisks; he is regarded as one of the most notable and builders in the history of Egypt. Ramses the Great built the temple of Ausar at Abedju, and the imposing rock temple facade at Abu Simbel.

Ramses II had many wives and sired over a hundred children. His favorite wife by far was Queen Nefertari, whose name means "Beautiful Friend." She died around the 24th year of her husband's reign and was buried in a spectacular tomb in the Valley of the Queens.

Ramses II died after a 67-year reign and outlived many of his sons. His 13th son, Merneptah, lived long enough to become his successor and ruled for a decade. Merneptah himself was no young man when he inherited the throne. He was one of several children born to Ramses II and Queen Istnofret, the King's second-ranking wife after Nefertari; Istnofret replaced Nefertari after her death. How either of the two main wives died is yet to be determined.

Ramses II is believed by many to have been the pharaoh mentioned in the biblical story of the Exodus. Others suggest that it was Merneptah. No evidence of the "Exodus" has ever been discovered in ancient Egyptian documents or inscriptions. However, Merneptah's possible link to the Exodus arises from his claim of victory over Israel on what is known as the Israel Stela: according to the text, Merneptah captured 9000 Israelites and killed another 6000.

Alexander the Great (356 - 323 BC)

As the son of King Phillip II of Macedonia, Alexander the Great succeeded in overthrowing Persian rule in Egypt during 332 BC and initiated the era of Greek dominance. This victory promoted him to Pharaoh, inaugurating the Macedonian Dynasty. A new state capital was established, in 331 BC, at a settlement previously known as Raqote, present day Alexandria.

Alexandria soon grew into a prosperous cosmopolitan city and cultural center: the city boasted an amphitheater, a gymnasium, a stadium and a museum known throughout the ancient world, plus an aqueduct and a hall of justice. It became an important commercial center and a trading post between Asia and Europe.

Alexandria became the intellectual hub of the eastern Mediterranean, and during Ptolemaic rule it evolved into the scientific and literary center of the world, where leading scholars, physicians, scientists, writers, artists, and poets congregated. In 280 BC, a medical school was founded. Ten years later, Ptolemy I Soter founded the renowned Library of Alexandria. The Ptolemies duplicated books from libraries in Athens and other cities and brought them to Alexandria; the collection is believed to have reached some 500,000 scrolls by 250 BC, making it the largest of the ancient world. There were great works on history, geography, mathematics, astronomy, geometry, science, medicine and philosophy. The eventual fate of the library is unknown; no remains have been found. Some believe it was ransacked and put to the torch in c. 412 AD.

Another of the Seven Wonders of Ancient World was also found in Egypt; it was the only one actually to have served a purpose and it was the last to perish. The Lighthouse of Alexandria was situated on the small offshore island of Pharos. It was an essential safety installation, with its beams of light guiding ships as they maneuvered along the hazardous coastline. For over 1000 years, its light could be seen for more than 35 miles. During the day, a bronze mirror at the very top of the lighthouse reflected the sunlight and in the evening, fire was used to throw light. Legend has it that the mirror detected and burned every enemy ship before it reached the shores of Alexandria. Construction is believed to have begun under the rule of Ptolemy Soter c. 290 BC and ended during the reign of his son, Ptolemy II Philadelphus, twenty years later. The architect was Sostratus. When it was completed, the monument was dedicated to Ptolemy Soter and his wife. The lighthouse was ravaged by earthquakes in AD 1303 and 1323; the rubble of what was once a 440-feet-high tower was used to build a fortress during the late 15th century of our era.

However, during Ptolemaic times, all was not well within Egypt.

It has been stated that, outside the capital, Egyptian commoners were reduced to second-class citizens in their own homeland as Greeks flocked to Egypt, attracted by its exoticism and prosperity. The population has been estimated at 3.5 million during the Late Period and 7.5 million by 100 BC. The natives were faced with heavy taxes and rulers who spoke a foreign language; they were barred from owning property and from holding public office in Alexandria. However, Egyptian deities maintained their status as the Macedonians, who ruled as pharaohs, integrated their gods with those of Egypt.

According to legend, Alexander the Great visited the temple of Amen and was told by the oracle that he was of divine birth. At that, he vowed to be buried in Egypt; and, indeed, when Alexander died from a fever (believed to have been malaria) in 323 BC, at the age of 33, his body was brought from Babylon to Egypt and he was given a true Egyptian burial with all the traditions and rituals of the past.

In 304 BC, his lieutenant, field commander and childhood friend, Ptolemy I Soter, proclaimed himself Pharaoh and established the final dynasty, which lasted nearly three centuries.

The list of pharaohs provided at the beginning to this book is based on data that scholars have compiled from several sources. The fragmented *Turin Canon Papyrus* provides a list written in Hieratic (a cursive or short-hand form of hieroglyphs) of rulers up to the 18th Dynasty. This scroll, housed at the Turin Museum in Italy, appears to have been written during the lengthy reign of Ramses II. A list of kings' names and dates, up to the 5th Dynasty, is also inscribed on the diorite *Palermo Stone* exhibited in the Cairo Museum. The *Abydos List of Kings* includes pharaohs starting with Menes and ending with Seti I. This valuable source of information excludes the pharaohs of the Amarna Period. Another important royal list, with 50 names still legible, is found on the tablet known as the *Table of Saqqara*. The *Table of Karnak* dates to the reign of Tuthmose III and provides the names of dozens of rulers, 48 of which remain legible.

The greatest body of data is obtained from *Manetho's King List*. At the command of Ptolemy I and II, in the 3rd century BC, Manetho comprised a chronological list, three books long, covering all the ruling kings and dynasties starting with King Menes and ending with the last native pharaoh, Nectanebo II. That invaluable work actually has never been found, but it is known from citations made in other early works; it has often been quoted, with occasional comments made by later historians and authors. Although it contains some contradictions and overlapping dates, Manetho's King List is an indispensable framework upon which to base our understanding of ancient Egyptian chronology.

Excavations have given us limited information about several of Egypt's queens. Few ruled Egypt in their own right, independent of their husbands; many had been princesses, the daughters of the pharaohs, and the men they took as husbands became king of Egypt so that they in turn became queen. Some queens were foreigners, some were commoners and some were members of the pharaoh's harem. Often, a pharaoh's first-born daughter would marry her brother or half-brother to keep the bloodline pure. The duties of the Queen of Egypt included managing the King's palace and harem; few actually wielded authority over state affairs. Here is a short list of some whose legacy has come down to us in modern times.

Neitkrety (Nitocris) - 6th Dynasty

Neitkrety was a beautiful queen of the late 6th Dynasty and is credited as the first known female to exercise political power in Egypt. In *Manetho's King List*, she is shown as the last pharaoh of this dynasty. She may have been married to Merenre; or perhaps to Pepy II. She is believed to have ruled Egypt with the primary goal of avenging the death of her brother, who was killed for committing a minor religious sin. According to legend, Neitkrety invited those whom she believed to

be responsible for her brother's death to a lavish banquet. The attendees all drowned when the waters of the Nile came gushing forth (from
a secret channel she had had built) and flooded the banquet chamber.
Neitkrety's reign was not long; she survived the event herself, but
shortly afterwards took her own life.

Neferu-Sobek - *12th Dynasty*

She was the last pharaoh of the Middle Kingdom. Three statues
and a sphinx belonging to her were discovered in the Delta. Neferu-
Sobek ruled for four years and is mentioned in three king lists.

Ahmose Nefertiri - *18th Dynasty*

Queen Ahmose Nefertiri was born to Seqenenre Tao II and Queen
Ahhotep of the 17th Dynasty. When Seqenenre Tao II died a violent
death, battling the Hyksos, Ahhotep (who lived until 90) is credited
with encouraging the dispirited Egyptian troops to continue the fight.
At Karnak, an inscription praises her for looking after the soldiers,
boosting their morale and pacifying Egypt. Ahmose Nefertiri married
Ahhotep's son, Ahmose, founder of the 18th Dynasty. She gave birth to
six children, including a son who became King Amenhotep I and a
daughter who became Queen Ahhotep II.

Shortly after Amenhotep I inherited the throne, Ahmose Nefertiri
died; they eventually were buried side by side. Ahmose Nefertiri was
the first to bear the prestigious title of "Wife of Amen." Her step-
daughter became a powerful woman, Queen Ahmose — by marrying
Tuthmose I, she was crowned as Pharaoh. At the temple of Hatshepsut,
Ahmose is illustrated as the consort of Amen, giving divine birth to
Hatshepsut.

Hatshepsut - *18th Dynasty*

According to legend, Amen-Ra proclaimed before the pantheon of
gods that Egypt would be ruled by a great queen. Tehuti came forth and
identified the woman as the wife of Tuthmose I, the beautiful lady
named Ahmose, whose name translates into "Born of the Moon." Amen-
Ra summoned Khnemu to fashion upon his potter's wheel the body and
ka of his daughter, who would be born of Queen Ahmose, and who
would become a great queen of Egypt.

In 1504 BC, at the age of 32, Queen Hatshepsut became the first woman to wear the Double or *Pschent* Crown of the Two Lands. Her name means "Foremost of the Noble Women."

Hatshepsut often represented herself as a man and even went as far as wearing the traditional male pharaonic garb as well as the royal false beard. As a woman, she had to conjure up a compelling rationale to ensure her right to claim the throne. Hatshepsut claimed to be of divine birth, specifically chosen by Amen-Ra, the King of Gods, thus rendering her worthy to all the gods of Egypt. Scenes of Hatshepsut's divine birth are displayed on the walls of her mortuary temple, where we see Amen approaching Queen Ahmose (in the form of Tuthmose I) for the purpose of conceiving Hatshepsut. An inscription carved at the chapel of her temple tells how Amen-Ra prophesied Hatshepsut's ascent to the throne, through a great oracle, proclaiming her ruler of the Two Lands. In another inscription, Amen-Ra is shown crowning her as pharaoh, further solidifying her claim.

Hatshepsut was a strong-willed woman who did not let anyone interfere with her plans or obstruct her ambitions. She began her reign with her half-brother as co-regent, securing the family line. However, this joint rulership ended with the death of Tuthmose II in 1504 BC. She then co-ruled with her stepson by a minor wife, Tuthmose III. During the second year of their joint reign, she initiated plans to become the sole ruler of Egypt, while Tuthmose III remained in the background. Her attempts were successful, and with Tuthmose III as co-regent in name only, she reigned alone from 1498 to 1483 BC.

Egypt prospered under her leadership and she became highly respected and admired by her people. The economy flourished and no wars took place during her reign. She proved her sovereignty by arranging and funding great public projects to restore temples and monuments that had been damaged or destroyed by the Hyksos. She also inaugurated several new building projects. In 1493 BC, during the sixth or seventh year of her reign, she ordered up a fleet of five ships and participated in a trade expedition to the land of Punt. This milestone event in her life is recorded on the walls of her temple. The expedition brought back huge cargoes of the fragrances for which Punt was noted, especially myrrh and frankincense. These were used in cosmetics as well as for incense for the temples, and possibly for medicinal purposes. She also brought back gold, ebony, ivory and exotic animals.

Upon her death in 1483 BC, her scorned successor Tuthmose III did everything in his power to erase all traces of her memory. He had her name carefully chiseled out from an inscription at the Temple of Karnak. Blocks were dismantled from her Red Chapel and re-used to build a pylon honoring Amenhotep III. Some of her monuments were also destroyed: her memory posed a threat to the male-dominated line of pharaohs. However, Queen Hatshepsut is remembered by Egyptologists and scholars as a remarkable woman, builder, tradesperson and pharaoh.

Tiy - 18th Dynasty

Tiy was Queen of Egypt by marriage to Amenhotep III. She was his favorite wife, and together they had several daughters and a son who became the Pharaoh Akhenaten. Tiy is honored as the first queen of Egypt to have her name credited with official deeds including the announcement of Amenhotep III's marriage to a foreign princess. She was a commoner by birth who lived with her son in Amarna before "going west" at the age of 48.

Nefertiti - 18th Dynasty

Nefertiti is believed to have been of nonroyal blood, perhaps of Nubian or Mitanni origin. Or, she may have been the daughter of Aye. Nefertiti possessed outstanding beauty and her names translates into "The Beautiful One Has Come." Akhenaten, however, referred to her as "His Mistress of Happiness." In honor of Aten, Nefertiti changed her name to Nefer-Nefraten, meaning, "Fair is the Goddess of Aten." She was "immortalized" when her magnificently sculpted head was discovered in the workshop of a sculptor named Tuthmose, bringing us a permanent memory of her lovely countenance.

Tuya - 19th Dynasty

Tuya was a commoner by birth who became wife of Seti I. Together they had a child who became Pharaoh as Ramses II. Tuya lived to see her son inherit the throne. Ramses II gave his mother royal recognition wherever he could; she was buried at the Valley of the Queens.

Nefertari - *19th Dynasty*

Nefertari was married to Ramses II as early as the first year of his reign, and was his chief or favorite wife. She is believed to have been of non-royal blood, born to a military official. When she died, he dedicated a temple to Nefertari and Het-Heru at Abu Simbel. However, it is her exquisite tomb in the Valley of the Queens that is recognized as one of Egypt's most beautiful constructions.

Istnofret - *19th Dynasty*

Istnofret ("Beautiful Isis") was the second in rank of Ramses II's many wives. She gave birth to several children, including Setna Khaemwast and Merneptah, Ramses II's successor. She became the chief wife when Nefertari died.

Twosret - *19th Dynasty*

Outliving her husband, Seti II, Twosret became the last pharaoh of the 19th Dynasty. Twosret, the last true native female pharaoh, ruled Egypt with Seti II's son Siptah, born from another wife. After his death six years later, she ruled independently, but with the assistance of a vizier and official named Irsu (or Bay?). Believed to be of Syrian descent, Irsu was not very popular with the people and was regarded as an opportunist. Twosret reigned as pharaoh for nearly two years. At Per Bast, many gold and silver vessels have been discovered with her name inscribed on them.

Cleopatra VII - *Ptolemaic Dynasty (69-30 BC)*

The last Pharaoh of Egypt was the Macedonian Cleopatra VII, who was born in Alexandria. Cleopatra, whose name means "Her Father's Glory," was a brilliant and charismatic woman who was devoted to Egypt. She excelled in many arenas, spoke the principal foreign languages, and had a good head for business. She was a born leader and had great ambitions for her country. Surprisingly enough, coins stamped with Cleopatra's face show that she was far from beautiful. Her very real powers of attraction stemmed from her intelligence, dignity, convictions, aspirations, and pride.

Cleopatra VII was the daughter of Ptolemy XII Auletes, who became known as the "Flute Player." Ptolemy XII had been a weak ruler;

he was actually overthrown in 58 BC and fled to Rome. It is believed that a year earlier, he had paid tribute to Caesar in order to keep Rome at a distance. This act gave Rome *de facto* dominance over Egypt at a time when the Roman empire was expanding in size and power. During his two-year absence, his wife Cleopatra V and eldest daughter Berenice IV took the throne. In 55 BC, Ptolemy XII Auletes paid enough tribute to the Romans to be allowed to return to Egypt. He reclaimed the throne with the help of the Roman General Pompey and had Berenice IV executed.

Ptolemy XII Auletes died in 51 BC and Cleopatra inherited the throne at the age of 18. Ptolemy Auletes had left Cleopatra VII and her brothers and sisters under the care of Pompey. Tradition dictated that she could not be sole ruler, so her 12-year-old brother Ptolemy XIII was appointed as co-regent. (Co-regency was first adopted by Amenemhet I of the Middle Kingdom. During the 20th year of his reign, he appointed Senwosret as co-ruler; Senwosret eventually succeeded him and became the second pharaoh of the 12th Dynasty.) Cleopatra's political aspirations drove her to push her brother aside, much as Hatshepsut had done with her half-brother nearly 1500 years earlier. It was Egyptian law that the male co-regent's name be placed first; but Cleopatra dropped his name from official documents. She even had her own portrait and name inscribed on coins without including her co-regent.

In 48 BC, Cleopatra VII was stripped of her power by her co-regent's advisor. She was driven into exile and she fled to Syria. Ptolemy XIII eventually drowned, and their then 11-year-old brother Ptolemy XIV was appointed as Cleopatra's co-regent.

She was well aware that Egypt's future depended upon amicable relations with the Romans, who were gaining the upper hand in the entire region. Cleopatra VII wished to rule Egypt as a partner to Rome, not as a conquered Roman province. In 46 BC, she ingeniously befriended the Roman general and military leader, Julius Gaius Caesar, charming him completely. They apparently took a two-month trip up the Nile, flaunting their new alliance. A year later, Cleopatra gave birth to Caesar's son. His name was Ptolemy Caesar (he was known as Caesarion, "Of Caesar"). At the age of four, the boy was established as Cleopatra VII's co-regent, upon the death of Ptolemy XIV (who died by poison). Many believe that Cleopatra killed him in order to establish Caesarion as next in line.

Caesar openly acknowledged Caesarion and appointed the child heir to the Egyptian throne. For two years, Cleopatra VIII and Caesarion lived in a villa outside of Rome, where Caesar was a frequent visitor. Hatred was growing among the Romans, Egyptians and Greeks. Caesar was already married to a woman named Calpurnia, and Cleopatra VIII was despised by most Romans and regarded as a cheating, ambitious mistress. Meanwhile, Egypt felt betrayed and abandoned by their ruler, who was already a foreigner, anyway, while the Greeks also felt cheated by Cleopatra's alliance with Rome. Caesar was considered a significant threat to Rome's well-being, in part because of his compromising involvement with the temptress from Alexandria. Three years later, he was assassinated by his senators in Rome. Civil war plagued Rome after Caesar's death. Cleopatra VII and Caesarion were left completely unprotected; they fled home to Alexandria. Cleopatra soon heard that Caesar had left no provisions for her and their child in his will; both were now in mortal danger.

Enter Mark Antony, a handsome young Roman soldier and Caesar's chief lieutenant. In 42 or 41 BC, Mark Antony sent for Cleopatra to meet with him in Tarsus (Turkey), to discuss her possible role in the murder of Caesar. Cleopatra VII, dressed as the Great Auset, sailed on a spectacular gilded barge symbolic of her rich land. The goddess must have been with her, for Mark Antony and Cleopatra VII enjoyed a magnificent feast and spent considerable time together. He followed the Queen back to Alexandria, to the great dismay of many Romans; and he remained in Egypt for a few months before returning to Rome.

In 40 BC, already captivated by Cleopatra VII, Mark Antony married Octavia, the sister of Caesar's nephew and heir Octavian. This marriage subdued the turbulent relations between the two men. Octavia bore Mark Antony two daughters; had they been sons, history may have gone rather differently. Octavia also raised Marc Antony's children by his deceased wife, Fulvia. Octavia must have been quite a remarkable woman in her own right, for after Cleopatra's death she also raised the children her husband had sired with her.

Cleopatra VII bore Marc Antony a son, who was named Ptolemy

Philadelphus, and a set of twins named Cleopatra Selene (the Moon) and Alexander Helios (the Sun). Marc Antony outraged the Romans when he gave his children large sections of eastern Roman territory. He did not see Cleopatra VII again until he returned to Egypt some four years later; he married her in 36 BC, having disavowed Octavia earlier the same year. Octavian, who later became Emperor Augustus, was offended by these acts. Relations were further stressed when Mark Antony had Cleopatra's VII name and image inscribed on Roman coins that were circulated throughout Mediterranean lands.

Octavian convinced the senate to declare war against Cleopatra. The Sea Battle of Actium, off the coast of Greece, ended when Cleopatra VII suddenly withdrew her fleet and returned to Egypt. She must have realized that Marc Antony was about to be defeated by Octavian's navy, led by his general Agrippa, or perhaps she thought that he was already dead when she turned back.

In Roman eyes, Marc Antony lost all respect as a result of his weakness for the Queen of Egypt. He died in 30 BC by his own hand, in true Roman style, by falling upon his sword. Now, Cleopatra VII had no option left but to exercise her charm upon Octavian. This time, her efforts fell flat. Octavian wanted nothing to do with her, either romantically or politically. At the age of 39, Cleopatra VII chose death over defeat and humiliation; she would have been exhibited in the streets of Rome as a triumphant acquisition. The general belief is that she took her life with the help of an asp, quite fittingly a symbol of Egyptian royalty and immortality. Egyptian religious beliefs proclaimed that death by an asp secured immortality. Her final act was a success, as she has never been forgotten.

Octavian actually granted her last wish by giving the Queen a spectacular burial and laying her to rest alongside Marc Antony. The three children they had together were dispatched to Rome to live under the care of Octavia. Caesarion was put to death by strangulation, so that he would not be able to claim Egypt's throne as the last ruling Ptolemy, nor make any claim over Rome as the son of Caesar. This act also eliminated any threatening ramifications resulting from Cleopatra's alliance with Caesar and permanently terminated the line of pharaohs in Egypt.

24. Battles and Warriors

The ancient Egyptians were more peace-loving than warlike, but Egypt's prosperity was an irresistible lure to its less-prosperous neighbors. They were often invaded and constantly had to deploy defensive strategies and counter-attacks. For divine protection during times of war, they relied on Montu, the hawk-headed solar god of war, and Nit, the goddess of warfare, who were believed to protect both the pharaoh and the soldiers.

During successful military campaigns, captives were taken and brought to Egypt as labor to build temples, raise dykes, cut canals and construct other public works in the service of the monarchy. However, when Egypt fell under foreign domination, late in its history, the social and political status of the natives dramatically declined. As an example of how much prestige and power Egypt lost during those turbulent times, a young Egyptian princess was sent abroad to marry a foreign king; in good times, no Egyptian princess had ever defied the ancient laws nor demeaned herself by marrying in another land other than her own. The story of Wenamen, a late 20th Dynasty official, is also illustrative. He was sent by order of Ramses XI on an expedition to Byblos to acquire timber for the building of Amen's royal barge. Wenamen encountered many tribulations and indignities; indeed, his request was rudely denied by the ruler of Byblos. Another ambassador of the same dynasty was not only robbed but had to pay dearly to recover his own goods.

A short history of conflicts

Egypt's first recorded battle took place c. 3100 BC, unifying the Two Lands and establishing the First Dynasty. Throughout the Old Kingdom, trade expansion was the main reason for military campaigns. During the 2nd Intermediate Period, Egypt was invaded by the Hyksos. During the New Kingdom, Egypt defended herself against the Hittites of Turkey, the Kassites of Babylon and the Mitannites of North Syria. During the 3rd Intermediate Period, the Libyans and the Kushites from Nubia threatened Egypt and during 671 BC, Egypt's most formidable enemy, the Assyrians, declared war. During the Late Period, Egypt was invaded by the Nubians, Assyrians, Persians and, in 332 BC by the Macedonian Greeks. The Ptolemaic Dynasty was established when the Ptolemy I Soter proclaimed himself Pharaoh in 304 BC. Ptolemaic rule came to an end with the Roman conquest in 30 BC.

The traditional enemies of Egypt were known as "The Nine Bows." Reference to this group goes as far back as Predynastic times. Although their precise identities have not been fully determined, they are assumed to have included the Libyans and the Nubians, the Hittites from Asia Minor, the early Assyrians, Bedouins, Mitannians and the Kassites. Egypt's enemies were often portrayed as subdued captives with their elbows and ankles bound.

Sticks and stones

In the early days, the Egyptians were not as well-organized nor well-equipped for warfare as their neighbors. During the Predynastic era, weaponry consisted of knives made of stone and needles carved from bone. In the Old Kingdom, both were made of copper, later replaced by bronze. Soldiers fought on foot with wooden or stone-headed maces, daggers, and spears, with leather shields slung over the shoulder with a leather strap. Ceremonial daggers with blades of copper or bronze were found in the tomb of Tutankhamen, and on his mummy a sheathed dagger of outstanding craftsmanship was placed, with a floral design on the handle, adorned with tiny beads of gold.

Over time, a solid military establishment was created. During the 6th Dynasty, General Weni, the royal chief official and commander serving under Pepy I, created a highly-organized military establishment that endured well into the New Kingdom. General Weni is credited with leading five military campaigns into Syria as well as with being the first man other than a pharaoh to be depicted in a relief, leading an army into battle. It is written that General Weni improved the morale and the military skills of Egyptian soldiers, supplementing their existing (mainly defensive) tactics with training in a more combative approach. General Weni eventually became overseer of Upper Egypt.

In around 2060 BC, King Montuhotep II led a series of successful military campaigns against the Libyans in the Delta and the Asiatics in Sinai. He took possession of Henen Nesut, the capital of the rival kings, and thus inaugurated the Middle Kingdom. By this time, Egyptian troops were carrying battle-axes, copper blades, and bronze spears, and the soldiers began wearing protective clothing made of leather. (It was not until the New Kingdom that the royal armies began wearing metal armor.) In a cemetery at Deir el-Bahri, the bodies of 60 soldiers were discovered, shrouded with the inscription and seal of Montuhotep II; the mummies reveal that they died of battle injuries.

Desert storm

The Hyksos, an Asiatic-Semitic people known as "Desert Princes" or "Shepherd Kings" ("Heka Khasut" in ancient Egyptian), slowly migrated into the northern delta region during the 18th century BC and gradually acquired dominion over the land, establishing their capital at Per-Ramessu (Avaris). The Hyksos formed relations with Nubia, in order to secure their southern border, and ties with Africa. There were five Hyksos kings between c. 1663 and 1555 BC. They settled at Per Ramessu and worshipped the desert god Set. The Hyksos worshipped Egyptian deities and maintained their culture and traditions, adopting local customs and not attempting to impose their own, while exercising power over the land within Egyptian boundaries.

The Egyptians despised the Hyksos and considered them barbarians; however, they actually exposed the Egyptians to many technological advances. Most important of all, the Hyksos introduced the harnessed horse and chariot. Until then, the Egyptians had fought on foot. As the development of improved weaponry was necessary for survival in this combative era, the Egyptians went a step further and improved the design of the chariot, making it lighter in weight. The driver was now placed closer to the axle, which was clad in metal in order to minimize friction. These alterations greatly enhanced the performance of the horse, since the load was very much lightened. The charioteer rode standing up, using leather straps for stability. The chariots were also used in sporting games where speed was an important factor. The open back of the chariot enabled the rider to jump out at a moment's notice. Four spectacular chariots were discovered among Tutankhamen's treasures. Although he led no military expeditions during his reign, his experience in the afterlife might be less peaceful, and he was provided with everything he might need.

Before the Hyksos arrived, Egyptian weapons were mostly small and feeble and little or no protective clothing was worn. Improved weaponry such as daggers, scimitars, and body armor, all came from the Hyksos, including the use of leather helmets in place of shoulder-length wigs and skull caps — or no head protection at all!

The bow and arrow was the Egyptian soldier's main tool of defense; the Hyksos introduced a much-improved version called the "composite bow." It was far stronger than the standard Egyptian wooden bow and could shoot much farther. Now, the soldiers of the new and improved army were trained to use the bow and arrow while racing along in horse-drawn chariots; and it was with the Hyksos' own weapons that the Egyptians were able to expel them a century later.

During the 2nd Intermediate period, the Hyksos King Ipepi, from Per Ramessu in Lower Egypt, sent an offensive message to Pharaoh Seqenenre II Tao in Uast. One version says that he strongly objected to the hunting of hippopotami. Another version says that he claimed that the hippopotami kept in the Pharaoh's royal pools were disturbing his sleep. The two towns being several hundred miles apart (pretty far for a hippo's grunt to travel), this allegation infuriated the Pharaoh. He took it as a personal insult and a war began. Shortly after, Seqenenre II Tao died of head injuries (apparently from a battle-axe); his mummy displayed a badly damaged skull when discovered in AD 1881.

After his death, his wife, Queen Ahhotep I, encouraged their two sons Kamose and Ahmose to continue the war in their father's name. Kamose and Ahmose were greatly aided by the cunning and merciless combat skills of the Nubian *Medjay* Force that served as infantry units. Kamose had no male heir and did not live to see victory over the Hyksos. That honor went to his younger brother, Ahmose, who successfully expelled the Hyksos from Egypt and restored the boundaries held during the Old Kingdom. It was a well-fought battle, won at high cost but in the end bringing great rewards: Ahmose's victory established him as the founder of the 18th Dynasty and the New Kingdom. When Ahmose died (c. 1515 BC), his son Amenhotep I took over his campaigns. Amenhotep I led his troops into Nubia and completed the job by defeating the Libyans as well.

Special awards such as the Golden Fly (a pin in the form of a gilded horsefly, scourge of war horses and other great beasts) were bestowed upon those who displayed outstanding bravery in battle. Queen Aahotep I received the Golden Fly for her participation in the war against the Hyksos. She lived past the age of 90 and was laid to rest beside her son, Kamose, at Uast. In her tomb, along with honorary awards was an axe made of inlaid gold, copper and semi-precious stones bearing the name of her son, Ahmose.

An inscription commemorating Kamose's victory is recorded on the Kamose Stela dated to the 17th Dynasty. The stela tells how Kamose led a successful campaign against the Hyksos and humiliated their King Ipepi. Kamose brought back chariots, weaponry and much valuable plunder.

Military build-up

During the 18th Dynasty, the Egyptian army expanded and became increasingly well-armed. By the New Kingdom, the army was comprised of three branches: archers, infantry and charioteers. The latter group was exclusive to the nobility and the upper class. During the New Kingdom, the Egyptian infantry fought with battle-axes, spears and daggers. Iron weapons replaced those of bronze.

The pharaohs of the New Kingdom were constantly engaged in battle expeditions and achieved a great increase of military power. Amenhotep I led the Egyptian army into battle in Nubia. Tuthmose III won the Battle of Megiddo, Ramses II fought in the Battle of Kadesh and Ramses III defeated the Sea Peoples.

Tuthmose III was a fearless warrior and a gifted commander. He triumphed over the Syrians in the Battle of Meggido; and he reached the furthest point south, just before the fourth cataract, to found the town of Napata in Nubia. During most of his reign, he fought to restore Egyptian power in Palestine and Syria. Tuthmose III conducted about 20 campaigns against the Syrians during the New Kingdom, earning him the title of the "Napoleon of Egypt" millennia later. He is regarded as one of the world's greatest military commanders. His mummy was discovered in the Valley of the Kings in 1881 along with that of Seqenenre II Tao.

Horemheb, who was appointed army commander by Tutankhamen, was the last pharaoh to rule during the 18th Dynasty. Prior to his death he named another military commander, Ramses I, as his successor since he had no male heirs. His descendant Seti I led a military campaign into Syria during the first year of his reign; he often took his young son Ramses II along on military campaigns, thus preparing him for a warrior's life and training him in battle strategies.

In turn, Ramses II gathered a force of 20,000 men during the 5th year of his reign (c. 1275 BC) and set out to regain control of former Egyptian territories in Africa and western Asia. His troops were divided into four units of 5000 men, and each division was named after one of the four great gods; Amen, Ra, Set and Ptah. On his way to battle, the Pharaoh was deceived by two undercover Hittites, and was led straight into a trap where enemy forces, an army twice the size of his, waited in ambush. Many Egyptian soldiers perished, but in a surprise, winning maneuver, Ramses II was saved by his personal guard and shield-bearer who led him by a route different from that of his doomed soldiers. As a result of this double deception, the Hittite King Muwatallis was forced to defend himself without warning.

Both rulers were losing too many men in this ongoing conflict, and King Muwatallis proposed a peace treaty nearly 15 years after the war began. During the 21st year of his reign, Ramses II accepted the proposal, and thirteen years later he sealed the pact by marrying the king's daughter, a Hittite princess. She was given the Egyptian name of Manefrure and became one of his Great Royal Wives. Although the war remained inconclusive, it was depicted as a proud Egyptian victory on the walls of the temples at Karnak and Luxor, at the Ramesseum and his temples at Abtu, Abu-simbel and Derr. At the Temple of Abu Simbel, Ramses II is shown riding his royal chariot in the Battle of Kadesh, courageously charging ahead toward the enemy, leading his men into war.

Ramses III, of the 20th Dynasty, waged and won three successful wars within a span of six years. He not only defended Egypt from the invasion of the Libyans but fought the earliest sea battle in recorded history, c. 1200 BC, against the Mediterranean Sea Peoples of Asia Minor. The Sea Peoples were not, in fact, well-equipped to fight and had vessels powered only by sails, while those of the Egyptians were furnished with both sails and oars. Egypt thus gained a new population of laborers and army grunts.

The Egyptian navy was actually engaged more in transporting troops and in escorting trading expeditions than in active battles. King Necho II of the 26th Dynasty is credited with forming the first Egyptian navy; he also built a canal between the Nile and the Red Sea, enormously facilitating trading expeditions eastward and southward. Warships were constructed that could hold up to 250 soldiers; they were well equipped and quite maneuverable. It was with such warships that Ramses III successfully defended Egypt from the invading Sea Peoples. Ramses III is considered the last great warrior pharaoh.

Bleeding from many wounds

The Libyans gradually increased in power and during the 3rd Intermediate Period, their king Sheshonq conquered Upper and Lower Egypt. Sheshonq was born into a family of generations of high priests based at Henen-Nesut and could hardly be considered a foreigner. He applied his military expertise and re-established trade with Nubia and Byblos. During the 22nd Dynasty, Sheshonq undertook a campaign of foreign conquest and invaded Palestine.

By c. 730 BC, Egypt was once again an easy target, as civil wars kept all attention focused inward. At this time, the Nubians gained the upper hand and ruled for nearly 70 years. By c. 674 BC, Egypt was attacked by the mighty Assyrians, thus weakening the Nubian grasp. This was repeated in 671 BC and 664 BC. By 525 BC, the Persians had taken over; they in turn were overthrown by the Macedonian Greeks in 332 BC.

The final battle took place at Actium, where decades of diplomacy and resistance came to an end; Egypt succumbed to Rome, becoming a mere province, and pharaohs ruled no more.

25. The Pyramids

A popular Arabic saying captures the essence of the oldest and last remaining wonder of the ancient world: "Man fears time, but time fears the Pyramids." Still standing nearly five millennia after they were built, the pyramids symbolize the origins of mathematics, geometry and astronomy. Without this combined intelligence, the pyramids could not have been designed. Indeed, it seems that the Egyptians may have been aware of the dimensions of the earth and incorporated those figures into their scale of measurement and the building of the Great Pyramid. The uncanny precision of these constructions is a stunning reflection of the sophistication of these people who lived in the very first days of the history of Western civilization.

The pyramids are generally oriented east/west. The Egyptians called them *mr*, but the Greeks named them "pyramidos" after the wheaten cakes, of that shape, eaten in Greece. The pyramids were modeled after the primeval mound from which all life originated, symbolizing the concept of rebirth, resurrection and immortality.

The rising and setting of the stars were measured and used to establish a true North. From this point, South could be derived, and East and West were calculated by using the midpoint of North and South. This is the earliest form of astronomy in ancient Egypt, and it enabled them to orient the pyramids very precisely.

Pyramid scheme

Explorations of the pyramids were expected to reveal great insights into the customs of the ancient Egyptians; in reality, more questions were raised than answered. Did the ancient Egyptians really know the exact dimensions of the earth? No explanation seems adequate, yet they seem to have been well aware that the earth is spherical and apparently they found the value of *Pi*, and, by carefully observing the movements of the planets, it seems that they ascertained the earth's circumference. They built the Great Pyramid so that the relationship between its circumference and its height is the same as the relationship between the earth's circumference and its radius at the pole.

Professor Charles Piazzi Smyth (scholar and Astronomer Royal for Scotland) measured the pyramid and calculated its vertical height. He came to the conclusion that that the pyramid gained 9 units in width per 10 units of height. When he multiplied the height of the pyramid by a 10:9 ratio, the result was 91,840,000 — just about the mean distance of the earth from the sun (which varies between 91,000,000 and 92,000,000 miles).

Sir Isaac Newton conducted research on the building of the pyramid, and he concluded that two different types of cubits must have been used: the standard cubit measures 20.6 inches but the second one — which he called the "sacred cubit" — equals the polar radius of the earth when divided by 10,000,000, that is (in today's equivalent), 25 inches. When the base length of the Pyramid is divided into units of 25 inches, the result is 365.2 — the number of days in a year. Indeed, they seem to have known what they were doing.

The pyramids were believed to be houses of eternity for the deceased pharaohs, serving as permanent places for their spirits to dwell, and as funerary temples. The pyramids served as memorials rather than actual tombs; no actual pharaonic remains have even been found inside or under a pyramid. Directly underneath the core of the pyramid were the burial chambers. Descending corridors were constructed at an angle leading to the chambers, which were sealed with solid stone. Of course, this did not suffice to keep tomb robbers away.

It has been suggested that the pyramids were great secret temples where the privileged classes underwent a mystical ritual that was believed to transform the deceased into gods; others believe the pyramids to have been the product of a colossal work project intended merely to keep the citizens occupied and unified by working toward a collective goal. Other theories assert that the pyramids are stone calendars and/or astronomical observatories.

Most of the pyramids are situated on the western side of the Nile within fifty miles of Cairo, in the Land of the Dead and the setting sun.

Hard rock

Ancient Egypt was rich in building material suitable for monumental construction. Large quantities of red, grey and black granite were quarried at Aswan and used to line the corridors and interior of the pyramid chambers. Limestone was quarried near Mennefer and was used for the outer surfacing; sandstone came from the cliffs in Upper Egypt.

These heavy blocks of stone are believed to have been transferred to the building site by rope, barge, and sledges hauled by gangs of workers. After being floated down the Nile, the barges or flat-beds constructed of imported timber were pulled by sleds or rolled on logs; animals such as horses were not used to carrying such heavy loads nor was the wheel in use at this time in Egyptian history.

The blocks were so meticulously aligned that a razor blade could not be inserted into the seams. Iron tools were not yet in use; copper was the best they had for tools such as chisels and saws for cutting the limestone blocks that formed the outer casing.

The basis of the pyramid was the *mastaba* or mortuary compartment that was customary during the First Dynasty. King Djoser of the 3rd Dynasty charged his vizier, Imhotep, with designing a new style of mastaba to shelter his eternal rest. Rather than using the traditional mud bricks, Imhotep had the (very solid) idea of building one mastaba over another, of imperishable stone until six layers of diminishing size were formed, reaching 200 feet in height.

His plan was built from local stone; however, fine limestone was used for the outer facing. Each side was aligned to the four cardinal points of the compass. The result was the first surviving man-made monument in history made entirely of stone; it is known as the Step Pyramid of Saqqara. The design of the pyramid symbolizes a flight of steps leading to heaven, a stairway to the stars where the deceased hoped to be reunited with Ausar and dwell among the gods. King Djoser's tomb chamber was constructed entirely from pink granite and situated at the bottom of a shaft sealed with rubble. This pyramid was originally surrounded by temples and royal courtyards.

King Sneferu (of the 4th Dynasty) built the next three pyramids, which were later perfected by his successors. The first was the Pyramid of Meidum, located five miles south of Saqqara. It is generally believed that Sneferu actually continued work started by his father Huni, the last pharaoh of the 3rd Dynasty.This pyramid originally began as a du-plication of the Step Pyramid, this time with seven layers.

The Bent Pyramid is situated at Dahshur. It began at a 54 degree, 31 minute angle and narrowed upward to a 43 degree, 21 minute angle. This tapering effect was intended to prevent the structure from crum-bling, as its weight would cause the limestone sides to crack. Therefore, this pyramid displays a "bent" or sloped appearance. The Bent Pyramid is also known as the South Pyramid.

The Red Pyramid is also located at Dahshur. When bathed in the desert sunset, the pink limestone casing flushes to a warm red. It was also known as the North Pyramid, as its entrance is positioned in a de-scending passage cut into the northern side.

Sneferu's son Khufu built the first, the tallest and the largest of the three pyramids at Giza. It is believed to have taken some twenty years for about 20,000 men using 2.3 million limestone and granite blocks to complete the structure. Each block weighed between 2.5 to 15 tons; enough to ensure stability and endurance. During the 13th century of our era, Arabs stripped the sheathing of smooth limestone away from Khufu's pyramid in order to build mosques in Cairo. The pyramid rests on a base covering 13 acres. Originally it rose to a height of 481 feet, but it is now 451 feet tall. This pyramid is unique in the fact that its chamber is quarried directly from the bedrock under the core of the pyramid.

Like the pyramids at Dahshur, it once contained a mortuary temple, and a great causeway connecting it to the valley temple. In old maps from the 19th century, the entire complex could still be seen. The square base of the pyramid has a perimeter equal to the circumference of a circle whose radius would equal the pyramid's height. The north and south sides are accurately oriented, missing true north by less than 1/10th of a degree. Clearly, the ancient Egyptians were skilled in taking precise astronomical measurements and then transferring this knowledge to earth. The Grand Gallery of Khufu's pyramid leading up to the King's Chamber is further aligned with the local celestial meridian, which was used to observe stellar movements. According to legend, Khufu designed his own burial chamber, situated below the pyramid, surrounded by a moat: Herodotus claimed that in the underground chamber, "a cut was made from the Nile" and the water from it turned this site into an island. No evidence of this has ever been found.

His son Khafre built the second, in order and in size, of the pyramids at Giza. His is the best preserved of the three and still displays pieces of its original limestone casing at the apex. Khafre's pyramid originally stood at 471 feet, that is, 10 feet lower than Khufu's pyramid; but the slope of its angles is 2 degrees higher than those of his father's pyramid and it is constructed on a higher plateau, so that it appears to be the tallest of the three. Khafre's complex consisted of the pyramid and a mortuary temple linked by a causeway to the valley temple.

His son Menkaura ("Established Spirits of Ra") is responsible for the third of the pyramids at Giza; it is the smallest one there, but still it rises to 218 feet. Menkaura died before his pyramid was completed; it was finished by his successor, Shepseskaf.

Each of the pyramids at Giza originally contained an adjoining mortuary temple situated nearby as well as a valley temple, causeway and cult chapel. A modern theory has created much controversy surrounding the origins of this complex: it has been suggested that the physical layout of the three structures mirrors the three stars forming the belt of the constellation of Orion, known as *sah* to the ancient Egyptians. This theory supports the idea that the pyramids are symbolic of a terrestrial map of the heavens directing divine energy to earth. The ancient Egyptians believed that life on earth was reflected or duplicated in the heavens. To the left of Orion is Sopdet (Sirius, the Dog Star). Sopdet was venerated as embodying the soul of Auset, as Sah (Orion) represents Ausar. Sopdet and Sah were believed to be the souls of the divine couple who together ruled the heavens.

It is true that Menkaura's pyramid is curiously positioned out of alignment with the two larger pyramids, and is slightly off to the left. However, one must question why the remaining stars of the constellation of Orion were not represented or mapped out by any other pyramids if that was the rationale.

Modern research has proposed that the shafts (originally thought to exist for ventilation purposes) might actually have had astronomical significance. The eight-inch square shaft of the King's Chamber of the Great Pyramid points directly to the celestial pole, and the King's southern shaft points to the three stars of Orion's Belt as it would have appeared c. 2500 BC. The shaft of the Queen's Chamber, which was never used as a burial chamber, pointed directly to Auset's constellation, Sopdet, at the time the pyramids were built. This information leads to the theory that the deceased's Ka was supposed to be able to leave the pyramid through these shafts and join the gods in the heavenly Kingdom of Amenti.

Who did it?

There is also much controversy surrounding the question of who built the pyramids. Were thousands of slaves exploited or was it a Herculean collective effort on the part of the Egyptians themselves?

Burial grounds situated near the pyramids have revealed the tombs of the actual builders. Often, extra materials (such stone and mud brick left over from the pyramids) were used to construct small mounds over the graves of the workmen, indicating that they were given true and proper Egyptian burials, whereas slaves were not. This would seem to support the idea that pyramid construction was regarded by the Egyptians as a religious and state duty, even an honor. The pyramid-builders may well have been employed by the state, the same as the other skilled craftsmen, unskilled laborers, and local villagers who worked during the off-season on public projects between July and November, when the annual inundation took place. The workers and farmers contributed to the growth of the land while earning a modest income. A large labor force was organized, with a supervisory structure, which led to the expansion and development of the nation of Egypt and the welfare and security of its people. The construction of pyramids not only guaranteed the immortality of the pharaoh but of the workers as well, since they were able to afford a proper burial from the wages received.

Proof that the workers received wages lies in the well-documented strike or work stoppage that took place during the 29th year of the reign of Ramses III (mentioned in the chapter on Labor and Crafts). Upon a stela the pharaoh had information inscribed showing how well the workmen were compensated — he speaks of a monthly salary, and storehouses filled with linen, oil, food and sandals for the workmen.

No records have been found providing information on how the pyramids were planned, designed or constructed and few references to pyramids are found in the surviving texts. Ramps built from the mud of the Nile were probably instrumental in the construction. A ramp would lead from ground level to the top of the first layer of stone, then a second ramp would lead to the top of the second layer of stone and so on, until the top was reached. Later, the men must have worked their way down, smoothing the outer blocks and then removing the ramps.

Remains of such ramps have been discovered at the Giza Plateau, where blocks of stone were dragged by teams of workers, with rope and wooden sleds, to each corner of the pyramid. Solid evidence of this theory exists in the funerary relief of the tomb belonging to a 12th Dynasty Nomarch named Tehutihotep. In this scene, a colossal statue of the pharaoh (weighing over 60 tons) is being pulled by four rows of men totaling 172 workers. A man is seen pouring water in front of the sled to make the ground slick, enabling the blocks to be slid along.

Down in the valley

By the New Kingdom, pyramids were no longer being built. Pharaoh Tuthmose I instructed his vizier Imeni to come up with a unique burial place for him, and Imeni discovered the best location in a deep canyon over guarded by a huge pyramid-shaped mountain or rocky outcrop on the west bank of the Nile. Today, it is known as el-Qurn, which is Arabic for "The Horn." To the ancient Egyptian, the topography closely resembled the hieroglyph for the horizon, the entrance into the Underworld. The site was located on the west banks of the Nile, hidden beneath the hills of Uast. Its fine-quality limestone, proximity to the fertile banks of the Nile and protection against vandalism (provided by the steep cliffs) made this the ideal royal burial grounds. This necropolis is now known as the Valley of the Kings and nearly 30 pharaohs followed Tuthmose into this eternal sacred resting place.

Starting with its association with the primordial mound from which they believed life had sprung, the form of the pyramid held great fascination for the ancient Egyptians; and starting from their monumental constructions, it still fascinates us today.

26. The Great Sphinx

The Sphinx silently guards the pyramids, doubling as a symbol of mysterious wisdom and eternal vigilance. Called *Hu*, meaning "The Protector" or *Horem Akhet* (meaning "Horus of the Horizon") by the ancient Egyptians, it was designed to protect the deceased by keeping evil spirits away from tombs.

The lion, to the ancient Egyptians, was the guardian of the gates of dawn. The Sphinx, as a solar symbol of Ra, faces east, taking in the first rays of the rising sun on the first day of spring. Like the pyramids, the Sphinx is also aligned to the cardinal directions. The word "sphinx" is believed to derive from the Egyptian "shesep ankh," meaning "living image."

The image of a Sphinx crops up often throughout Egyptian history. The king was often portrayed as a sphinx as he defeated his enemies. An avenue of ram-headed sphinxes connects (and once guarded) the temples of Luxor and Karnak, where the statue of Amen was carried during the annual Opet Festival. During the New Kingdom, the Sphinx was worshipped as symbol of kingship. Ramses II built a granite altar between the lion's paws.

A mysterious feat

Fantastically, the Sphinx is carved out of a block of solid bedrock emerging from the desert sand of the Giza Plateau. Its lower body is constructed from huge blocks of stone that were quarried nearby. The body of the Great Sphinx is 240 feet long and 66 feet high, with a human face measuring nearly 14 feet in width, wearing the traditional Nemes headdress. The Sphinx once wore the false beard of royalty; a few fragments were discovered between its paws during the 19th century AD.

A mysterious face

With the body of a lion and the head of a man, it was believed to be carved in the image of Ra-Harakhte, or Ra of the Horizons. Some say the Sphinx's face is that of King Khafre of the 4th Dynasty, whom it strongly resembles and whom it appears to guard. The Sphinx was symbolic of Khafre's immortality as the sun god.

In 1996, after analyzing the angles, size and proportion of the head of the Sphinx, an American specialist concluded that it did not match Khafre's. The resemblance was closer, it appears, to his half-brother, the Pharaoh Djedefre Radjedef. Djedefre was a 4th-Dynasty king also known as Rdjedef. Khufu was succeeded by Djedefre, his son by a lesser wife, who ruled only for four years. Djedefre is believed to have been responsible for the death of his brother Kewab, eldest son of Khufu and next in life for the throne. Djedefre married Kewab's widow, Princess Hetepheres II, who became queen. Djedefre's pyramid is situated five miles north of the Giza complex at Abu Rowash. He is remembered as the first king to call himself the "Son of Ra."

Much controversy has brewed over whether it is Khafre's image that is immortalized through the Sphinx. Some believe that Khafre merely repaired and re-designed the Sphinx during his reign in the 4th Dynasty. They maintain that the head, disproportionately small, shows far less deterioration that the rest of the body, indicating that the Sphinx's head must have been built at a different time and of better-quality stone. No inscriptions have been found crediting Khafre as the builder of the Sphinx, although a stela has been found that tells of

Khufu ordering a temple to be built near it — this clearly indicates that the Sphinx was already built when Khafre inherited the throne from Khufu. Was it actually built far, far earlier?

A first face lift

Contrary to popular belief, the nose of the Sphinx was not destroyed by Napoleon's army. According to an Arab historian, the Sphinx's nose was destroyed by the Turks after their conquest of Egypt in AD 1517. The Sphinx is badly eroded and has undergone numerous restorations over the millennia. The most important act of restoration upon the Sphinx is inscribed upon a stone tablet 14 feet high. This tablet, known as the "Dream Stela," tells of a dream that took place 34 centuries ago. The story begins with a prince named Tuthmose, son of Amenhotep II.

One hot afternoon, Tuthmose lay down to rest by the feet of the Sphinx, sheltering in the shade after an arduous day hunting under the heat of the African sun. He dreamt that Ra-Harakhte, personification of the Sphinx, spoke to him in a great voice and commanded the hunter to remove the sand that was slowly obliterating him. If he successfully performed this feat, the prince (who hoped one day to wear the Double Crown of Upper and Lower Egypt) would prosper and be forever guided and protected by the Sphinx. Needless to say, when the prince became Tuthmose IV during the 18th Dynasty, he made Ra-Harakhte's request his first royal action. The Pharaoh cleared away the sand covering the Sphinx and repaired the blocks of stones that had fallen. Tuthmose IV, chosen by the great deity Ra-Harakhte himself, is known as one of the greatest of pharaohs. There is no evidence to tell us what became of his older brother who was, in fact, next in line to the throne; some believe that the "dream" was merely a product of his imagination created to gloss over the fact that he had murdered his brother. Certainly, if the gods had chose him as successor (as was the case with Hatshepsut), who could object? Tuthmose IV proudly inscribed this story upon a red granite stela and placed it between the front paws in memory and gratitude to Ra-Harakhte, the Sphinx.

Her age is a mystery, too

The body of the Great Sphinx exhibits patterns of extreme water erosion, indicating that it must be much older than previously thought. The head displays erosion principally due to blowing sand. Erosion by water could only have been produced by torrential downpours and exceptionally high floods, such as might be expected to have ensued at the melting of the Ice Age 12,500 years ago. This unique type of weathering, with its pattern of wavy surfaces, had to have been made when the Sahara was green and fertile and contained many lakes, subjecting it to flooding. If the Sphinx had been built c. 2500 BC by Khafre, only straight patterns of sand and wind erosion would be evident, due to the arid climate of the Sahara since the days of Khafre's reign.

Furthermore, the Sphinx is believed to be an astronomical marker for the vernal equinox. During 2500 BC, when earlier theories suggested it had been built, the sun rose in the constellation of Taurus during the spring equinox, bringing in the Age of Taurus. That being so, the Egyptians in their esoteric beliefs would have constructed the Sphinx to face the constellation of Taurus, the Bull, and most likely would have carved the head in the shape of a bull, an animal that they venerated highly. The Age of Leo came on between 10,970 and 8810 BC; at this time during the spring equinox, just before dawn, the lion-shaped Sphinx would have faced its celestial counterpart, the constellation of Leo, which would account for its shape.

Regardless of when it was originally built, the magnificent Sphinx has continued to proudly guard the Giza necropolis for the last four and a half millennia. Many legends surround this great monument. For centuries, travelers have been seeking wisdom from the lips of the Sphinx. After all, it is considered to represent Hu, a god of wisdom and an aspect of Ra. Some like to believe there are underground passageways and hints of a lost civilization hidden below the right paw, but there is no archaeological evidence to support that notion — although recent excavations have discovered several tunnels.

What goes on four legs at dawn, two at noon and three at dusk? The answer to the Riddle of the Sphinx lies inscribed between its paws in the form of a stela honoring the composite deity Kephera-Ra-Atem. Kephera represented as a baby as the sun rises, crawling on all fours; Ra as a man in his prime at midday, standing on two legs, and Atem, as the old man supported by a cane, at sunset. Man and the Sphinx as a divine solar symbol are incorporated in the Riddle of the Sphinx. The sun was of such high symbolic relevance to the ancient Egyptians that they deified its three major stages.

Heavenly observations played a vital role in the construction of the pyramids and the Sphinx, and in the building of temples as well. Temples were aligned with the principal fixed stars and the earth's cardinal points; and they served as observatories for the astronomer priests. Time was recorded by the passage of the stars as viewed from the roofs of the temples.

During Predynastic times, temples were simple huts. First built of perishable sun-dried mud brick, they gradually evolved into buildings of durable granite, limestone and sandstone. Blocks of stone were extracted from quarries by hammering wooden wedges into cracks, and soaking them; they would expand and split the rock. When it came to building, these stones formed the temple roofs; they were supported by columns, on a dirt floor. The skilled engineers and architects employed by the government planned and constructed temples on a large scale; they must have had a pretty solid knowledge of mathematics.

The ancient Egyptians were highly skilled in stone working. The Early Dynastic period and particularly the Old Kingdom are noted for their rapid and impressive development of architecture, specifically in tombs and temples built from stone. Spectacular rows of columns were fashioned from limestone and granite. These imposing structures of exquisite craftsmanship were designed in the form of papyrus bundles or stems, lotus buds and palm flowers symbolizing fertility. Often, they were decorated with scenes of worship and inscribed with hieroglyphics. A stone wall carved into the shape of a row of defiant and rearing cobras, the symbol of royalty and Lower Egypt, magnificently adorns the top of a small tomb situated near Djoser's Step Pyramid. Rows of pillars graced the entrance to the flat, rectangular temples, forming magnificent and imposing corridors. Other columns embellished gardens and terraces that opened onto shrines and courtyards.

Temples were entered through a pylon that served as a monumental entrance and ceremonial gateway, placed at the front of the building. The shape of the pylons was symbolic, reminiscent of the horizon (sign of eternity), and they were aligned in such a manner that the sun rose and set between the twin pillars representing the two mountains that make up the sign for "horizon." Temples were usually surrounded by a mud brick enclosure and were oriented east-to-west, so that as the sun rose it would pass through the pylon and extend its rays into the sanctuary housing the sacred statue of the deity. The temple complex would also contain living quarters, a school, a pool, workshops, granaries and store houses.

During the Middle Kingdom, royal palaces were constructed out of perishable brick and wood; none has survived, only the stone temples. The palaces were rectangular structures built with high walls and ornamented with towers to house the pharaoh and his entourage. From reliefs we can see that the palaces contained gardens, twin gateways, great halls and two administrative centers — one for Upper Egypt, one for Lower Egypt.

Architectural achievement, along with art and literature, reached great heights during the 18th Dynasty of the New Kingdom. Architects planned their constructions so meticulously that the stones fit to hairline precision. After the heavy construction was completed, artists adorned the walls and pillars from top to bottom with carvings and painted scenes.

Knowledge of geometry is evident as the workers were able to determine the volume of a pyramid and a cylinder. They knew that the area of a rectangle equaled its length multiplied by its width. The area of a circle was calculated according to the length of its diameter; still, theirs was a simple arithmetic of adding and subtracting. For dividing and multiplying, they used a table to find the answer.

The ancient Egyptians developed a decimal system of numeration to support their calculations. The numbers from one to ten, in their masculine forms, were known as:

1. ua
2. sen
3. hmt
4. ifdw
5. diu
6. seresu
7. sefej
8. hmnu
9. pesdu
10. medu

Their numerical system did not include zero; they counted by tens using seven different symbols. A vertical stroke denoted the number one, while five strokes represented five. An upside down letter "U" represented the number ten. A coiled rope stood for a hundred (known as *sha*), while a lotus plant represented a thousand, or *ja*. A vertical finger with the upper phalange slightly bent represented 10,000 (*djab*) and 100,000 (*jefenu*) was expressed with the symbol of a frog or tadpole. A man kneeling upon one knee with arms raised above designated 1,000,000 (*heh*). The Shen symbol of infinity represented the number 10,000,000, called *senu*. The highest number was always written in front of the lower number, they were usually read left to right.

When Set destroyed the Eye of Heru (or Wadjet) and tore it into pieces, it not only became a potent healing symbol but the pieces were used to determine fraction measurements. Its name translates into "whole" or "healthy." The Wadjet was used mainly for measuring quantities of grain, and is believed to have been introduced for this purpose during the 19th Dynasty.

When you convert the fractions 1/64, 1/32, 1/16, 1/8, 1/4, and 1/2 to a common denominator, 64, the sum of the numerators is 63; adding the fractions, then, gives a total of 63/64. Tehuti — as healer of Heru's eye — magically provided the missing and final fraction of 1/64, bringing it to completion.

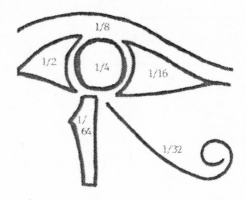

The *Rhind Papyrus*, apparently written during the 15th Dynasty by a scribe named Ahmose, shows examples of ancient Egyptian mathematics including the use of fractions. Ahmose himself copied this text from older writings. Although their calculating methods are considered somewhat inferior, particularly in comparison to chat of the Babylonians, what the Egyptians accomplished with their system is truly remarkable.

Seshat, consort of Tehuti, as goddess of measurement and writing, was also worshipped as patroness of mathematics and architects. Ptah, was the major patron and protector of craftsmen, builders and architects.

It has been written that the Karnak Temple honoring Amen, Mut and their son Khonsu (the Theban Triad), covered an area of five acres — at the time, it was the largest religious structure ever built. It boasted more than 130 columns 80 feet high. Decorated pillars supported the ceiling of the Hypostyle Hall, and an avenue of ram-headed sphinxes led to the entrance of the first pylon (rams were sacred as the symbolic animal of Amen, and sphinxes honored Ra, the solar god). Small figures of Ramses II are carved beneath the rams' heads. During the Opet Festival, Amen took the form Menu, the fertility god, as he visited the Temple of Luxor (which some refer to as his "southern harem"). Construction of this temple began during the Middle Kingdom and was completed by the New Kingdom. Nearly every pharaoh who ruled during this period made additions to the grand temple complex; they and their architects delighted in refining and improving upon the work of their predecessors and ancestors.

Queen Hatshepsut built a set of obelisks that stand in front of a pylon of Amen's sanctuary. Tuthmose III added two pillars to the temple during the 18th Dynasty. Ramses II constructed the great columnar or Hypostyle Hall at Karnak during the 19th Dynasty. The majestic "Avenue of the Sphinxes" built by Nectanebo I (30th Dynasty) connects the Temple of Karnak to the Temple of Luxor, situated one mile south. It has been estimated that this avenue was 20 feet wide, two miles long and lined with 1400 human-headed sphinxes, 700 on each side, spaced about 15 feet apart. Each sphinx measures 10 feet long and four feet high.

The Temple of Luxor, dedicated to Amen-Ra, was begun c. 1380 BC under Amenhotep III. Tuthmose III added chapels, and in the 19th Dynasty, Ramses II appended colossal statues, a pair of obelisks, a magnificent pylon gateway and an open colonaded courtyard. Tutankhamen, Horemheb and Alexander the Great also made contributions to this great temple complex.

Obelisks, known as *tekhen*, were colossal upright single blocks of highly polished stone, tapering into a point at the very top in the form of the pyramidion. The apex was also known as the sacred Ben-Ben, the primeval mound from where all life sprung. Obelisks were placed in pairs and were inscribed with hieroglyphs; their purpose was to pay homage to the great solar gods while symbolizing fertility.

The earliest obelisk is believed to have been made c. 1900 BC. The pyramidion was often gilded or made from copper and electrum imported from the Kingdom of Kush, to capture and reflect the rays of the rising sun as it pierced the sky. Constructed from a single slab of hard granite from distant quarries, obelisks could weigh up to 150 tons. The average height was about 70 feet; however, some were as tall as 160 feet and weighed over 400 tons. Copper tools were too soft to work with the hard granite, and iron was as yet rarely used in the making of tools, so it is believed that obelisks were carved and shaped, polished and smoothed by pounding with dolerite, a stone that is even harder than granite. Dolerite was also likely used to inscribe the hieroglyphs. An inscription exists showing a mason pounding a block of stone with a smaller one.

Archeologists have recreated Egyptian construction sites, trying to test their theories as to how these massive and fragile monuments were raised to an upright position at their final destination. Fortunately, the ancient Egyptians left a few clues. Once the obelisk was completed, it was transported by boat to its final destination. At the Temple of Hatshepsut, a relief shows two obelisks lying on the deck of a boat, being transported from Aswan to the Temple of Amen at Karnak. A ramp would have been built, and a sled would have been dragged along a path leading from the boat to the final site. All obelisks stand on base stones that reveal carved notches; these, apparently, were used as turning grooves to pivot the obelisk into place. The base stone was placed in a pit and the obelisk was dragged (up a ramp) to a position above. Men, maneuvering the obelisk with ropes and levers, lowered its bottom end and directed it into the turning groove in the base stone, then tilted it forward to an upright position. It is very possible that the pit was actually a sand pit; mud bricks covered holes at the bottom of the sandpit, and could be withdrawn at the critical moment to allow the sand to slowly poured out through slots. The obelisk was then able to gradually sink into its designated place. As it descended into an upright position, it was edged into a vertical position by men pulling on ropes at the very last minute. Evidence also exists that the sand method was used to lower a certain sarcophagus into its tomb. The erecting of an obelisk would have been an enormous exertion and, at the same time, a delicate task, requiring hundreds of men using their combined skill, strength, enthusiasm, dedication, and perseverance.

After months of strenuous effort, what a splendid moment it must have been when the monument was finally raised to greet the sky.

Senwosret I raised a 67-foot obelisk marking the temple of Ra at Iunu. Tuthmose I carved a pair for Karnak, and Tuthmose II quarried a 137-foot obelisk weighing nearly 1200 tons. It was reduced to 105 feet but still lies unfinished at the quarry.

During the 16th year of Hatshepsut's reign, she erected six obelisks and one of them can still be admired; it stands 97 feet high at Karnak. Hatshepsut is credited with erecting many great monuments throughout her reign; she ordered construction and restoration projects throughout the land. She built a palatial temple composed of three terraces rising into the cliffs of Deir el-Bahri, overlooking the west bank of the Nile. The mortuary temple was dedicated to Het-Heru and served to keep Hatshepsut's name and memory alive. This temple is one of the most beautiful and distinct of all the architectural wonders in Egypt. It is here that Hatshepsut recorded her divine conception, birth, and coronation, the erection of the obelisks and the successful trading expedition to the land of Punt.

It is believed that 500 years earlier, during the 11th Dynasty of the Middle Kingdom, Pharaoh Mentuhotep II built his mortuary complex at the very same spot where Hatshepsut's is located. The queen added onto it, duplicating the temple and expanding the complex.

Senenmut, a commoner by birth who rose to the position of high official during the 18th Dynasty, is believed to have been her lover and confidant. He certainly played an important role in Hatshepsut's life, including tutoring her little daughter, Nefrura. Known for his architectural skills, Senenmut designed Hatshepsut's mortuary complex. He was bold enough to have inscribed his own name and image on her temple. However, both Senenmut and Hatshepsut's names were destroyed by her successor, Tuthmose III.

Tuthmose III erected two obelisks at the Temple of Ra at Iunu. Since the 19th century of our era, one stands in London and the other is in New York City's Central Park. Most of the obelisks in Egypt have been destroyed or taken away, by Persians, Turks, Europeans and Americans alike.

Amenhotep III (18th Dynasty) built a spectacular funerary complex at Western Uast. The only surviving remnants of this temple are two 70-foot statues known as the Colossi of Memnon.

The most prominent and celebrated architect of ancient Egyptian history is Imhotep, builder of the first stone monument; the best-preserved architectural works are those of Hatshepsut, Tuthmose III, Seti I, Ramses II, and Ramses III.

Many of the great ancient structures still standing were built c. 1290 BC under the direction of Ramses II, who undertook many lavish, grand scale construction projects. With the Ramesseum, at Uast, he completed his father's spectacular funerary temple on the west bank of the Nile, at Luxor, and dedicated it to Amen. Ramses II began work on the Ramesseum shortly after his ascension to the throne and it was completed around the 22nd year of his rule. It consisted of two temples, two pylons, two courtyards and the great pillared (or Hypostyle) Hall. On the northern wall of the Hypostyle Hall, a temple was built dedicated to his mother Tuya and his favorite wife, Nefertari.

In 1269 BC, Ramses II ordered the construction of four 65-feet-high seated statues of himself cut into the living rock. These images not only adorned the temple but served as their sentinels. The memorial carvings in the granite cliffs of Mount Rushmore in South Dakota must have been inspired by the architectural genius of Ramses II as displayed at Abu Simbel. The temple is dedicated to Amen-Ra, Ra-Harakhte and Ptah. It is precisely oriented so that, twice a year, the first rays of the morning sun shine down to illuminate the rear wall of the innermost and holiest chamber where the statues of the four gods are seated. Nowadays, this remarkable sight can be enjoyed on February and October 22nd.

Next to the great Pharaoh's legs are his Queen Nefertari and their children, represented in diminutive form to emphasize the magnificence of the pharaoh. The complex contains a smaller temple dedicated to Nefertari and Het-Heru. Nefertari's tomb, in the Valley of the Queens, is the most elegant and refined; its superb artwork and color have been preserved and restored.

In the 1960s, the two magnificent rock-hewn temples of Ramses II were relocated at Abu Simbel to save them as the waters rose due to the construction of the Aswan Dam. The statues had to be cut out piece by piece and set onto a higher level and re-inaugurated in the fall of 1968. At Abedju, Ramses II built his own mortuary complex dedicated to Ausar, Auset, Ptah, Amen-Ra, Heru and Ra-Harakhte. This is considered the greatest building of his reign and of the history of ancient Egypt. It is here where the *Abydos King List* was found. Ramses II also erected the avenue of ram-headed sphinxes crouched in front of the temple of the (ram-headed) god Amen at Karnak; this was Egypt's most important shrine during the New Kingdom. In addition, Ramses II sponsored building projects down in Nubia, where he constructed six temples. His so-called victory at the Battle of Kadesh is inscribed at the Ramesseum and at the Temple of Abu Simbel. His Syrian, Libyan and Nubian conquests were also commemorated there, along with his marriage to the Hittite princess. The more he built, the mightier he became, as a man and as a legend.

Medinet Habu is the mortuary temple complex of Ramses III. He duplicated his predecessor's Ramesseum in the sense that it was composed of a palace, temple, two pylons, storehouses and accommodation for priests. This complex was to become the last of the great architectural achievements of the Ramessid Era. The Ramesseum and Medinet Habu are among the largest mortuary temples of western Uast.

Temples continued being built during the Ptolemaic era. The Temple of Edfu dedicated to Heru and the Temple of Denderah honoring Het-Heru are magnificent works of late Egyptian architectural art. At the northern entrance to the courtyard of the well-preserved Temple of Edfu stands one of the original statues of a falcon, the sacred animal of Heru. The temple of Denderah is best known for the zodiac depicted on the ceiling, believed to have been constructed during the first century of our era, under the reign of the Emperor Tiberius, when Rome already ruled over this proud civilization.

28. ART

Most of our information about life in ancient Egypt comes from the detailed illustrations they so fortunately left behind. Countless scenes of everyday life and the activities they hoped to experience in the afterlife adorned temple and tomb walls. They didn't create these pictures for our sake, nor for the sake of "Art," but rather to promote immortality and provide guidance into the next world. These instructional drawing were intended to assist the dead in participating in these mortal activities in the hereafter.

Frequently, the figure was illustrated in the prime of his life, playing sports, making music or giving offerings to the deities. Many colorful scenes show the Egyptians dancing, playing, or eating, worshipping or mourning, sailing, fishing, or hunting; others portray people at work: baking, weaving, washing, farming and harvesting, building, and fighting in battle. One of the oldest existing artworks is a fragment of a frieze now called "The Geese of Meidum," found in the tomb of Princess Itet and dating back to c. 2700 BC.

Masterpieces of vivid color and imagery were created throughout Egyptian history. Details were meticulously drawn and the overall style is graceful and elegant. The artist's confidence was clear in the splendor of his work; his imagination, however, was seldom explored freely, as he had to conform to the specifications dictated throughout the past. Art was public and had to be legible to the viewer. The artist remained anonymous; it was his professional duty to provide this service.

During the Middle Kingdom, draftsmen were known as "scribes of outlines"; they drew freehand, while apprentices mastered the rules of proportion by first drawing grids, in red. On funerary wall reliefs, a chisel was used to engrave the image and hieroglyphs, which were later filled in with colors by a colorist, so there were two types of painters in ancient Egypt: the outliner or draftsman, and the colorist.

Paints were composed of mineral pigments in powder form and water mixed with clay, glue, wax, gum and egg white. Various resins were added as bonding agents. A reed pen or a brush of soft bristles, made of a wooden stick with a tip of frayed plant fibers, was used to apply the colors. Some artists covered their finished works with a coat of transparent varnish made from beeswax or the diluted gum of the acacia plant in an attempt to preserve the colors; this may have brightened the look in the short run, but by our era it has had the opposite effect.

The artist's palette consisted of white (*hedj*), achieved by mixing chalk or powdered limestone or gypsum with honey. Galena, charcoal, carbon, burnt animal bones or burnt wood gave them black (*khem*); this could be softened with limestone to produce grey. Malachite, found in the eastern delta region and in the Sinai, and other copper ores, were used to obtain green (*wadj*). Both red (*descher*) and yellow (*ketj*) were derived from ochre. Brown was achieved from iron ore mixed with red and yellow. For blue (*irtyw*, or *khesbedj*) they could use finely crushed faience or glass, as well as copper frit, or powdered lapis or azurite.

The flesh of a man was colored a reddish-brown while woman was drawn in a soft yellow or pinkish brown. This indicated that men primarily worked outdoors while women's work kept them indoors. Black was the color of resurrection as it symbolized the black soil that parched in the sun and then was given life by the Nile. A god depicted in black exhibited his funerary status and relations. A deity would be drawn in blue to emphasize his divine powers. Green was symbolic of youth and renewal.

By the New Kingdom, more realistic hues began to appear. Animals were painted in their natural colors, as much as possible. Water and celestial objects were drawn in blue, the color of the Nile, the heaven and sky. Priests were also drawn in blue, a color regarded as spiritual and holy. Gods were often illustrated in gold, symbolic of the flesh of Ra. Nubians were depicted in dark brown.

Different perspectives

Objects and creatures were drawn without any indication of perspective or depth, in two dimensions, as if they were spread out on a flat surface. If the artist was commissioned to paint a pool with fishes, he would draw a perfect rectangle for the pool and draw the fishes in an equal, repetitive, uniform fashion over the pool. A box filled with offerings would be indicated by depicting the offerings above the box, each in its true and whole shape, without overlapping and hiding any portion. The viewer knew how to interpret the spatial relations of the items. Art, like hieroglyphs, had to be read, as it contained a message.

What was visible was considered to be eternal, so for principal characters, as much of the body as possible had to be indicated. Faces and figures were drawn mostly in profile, with frontal views added where necessary to provide full information. If the head were drawn facing forward, the definition of the nose would vanish and therefore would cease to exist; and the nose was important, as affection was often expressed by rubbing noses together. The nose was also symbolic of joy, and was used in profile view as the determinative for the hieroglyph expressing "to kiss." However, the eye on the side facing the viewer could be depicted frontally. The shape of the shoulders, too, was best defined in frontal view, and one arm would be lost in a literally correct side view. Besides, the Egyptians were very fond of jewelry and if the upper body were drawn in profile, no one could appreciate the outline and detailed craftsmanship of their necklaces and pectorals, thus rendering the illustration much less aesthetically pleasing to the viewer and less satisfactory to the subject.

The legs were drawn in profile, indicating motion and life. The figure of a man was usually drawn facing the left, with the left leg forward so as not to suggest incompleteness by hiding the other leg. The man was in motion, hunting and fighting, while a woman's feet were usually shown together, symbolic of her staying put, at home.

Those of lower status could be treated more casually. Prisoners and foreign deities such as Qetesh, a Semitic goddess of nature, were drawn in full frontal view, at best. Laborers, peasants and servants, inconsequential in contrast to nobles and royalty, were usually drawn in full profile or with their backs to the viewer, in a natural manner.

Although a man was rarely portrayed with an arm around his wife, the woman is usually positioned sitting by the husband's leg, with one arm around his shoulder or waist. The painted limestone sculpture of a dwarf named Seneb (who bore the title of "Head of the Royal House of Weaving") and his family, who lived during the 6th Dynasty under Pharaoh Pepy II, shows him seated in the scribal position. Sitting by his side is his wife Sentyotes, with one arm tenderly placed around his right shoulder and the other arm affectionately touching his left arm. Smaller renditions of their son and daughter, wearing the side lock of youth, are shown below Seneb.

Drawing a pharaoh in proportion to his family would diminish his real stature in life, which was far more than a physical dimension. His status and prestige had to be represented as well as his body. Size represented authority, strength and dominion. The gigantic statues at the temple of Ramses II best illustrate this tradition, as he is accompanied by much smaller figures of his wife and children.

Statues were sculpted to appear as lifelike as possible, as they were intended to come alive (or at least to support the spirit of the person depicted) and live eternally. Figures were carved from alabaster, granite, limestone, diorite, sandstone, basalt, and quartzite, as well as from clay, wood, ivory, bronze and gold. Statues were placed in tomb as objects of worship and recipients of daily offerings. The sculptor carved the individual's name on the statue to assist in recognition and identification.

Scribes were always represented seated, in a traditional cross-legged position, prepared to write — with a sheet of papyrus placed upon the knees and a reed pen in hand. Seated statues were always sculpted to face the front and statues of standing male figures or deities were sculpted with one foot forward.

During the Middle Kingdom, a type of statuary art known as "block statues" emerged. Only the head emerges from the figure of the body, which is carved in the shape of a block. A block statue of Seneb shows him in a seated position, with his arms folded and resting upon his knees under his chin. The cube-shaped body was then inscribed with hieroglyphic inscriptions.

Sculptors achieved exquisite and outstanding visual effects in their masterpieces by implanting eyes made of painted crystal or obsidian, a dark green or black glass formed by volcanic activity that produced a most realistic and startling effect. A life-size sculpture of the High Priest Rahotep alongside his wife Princess Nofret (who lived c. 2600 BC), was believed to have frightened away prospective thieves in AD 1871. The thieves were so shocked by the vivid inlaid eyes, which seemed to move under the light of their candles, that they dropped their tools and weapons, fleeing in terror.

One of the most beautiful examples of art from ancient Egypt is the painted limestone bust of Nefertiti that was found intact, in Akhetaten, at the workshop of a sculptor named Tuthmose. The color and detail are remarkable; they were perfectly preserved by the sand and dry climate for over 3000 years. The bust was discovered in 1912, lying upside down amidst broken sculptures and rubble.

Tuthmose's studio was nearly completely destroyed. Most sculptures in Akhenaten were viciously smashed in an effort to destroy the image so that the persons in question would be permanently forgotten, and thus non-existent. For, once the body was destroyed, the statue not only guaranteed immortality to its image but served as a dwelling place for the soul of the deity.

Once a revolutionary, always a revolutionary

The rules of art remained quite constant throughout the history of ancient Egypt, but during the New Kingdom, art reached its highest peak. The greatest change came from King Akhenaten, who seems to have enjoyed shocking the public. He revolutionized not only religion but art. Akhenaten gave rise to what is now known as the distinctive style of "Amarna Art," named after the capital city that he founded. This style differed not only in subject matter but in human proportion as well. Traditional methods of art were completely abandoned under his reign. Until then, figures were drawn in an idealized youthful and attractive manner, the way the ancient Egyptians wished to remain and be remembered as age, illness and physical deformities were absent in artistic portrayals.

In the Amarna style, the perfection of the human body was no longer a dominant factor. Realistic and natural human traits and forms, even if unattractive, began to emerge as illustrations were drawn in an intimate, informal, creative and innovative style. The great Pharaoh himself was believed to have been somewhat disfigured, and that trait shows up in all his artistic representations. His Queen Nefertiti and their six daughters were also portrayed in a distinct manner. The style consisted of elongated skulls, narrow eyes, long necks, thin arms, short legs, exaggerated thighs and protruding bellies.

Akhenaten was the first pharaoh to be illustrated as a family-loving man, engaging in such tender activities as playing with his beloved daughters and expressing devotion to his queen. Until then, pharaohs were most often depicted in dignified poses or engaging in battle and conquest, or returning home in triumph — scenes emphasizing their masculine nature and successful leadership.

The Amarna Style prevailed throughout the 17 years of King Akhenaten's reign, but quickly lost favor upon his death. However, some traces of this style can be detected during the early part of the reign of Tutankhamen, perhaps out of respect for his father-in-law. On the back of Tutankhamen's spectacular pharaonic throne, his beloved Akhesenamen is shown tenderly touching his shoulder. This clearly duplicates or continues the relaxed and intimate manner of the Amarna style. A unique trend in a highly traditional field, Amarna art represents the apex in Egyptian artistry and conveys a delightful sense of creativity, freedom and talent.

Many impressive literary works from ancient Egypt have survived for thousands of years. Narratives, prayers, hymns, myths, proverbs and poems were composed as well as travel and adventure stories. Autobiographies, passionate and poetic love stories and highly imaginative fairytales have been preserved, although the authors' names have not.

The literature produced during the 20th Dynasty is considered to be among the finest. Great skill in expression together with humor, irony, metaphors, word-play add charm to the writing. These enchanting works soon spread to other lands, inspiring many other writers.

Literature was divided into two categories: sacred and non-religious writings. Sacred texts were written to guide the deceased through the dangers of the Underworld on his way to join Ausar in Amenti. This category was composed of mythological, astronomical and magical writings as well as rituals, hymns to the deity and funerary texts. The oldest surviving Egyptian writings are the Pyramid Texts, carved inside the pyramids of the Old Kingdom; they are most commonly referred to as *The Book of the Dead*.

Private tombs were often inscribed with an account of the deceased's biography and achievements. Non-religious writings included narrations of significant events in their lives, including personal tragedies, adventures, fears, hopes, joys and sorrows.

Some of the finest writings came in the field of romantic and lyrical poetry, the Egyptian's most individualistic form of creative expression. King Akhenaten's glorious hymns to his solar deity Aten are fine examples.

Literature emerged during the 12th Dynasty. Until then, stories were told and passed down verbally through generations. At this time, the narrative tale was developed into a fine craft. Eight dynasties later, romantic poetry and fables developed into a distinct literary genre.

A highly developed literature of wisdom emerged, expressing the philosophical thoughts of the day. Many writings served as instructions based on the laws of Ma'at — the virtues, values and moral guidance by which ancient Egyptians were to live. These virtues consisted of righteousness, modesty, respect, honesty, fairness, moderation and kindness. The *Instructions of Hardjedef* contains a code of ethics. Hardjedef was a 4th Dynasty sage who compiled these thoughts for his son to live by. *The Instructions of Ptahotep*, also written during the Old Kingdom, is a text comprising the ethical observations of Ptahotep, a 5th Dynasty sage and vizier.

The truth will out

A wonderful story entitled "Truth and Lie" or "Ma'at and Gereg" clearly demonstrates the rewards of being truthful. In the times when Ra ruled as a mortal over Egypt, there lived two brothers. One brother named "Truth" was pure of sin and lived by the laws of Ma'at, while his brother, "Lie," possessed the darkest of hearts and knew sin intimately.

One day, Truth requested the use of a knife from his brother Lie. Lie hesitated but eventually gave in. When the day ended, Truth realized he had misplaced his brother's knife. Truth begged Lie for forgiveness and promised to replace it immediately. Lie replied that it was "unique and irreplaceable." Truth said that it was an ordinary knife, and that he would replace it with an even sharper and bigger one. Lie insisted on his devotion to his suddenly remarkable knife. Truth felt helpless.

Lie brought Truth before the Nine Gods of Iunu to be judged. Lie persisted with his untruthful claims and Truth remained bewildered at the extent of his brother's falsehood and accusations. Truth simply stood there in awe and the gods ruled in favor of Lie, as Truth did nothing to defend himself.

When Lie was asked by the gods what punishment should his brother suffer, he replied that all his property should be given to him, that Truth should become Lie's servant, and that his eyes should be struck out.

When all this was granted and Lie saw his brother blind, he experienced his first bout of guilt. He could not bear the feeling, and ordered Truth be killed. Meanwhile, Lie's men felt deep compassion for their former master and, rather than executing him, decided to abandon him deep in the rugged mountains with some provisions. The gods would have to have the final say on the destiny of Truth.

Truth wandered through a valley, groping his way, as his food and water slowly dwindled. He lay down to rest and hoped that death would take him. Before long, a beautiful woman and her entourage came traveling by and discovered the helpless, blind young man on the verge of death. He was taken to her estate and bathed in oils, fed the finest of foods and dressed in clean linen robes. He was given the job of "Doorkeeper," but soon he and his hostess became lovers.

As a result, in due course, she gave birth to a young boy. He grew into a strong and handsome man, but did not know who had fathered him. One day, when he was old enough to inquire, he begged his mother to tell him who his father was. She pointed at Truth who was sitting, guarding the gates to her estate. She explained to the boy that she loved Truth dearly — but sadly, the law did not permit a noblewoman to marry a blind servant.

The boy's anger rose to a mighty level and he spoke defiantly to his mother for the first time. He stated that his father would no longer sit as a servant and guardian of the gates. The boy went to Truth, led him by the hand into the estate, and clothed him as a nobleman. This act of bold kindness made the mother extremely proud and she in turn was inspired to hold an elaborate feast in honor of Truth. During this soirée she revealed to all that the blind servant was not only the boy's father but the love of her life.

Presently, the boy came to wonder how such a good man could have suffered the terrible fate that had befallen Truth. Truth had no choice but to tell his son the whole story of how Lie tricked him. This enraged the boy, who vowed vengeance over his uncle.

The following morning, the boy chose the finest and biggest ox and set off to the estate of Lie. On his way, the boy approached a herds-man and explained that he had business to attend to for a few days and could not take the huge ox with him. He asked if the herdsman would watch the animal for a few days until he returned. The boy paid the herdsman handsomely, and confidently made his way into town.

Meanwhile, Lie visited the herdsman to select a new ox for his farm. He immediately spotted the large ox and desired it for a feast he was planning. The herdsman protested that it was not for sale and that he was merely watching the beast for a traveling merchant. There was no resisting, however, and seeing no choice he reluctantly gave in.

The next morning, Truth came to retrieve his ox and noticed that it was gone. The herdsman nervously stuttered that he could have his pick of any oxen in his possession that belonged to a man named Lie.

The boy's rage was mighty and he brought his case to the Nine Gods of Iunu. The boy said that the ox was ten feet tall and "unique and irreplaceable." Lie spoke calmly and stated that the ox was slightly lar-ger than others, but not ten feet tall! The Gods were also astonished by the boy's claims about this gigantic ox, for no such animal has ever been seen by man or gods. Now, the boy retaliated and asked the gods if they had ever seen a blade such as the one Lie had described years before. The boy revealed his identity and exposed the trickery and falsehood of Lie before the Nine Gods.

The Nine Gods then turned their gaze on Lie, as he begged for for-giveness. Sure that Truth had been put to death by his men years ago, he cleverly proposed that, if Truth was still living, then he should suffer the same fate that Truth had endured. The gods were pleased with his confession and choice of punishment.

Meanwhile, Truth was fetched from the estate and brought into the presence of all the assembly. Lie was horrified at the sight of his brother, and more horrified still to find himself being dragged off to his self-pronounced sentence of death. Truth not only reclaimed his estate and wealth but the gods were kind enough to restore his eyesight. Re-instituted as a nobleman, he went on to marry the mother of their most remarkable child.

The Middle Kingdom is known as the "golden age of literature" when other genres of writing emerged. The works produced during this time were likely duplicates of much older works of the Old Kingdom. Over the centuries, these works were often copied by schoolboys as training exercises.

Egyptian works often included tales of the deities, collections of wise sayings or proverbs, moral and worldly observations and several versions of the Story of Creation. Many legends and hymns were also inspired by the sun and the Nile, the sources of life.

Wisdom literature was tinged with politics, emphasizing the pharaoh's status and power. Scientific treatises, such as the Mathematical *Rhind Papyrus* and medical texts such as the New Kingdom *Ebers Papyrus* provided a wealth of information on these matters. From the Old Kingdom and on, such works were compiled, collected, improved upon, and consulted through the centuries.

Stories often ended with a moral message. One of the most famous works of the Middle Kingdom is the "Story of Sinuhe," a story that captures the Egyptian's love for his homeland. "The Treasure Thief" expresses admiration for cunningness and the customary happy ending. "The Shipwrecked Sailor" bears a similarity to later works such as "Sinbad the Sailor"; both stories involve a shipwrecked sailor's experience on an island inhabited by a giant serpent. Another tale set during the reign of Ahmose II (of the 26th Dynasty) parallels "Cinderella"; both stories involve a red slipper and the quest for the woman whose foot it fits precisely.

A captivating tale

Another popular story called "The Taking of Joppa" bears a strong resemblance to "Ali Baba and the Forty Thieves," of *The Arabian Nights*. Fragments of the tale were inscribed upon what is known as the *Harris Papyrus*, dating to the New Kingdom. The story is set during the reign of

Tuthmose III, an 18th Dynasty pharaoh. Many Egyptian soldiers who were stationed in Joppa, a city in Palestine and an important stop on the trade route to the east, perished when the Prince of Joppa rebelled against Egypt. Naturally, the Pharaoh was less than pleased, and he called upon his officials, scribes and noblemen to come up with a plan for dealing with Joppa. Silence reigned, as all pondered the situation.

Then a general named Tehuti, with a reputation for being crafty and fearless, stepped forth and proposed a plan. Tehuti spoke of a magical staff that belonged to the Pharaoh, a wand that could render an object or person invisible, or could be used to change one's appearance completely. In his plan to take Joppa, Tehuti requested 200 of the Pharaoh's most valiant soldiers and the temporary use of the wand. The men were to be concealed inside 200 large barrels and loaded onto mules to be sent to Joppa.

Bending his charisma and persuasive powers upon the Pharaoh, Tehuti gained his confidence. The Pharaoh admired his ingenious plot, and Tehuti was granted all the support he would require. In turn, he promised to conquer Joppa and avenge Egypt.

Tehuti took the first step and forwarded a message to the Prince of Joppa. In the letter, he claimed that he had become disenchanted with Egypt and renounced his allegiance to the Pharaoh. He said that he was fleeing Egypt, as his life was in danger after falling out of grace with the Pharaoh. As a result, Tehuti offered his loyalty and services to Joppa.

The general's reputation preceded him; the Prince had heard many stories, and while he was suspicious he was also eager to have such a cunning general on his side. Tehuti closed his letter with mention of the Pharaoh's magic wand, which he promised to give to the Prince as proof of his new allegiance to Joppa. The Prince took the bait, and a meeting was arranged at the Prince's headquarters in the field.

Together, Prince and General broke bread and drank copiously. Newfound friendship may be pleasant, but the Prince's curiosity soon got the better of him, and he was impatient to have proof that the magical staff existed and was in Tehuti's possession. The General obligingly brought out the magical staff — he raised it high and brought it crashing down on the head of the Prince, who fell to the ground. Tehuti called upon the magic to change his own appearance to that of the Prince of Joppa, while he bound the latter and threw him into a large skin bag.

Tehuti, now disguised as the Prince, told the guards stationed outside the tent to keep an eye on the Egyptian general, who was tied up inside the skin bag, having made an attempt on the life of the Prince. Then he called for the 200 mules, each laden with a heavy barrel, for he claimed that they contained the booty of Tuthmose III.

Once the mules were inside the city limits, the 200 armed soldiers leapt out, slew the guards of Joppa and proceeded to take over the entire town. The remaining warriors of Joppa surrendered to Egypt for fear their Prince (who remained unconscious and bound) would be decapitated. Many residents of Joppa were brought to Egypt to serve in the homes of the wealthy as slaves and servants; Tehuti was promoted to the highest official position in the land of Egypt.

Some of these themes show up in other early stories. For instance, in "Ali Baba and the Forty Thieves," men are also smuggled in barrels; however, they are armed thieves who end up suffering a horrible fate.

He who laughs last

We conclude this chapter with a story entitled "The Tale of Two Brothers." Written during the 19th Dynasty, it is believed to have graced the library of Seti II. It is a story of betrayal and faith, magic, and two brothers named Anpu and Bitou who come to rule Egypt. The story bears a strong resemblance to the Biblical story of Joseph and Potiphar's wife, as both tales involve the rebuked advances of a brother's wife resulting in the innocent brother's incarceration.

Anpu, the elder brother, lived fairly well. He was married and owned a comfortable home, with many cattle and a large field. Bitou, his younger brother, worked for him; he had a great talent for managing cattle, so much so that he was able to communicate with the animals. One day, Anpu's wife tried to seduce Bitou, but he rebuffed her advances. He was horrified by this act betrayal, and he explained to the angered woman that he not only loved Anpu as his beloved brother but respected and loved him as a father as well. Bitou and his sister-in-law agreed to never speak of this incident again. However, at sundown, she broke her promise. Anpu's wife cried that Bitou had attacked her while she was brushing her hair. She claimed to have rejected his advances and demanded to know how he could do this to his elder brother, who had treated him like a son. Anpu was overcome with rage and resolved to kill Bitou.

Meanwhile, the cattle under Bitou's care warned him of his sister-in-law's deceit, and told him of Anpu's anger and intentions. Bitou fled his brother's home and prayed to Ra for help and guidance. Just before Anpu caught up to him, Bitou begged him for a chance to tell him the truth. At that very moment, Ra caused a river full of crocodiles to rise between the two brothers, separating them from each other. For now, they were able to communicate at a safe distance. Bitou explained the whole story as it truly happened; at first, Anpu did not believe him. Bitou convinced him of his innocence, as proven by the fact that Ra created a river between them to allow Bitou the opportunity to tell his brother the sad truth.

Anpu considered his brother's words, which he wanted so much to believe. Meanwhile, his anger slowly began to wane. Bitou then took a knife, plunged it into himself and fell to the ground. He would rather die and prove his innocence than live with guilt in the eyes of his beloved elder brother. Anpu was stricken with horror and deep sadness by this act; he was, by now, quite convinced of his brother's innocence.

Before he died, Bitou recited a spell which enchanted his heart and sent it to dwell in the highest branch of an acacia tree, thus preserving his life. He instructed Anpu that, if the branch should ever fall, he was to place it in water. Anpu would know when Bitou's heart fell, as his beer would then froth and overflow in the goblet from which he always drank. And with that, Bitou went off to dwell in the Valley of Acacia, where his heart now resided.

Upon returning home, Anpu was deeply distraught over his brother's departure. So affected was he that he ran a spear through his faithless wife. Her tormented soul knew no rest as she searched for a new body. Meanwhile, the gods felt sorry for the two honorable brothers and Khnemu fashioned a wife on his potter's wheel for Bitou. She was a beautiful girl named Bint Nefer, and he instantly fell in love with her. However, the Seven Hathors declared her fate to be most sudden and unfortunate.

The wicked soul of Anpu's wife had found a new home in Bint Nefer. Bitou told his new wife that his heart was resting high in the acacia tree. Whoever found it would have to fight Bitou.

Bint Nefer told every man she encountered of the location of her husband's heart. Bitou fought with them all and was victorious in each and every battle.

One day, the Pharaoh encountered the beautiful girl and desired to make her his wife. However, she told him that her husband was evil and the only way to destroy him was to cut down the acacia tree that nestled his good heart. Without hesitation, the tree was cut down and Bitou fell dead to the ground. It was not long after that Bint Nefer became the King's wife.

Anpu, who had grown into a solitary, bitter man, was holding a cup of beer when it began to foam and overflow. Anpu knew what had happened and went to the Valley of Acacia to retrieve his brother's heart and body. He searched for years without finding it; then, one day, he came across an acacia tree lying on the ground. His foresight advised him that this was no ordinary tree and, indeed, it held his brother's heart. He took it and placed it in water. During the night it came back to life and Anpu placed it back in Bitou's corpse. Bitou coughed and breathed life once more and the two brothers embraced.

Then Bitou changed himself into the shape of a bull, covered with the most unusual markings; now Bitou was ready for vengeance. He began to devise a plan. He instructed his brother to ride upon his back and travel to the King's palace. Here he was to give the young bull to the Pharaoh as a gift.

When they arrived, the Pharaoh was so pleased at the sight of the unusual bull that he gave Anpu many riches and sent him home. The bull received the best of care and attention, and was pampered to the fullest.

Bint Nefer's selfishness and curiosity were piqued; she went to visit the remarkable bull. The animal spoke in the voice of Bitou and revealed his true identity and intentions of revenge. The terror instilled in Bint Nefer was overwhelming. She spoke to no one of this but went to the Pharaoh. She requested the bull to be slaughtered as she was hungry and craved its meat. At first the Pharaoh hesitated, but he could not deny any of her wishes; he was completely enchanted by her outward beauty. The bull was slaughtered and Bint Nefer ate the liver. This, she thought, was surely the end of Bitou.

However, two drops of blood splattered when the bull was killed. At that exact place, two towering persea trees grew out of the two drops of blood and they grew to adorn the entrance to the king's palace.

One day not too long later, Bint Nefer decided to rest by the persea trees. When she was most relaxed, the trees revealed their identity to her once more. Bint Nefer begged the Pharaoh to cut down the persea trees in order to be used as material for new royal furniture she suddenly desired. Again, the Pharaoh hesitated but gave into her peculiar whims, her devious intentions veiled in beauty.

As fate would have it, while the trees were being chopped down, a tiny sliver of wood went flying and found its way into Bint Nefer's mouth — and she swallowed it.

Nine months later, she gave birth to a boy, who rose to become Pharaoh. One day, the boy Pharaoh summoned to his side all the sages, nobles and officials of the land, along with that of his mother, Bint Nefer. The Pharaoh revealed that he was Bitou, thrice-slain by Bint Nefer. It was decided unanimously that she pay for her crimes and live the fate the Seven Hathors had declared.

Bitou reigned as Pharaoh for twenty years. His elder brother Anpu was his loyal right hand man. Upon Bitou's death, Anpu was named pharaoh and Egypt continued to prosper.

Certainly, the vast majority of ancient Egyptians could neither read nor write, even if the literacy rate was higher than in neighboring countries. A member of any social class who learnt these skills was highly respected among his or her people. Literacy was a means of escape from the drudgery of harsh manual labor.

Ancient Egyptian is second to Sumerian as the oldest of recorded languages. Different styles of language have been identified, starting with Old Egyptian, spoken during the Old Kingdom and used to write upon inscriptions. In the 1st Intermediate Period and the Middle Kingdom, the language spoken was Middle Egyptian. This is the classical phase of Ancient Egyptian. Great literary works and monumental inscriptions were inscribed in Middle Egyptian until the late Greco-Roman period. By the New Kingdom, the adopted language was New or Late Egyptian. Nevertheless, writings were still inscribed in classical Middle Egyptian.

Historians have discovered that Queen Cleopatra VII was fluent in at least seven languages, including Egyptian. She is the only ruling Ptolemy to speak the native language of Egypt. She also spoke Ethiopian, Hebrew, Aramaic, Syriac, Parthian (Persian) and Trogodyte.

Tehuti is credited as being the inventor of hieroglyphic writing.

His counterpart Seshat was revered as the goddess of writing. One of the most oldest, beloved and important gods of Egypt was Ptah. Ptah was known as the "First of the Gods" and "Lord of all Truth." He was the patron god of Mennefer where his cult center was established by Narmer c. 3100 BC. His temple was called Het-Ka-Ptah, translating into "Temple of the Soul of Ptah." The Greeks corrupted these words into "Aegyptos," thus giving us the origins of the word "Egypt."

The need for writing arose from the growing administrative and bureaucratic requirements of a newly unified Egypt. The earliest samples of the use of hieroglyphs comes from inscriptions on labels and pottery items from the royal necropolis at Abedju dating as far back as the start of the Dynastic Period c. 3100 BC, or perhaps even earlier.

Pictograms formed the first hieroglyphs which evolved into a combination of symbols, merging art and language together representing ideas, sounds and objects.

They called their writings *medu neter*, which translates into "words of the god." Once inscribed, the symbol was given a voice and a life. As long as it remained inscribed, what was written was immortal. The names of such controversial Pharaohs as Hatshepsut and Akhenaten were maliciously destroyed and removed from all inscriptions by their ambitious successors for the purpose of condemning them to be forgotten, condemning them to non-existence.

As there were more than one way to write a specific word, hundreds of determinatives were used to facilitate in interpreting their individual meanings. As with most words used in describing this history, even "hieroglyph" is of Greek origin; it translates into "sacred carvings." Hieroglyphs were used mainly for decorative, formal, sacred and religious writings or inscriptions as they were carved upon stone and pottery. Civil writings, royal documents of lasting significance as well as the recording of historical events were also written in hieroglyphs.

Another form of writing was hieratic. This script was used for recording literary, scientific, administrative and daily correspondence. Hieratic was a simpler and more cursive writing derived from hieroglyphics which evolved c. 1780 BC. Hieratic is to hieroglyphs what hand-writing is to printing. Hieratic was written with ink on papyrus, potsherds, wood, leather or limestone flakes. This script was used until the end of the New Kingdom. The Greek word "hieratic" translates into "priestly writing," as it was the priests who wrote in hieratic when copying business, sacred and literary texts where speed was wanted. Scribes who were efficient in hieratic writing as opposed to mastering hieroglyphic writing were given lesser-ranked functions such as recording administrative duties.

Demotic was another type of script that appeared towards the end of the Late Period. In Greek, "demotikos" translates into "common" or "popular." Demotic evolved c. 700 BC from hieratic and was written faster and more cursive. This writing was used for daily, commercial, administrative and legal purposes. Religious texts continued to be written in hieratic and sacred inscriptions carved on stone remained recorded in hieroglyphs. However, demotic came to be used in literary compositions as well as royal decrees inscribed upon stelae. Demotic was the last of the ancient Egyptian languages to be written and like hieratic, was read from right to left.

Papyrus was first used at the end of the 1st Dynasty; an unused roll was discovered in a tomb at Saqqara. However, the earliest written papyrus to date is from the 5th Dynasty. Papyrus was produced from the sheets of the exterior of the plant stems which were soaked in water and pounded until flattened. The strips were then layered crosswise and overlapped into producing sheets. The juice from the stems when pounded served as an adhesive as the sheets were glued together at the ends. The sheets were then dried in the sun and the result was the equivalent of our books. For less formal documents, an ostracon — a limestone flake, or a flat stone or broken piece of pottery, was a less costly and effective substitute for papyrus. The word "papyrus" comes from the Egyptian word *paperao*, the name for the plant.

In ancient Egyptian, *per* means "house." Cities such as Per Bast, Per Ramessu and Per Ausar were named so for obvious reasons. The word "pharaoh" originally meant "great house" as it derived from per (house) aa (great). The pharaoh did indeed "house" the spirit of the gods. During the 3rd Intermediate Period or early New Kingdom, this word evolved to mean "ruler of Egypt," as the pharaoh was regarded as the "great house" who sheltered his people. From this point on, the king was pharaoh. However, references made to earlier kings by this author are referred to as pharaohs to maintain simplicity and uniformity.

From the 5th Dynasty and on, pharaohs were given several official names and titles. These consisted of the Prenomen, the name given to the pharaoh at coronation. This royal name usually followed the title of "Nwst-Bity" or King of Upper and Lower Egypt." It was believed to have been implemented late into the 3rd Dynasty upon the pharaoh's coronation of the double crown. In hieroglyphics, this title was inscribed with the sedge plant or nwst of Upper Egypt, and the bee or bity, representing Lower Egypt. The Prenomen of Ramses II was User-ma'atre-Setepenre, which translates into "Strength and Ma'at of Ra-Chosen by Ra."

The name at birth or Nomen, such as Ramses, was often followed by the honorable title of "Sa Ra," which translates into "Son of Ra." The king also held a Heru-name, which designated the pharaoh as a mortal embodiment of Heru. The Heru-name was instituted by kings of Upper Egypt during the Early Dynastic period.

Vowels, regarded as most sacred in ancient Egypt, were omitted from hieroglyphs. Vowels were considered to be the divine spirit of words and to make them visible was sacrilege. Only the priests possessed the true knowledge of their actual sounds while they were chanted in their solemn hymns. The absence of vowels from the ancient Egyptian alphabet is the reason why certain deities are often written in various ways such as Ra and Re and Amen, Amon or Amun. We have no way of knowing what the language of the ancient Egyptians sounded like.

During the Middle Kingdom, 700 different symbols were in use and by the Ptolemaic Period, over 6,000 hieroglyphs existed. The alphabet consisted of 24 characters representing consonants which formed the words and could be written from left to right, right to left or top to bottom. Generally, they were written from right to left. The correct direction was determined by reading the text towards the faces of the human or animal figures.

Hieroglyphs were divided into two categories, symbols with pictorial meanings called ideograms and those with phonetic values called phonograms. Not only were there symbols for uniliterals, the alpha-

betic signs below, but symbols for determinatives, and hundreds of bi-
literals and triliterals as well. When the symbol was meant to represent
what the picture actually depicted, a single upright stroke was added.
Three vertical strokes indicated the plural form of the written word.
The feminine form of a word ended with the letter "t."

A			N		
B			O		
C			P		
D			Q		
E			R		
F			S		
G			T		
H			U		
I			V		
J			W		
K			X		
L			Y		
M			Z		

Occasionally, more than one glyph was used for the sound of a
letter such as "A," "H," "S" and others. As no hieroglyph exists for the
letter "V", the letter "F" being the closest in sound, it is used in transliteration. The hieroglyph for the sound or letters "K" and "Q" are one in
the same, as are "U" and "W" as well as "C", as in "city" and the letters
"S" and "Z." From this alphabet, the English reader is now able to read
and write hieroglyphs through transliteration. The letter "L" was not
used until Late Egyptian history. The vowels listed above were actually
semi-vowels which were inserted when speaking.

Hieroglyphs were carved upon limestone and drawn in an aesthetically pleasing manner called "graphic transposition," leaving as

little blank space as possible. There was no system of punctuation within hieroglyphic writing.

Although it may have been spoken last, the name of a deity was always inscribed first in respect to its divinity. This is called "honorific transposition." An example would be the name of the Pharaoh Akhenaten, which was written as "Aten Akhen," placing the name of the deity first.

In etymological analysis, many English and European words have their origins, or at least a historical parallel, in ancient Egyptian; just a few are indicated in the following list.

Paperao - paper/papyrus
Hebeni - ebony
Djobe - adobe
Hibu - ibis
Mut - mother
Nut - night
Deshret - desert
Khem - chemistry, alchemy
Fellahin - fellow

Some scholars conjecture that the English title "Sir" stems from the most honored deity, Ausar (Wsir/Osiris). Indeed, the Egyptian word for an "official" was *ser*.

It is easy to see why cats were called *miw* and wine was known as *irp*. According to Webster's Universal Dictionary, the meaning of the word "Caesarion" is derived from the manner in which Julius Caesar came into this world. And, contrary to popular belief, the word "Gypsies" does not refer to Egyptians. This is the name given to Indians who migrated to Europe late in the 15th Century of our era, who were thought to have been of Egyptian origin.

Scribes underwent many years of intensive training before mastering the skill of writing. Their tools consisted of a wooden or stone palette holding two cakes of ink and a pot filled with water, with a set of reed brushes made from plant shoots. The ink was derived from plants such as the juniper and was mixed with gum, water, vegetable sub-stances, copper and earth. Black ink was obtained from charcoal and soot. Red, used to record titles, punctuation in hieratic, beginnings of paragraphs, chapter headings, and evil deeds, was obtained from ochre. In the tomb of King Tutankhamen, reed pens, an ivory palette and two ink pans were discovered. Also found was a wooden pen case carved in the shape of a palm column, overlaid with gold and inlaid with colored glass in order for the Pharaoh to write in the afterlife.

During the Old Kingdom, the artist or scribe drew a black line through each red hieroglyph in order to neutralize the harmful influ-ence it was believed to emit. A horned viper, the symbol for the sound "F" as well as the masculine pronoun "he", "his" or "him," was often in-scribed with its head severed from the body to prevent it from exerting evil influences. Apep was believed to be most deadly and his name had to be magically destroyed. In the tomb of Seti I in the Valley of the Kings, a knife is drawn severing Apep's head, as seen in the determina-tive of his name. For this same reason, the feared crocodile, was often drawn with a harpoon or knife spearing its body.

The last known hieroglyphic inscription was discovered at Philae, dated 394 AD. By the 4th Century of our era, hieroglyphic writing was believed to be anti-Christian, pagan in nature. It is interesting to note, however, that the name of Amen, the Creator and King of Gods, is still uttered after the Lord's Prayer.

In 391 AD, the Byzantine Emperor shut down all Egyptian temples as pagan centers of worship. The Serapeum was destroyed, as were many other Egyptian shrines. The last men to use hieroglyphs were the few remaining Egyptian priests to survive. When these men died, so did the ability to interpret and write the sacred carvings of ancient Egypt.

Between AD 100 and 640, a new language emerged in Egypt. It especially developed and gained in popularity c. 300 AD. This new lan-guage was comprised of the Greek alphabet, with six additional signs representing Egyptians sounds derived from Demotic which were ab-sent in the Greek alphabet. This language is known as Coptic, a word derived from the Arabic word "Qibt" (their name for Egyptian Christians). Some believe that the word "Qibt" in turn was derived from the Greek "Aegytpos."

Coptic slowly died out and was replaced by Arabic. However, it still remains the language of the Coptic Church in Egypt. An approximate 10% of the Egyptian population is currently fluent in Coptic.

Cracking the code

In AD 1799, a crib sheet that would enable the deciphering of hieroglyphic writings was literally stumbled upon one day in Raschid, located on the Rosetta branch of the Nile. It came in the form of a stone, accidentally discovered by one of Napoleon's officers.

This black polished basalt tablet came to be known as the Rosetta Stone; it held the key to unlocking the sacred mysteries of the forgotten past. It weighed nearly 1500 pounds and measured about 3 feet in height with a width of over 2 feet and thickness of 11 inches.

The text consisted inscribed upon it was a description of a temple endowment decree, dated March 27, 196 BC, addressed to King Ptolemy V Ephiphanes, on his last anniversary as Pharaoh. The tablet held the same text written in three different languages and contained words of gratitude from the priests of Mennefer to the 13-year-old Pharaoh for his generosity to the temple.

As the same text was recorded in ancient Greek and Demotic, its hieroglyphic interpretation was guaranteed. However, the uppermost hieroglyph text contained the least amount of symbols, as it was the most damaged of the three languages. The missing pieces have never been found.

It took no less than 20 years for the translation work to be completed. The first breakthrough was accomplished by Englishman Thomas Young (1773-1824). By the age of two, he was already reading and by the age of 14, he was fluent in at least 12 languages. Young was a brilliant physicist, mathematician and linguist who made several important discoveries in the deciphering of hieroglyphic writing. His greatest achievements were in the field of physiological optics.

Young was first to conclude that hieroglyphs may represent sounds combined into words. He also concluded some of the demotic symbols and hieratic were derived from hieroglyphic writings. He cor-rectly assumed that hieroglyphs contained both alphabetic and sym-bolic qualities. Young was not fluent in ancient Egyptian and this fac-tor greatly limited his progress. Nevertheless, Young did decipher the true meanings of several ideograms and letters. He was also correct in deducing that royal names were inscribed inside cartouches. From this, he deciphered the names of Ptolemy and Cleopatra. Both names were compared and noted as they both contained the letters "p, t, o, l, and e". Their hieroglyph equivalent was determined and other words were in-terpreted from these two names.

Young's results were published in 1819 and forwarded to a French-man named Jean Francois Champollion (1790-1832). Champollion was a child prodigy who taught himself to read at the age of five. He eventu-ally learnt Greek, Coptic, Hebrew, Chaldean, Sanskirt, Arabic, Syriac, Persian, Pali, Parsi and Zend — before the age of 17. According to leg-end, when Champollion's mother was about to give birth to him, a spirit or astrologer came to her bedside and revealed that the child "would be the one to bring light on the centuries of the past."

Greek and Demotic were known during the 19th century and both texts of the Rosetta Stone were discovered to be identical. It was natu-ral to assume that the hieroglyphic text also contained the same infor-mation. However, Champollion originally disagreed with Young over the idea that hieroglyphs combined both ideograms and phonetic char-acters. Champollion believed that they were merely ideograms, rather than alphabetic, and went on to publish this theory in 1821. It was only later, while investigating Young's theory with a more open mind, that he was able to make great progress. Champollion was also fluent in Coptic and eventually succeeded in translating the entire text of the Rosetta Stone. The value of Young's work was almost equal to that of Champollion, who took it to completion and published in 1828, but Champollion never gave Young the credit he so much deserved.

The Rosetta Stone is currently residing in the British Museum.

31. MEDICINE

Medical science is considered to have been founded in ancient Egypt, and they were the first to apply and record the results of surprisingly advanced medical practices. The first known treatise on surgery is dated to the 1st Dynasty.

The short life span of the ancient Egyptian was due to such diseases as tuberculosis and respiratory ailments as bronchitis and pneumonia. They also suffered from parasites absorbed through unclean waters, the dangers of childbirth, snake bites, polio, tumors, rheumatism, scoliosis, appendicitis, meningitis, small pox, malaria, measles and cholera.

Aspiring doctors underwent many years of hard training at the temple schools, where they were taught how to cure illnesses and set broken bones. The latter were treated with rational, medical methods such as plant, animal, mineral substances and surgical techniques, although the unfamiliar or unknown was remedied with magic or *Heka*. Intricate surgery, dream analysis, faith healing, amulets, herbs and recipes consisting of the most ghastly ingredients were used in curing illnesses.

From funerary work, the process of mummification, first-hand knowledge of human anatomy was acquired, and autopsies were performed as part of the learning process of the healers. Doctors were trained and specialized in particular fields, such as the head, internal maladies, gynecology and ophthalmology; texts were consulted and observations made.

Female doctors exercised their skills and knowledge under the supervision of Lady Pesheshet, the earliest female physician in history (5th Dynasty). Perhaps the earliest ophthalmologist was named Iry; he was an oculist and physician to royalty during the 6th Dynasty. It is interesting to note that *irty* was the ancient Egyptian word for "eyes" or "to see."

Dentists filled teeth with mineral cement or a mixture of resin and malachite. Loose teeth were bound with silver or gold wire as examined mummies have proven. It appears that silver wire was used during the Late Period. Dentists were in high demand — tooth decay was a great problem, as a result of consuming bread and cakes mixed with sand from the grinding process. Studies of mummies dated to the 4th Dynasty show surgically-produced holes under a molar that was used to drain an abscess. The mummy of Ramses II has proven that he suffered from gum disease and advanced tooth decay. One dentist named Hesy-Re, who lived c. 2600 BC, was also a vizier and high official under the reign of Djoser and during the time of Imhotep. His extensive titles included "Chief Dentist" and "Greatest of Physicians and Dentists."

The highly respected and highly skilled physicians were few and mostly at the disposal of the upper class, except during the reign of Akhenaten when physicians were ordered to offer their services free of charges to the poor.

Imhotep, the famed architect, was also a skilled physician. Two thousand years after his time, he of non-royal blood was immortalized and deified by the Greeks as the "Patron of Medicine." Shrines and temples were built and dedicated to Imhotep. He was not only the physician to the people, but to the gods as well. Clay models of one's diseased body part were often placed in Imhotep's temple for him to cure. Additionally, he was thought to heal and send relief of pain to the sick while they slept.

Surgery was successful in the treatment of broken bones as well as in the brain area, where intricate operations were practiced. The pulse was referred to as "the voice of the heart," as the ancient Egyptians were cognizant of the fact that the heart and pulse were synchronized.

Get it in writing

Papyrus records of antidotes and cures have been discovered which give a pretty good picture of the medicinal beliefs and practices of the times. These texts were frequently consulted as reference material for treatments which demonstrated the ancient Egyptian knowledge of medicine, healing, anatomy and autopsy.

One such papyrus, dated 3600 years ago, tells of 100 remedies and antidotes. Over half involved the use of soothing honey which cleansed, dried wounds and accelerated the healing process. The *Ebers Papyrus* contains nearly 900 prescriptions, charms, spells and invocations for any ailment. It is dated c. 1534 BC, however portions of the text hint of much older origins, dating back to the start of the 1st Dynasty. This papyrus discusses twelve cases with the relevant spells and has an entire section devoted to diseases of the eye.

The *Edwin Smith Papyrus* was written c. 1700 BC and contains 48 surgical operations, scientific diagnosis and treatments for wounds, fractures, dislocated and broken bones. These injuries were understood and treated with clinical methods. Magic was almost exclusively absent in this papyrus. However, it is believed that the data contained is also based on older texts written during the 3rd Dynasty. Some scholars believe that Imhotep himself authored this text.

The *London Papyrus* includes medical and magical wisdom believed to have belonged to the Pharaoh Khufu of the 4th Dynasty. The *Kahun Gynecological Papyrus*, dated 1825 BC, deals with such treatments as contraception, detecting pregnancies, evaluating fertility, determining a baby's gender, bladder problems and all medical cases related to pregnancy and the female reproductive system.

Medicines

Many of the ancient Egyptian herbal treatments were highly prized and soon spread throughout the Mediterranean area as they were practiced with successful results. Belladonna, poppy and thyme were effective pain relievers and sedatives. Powdered root of the man-drake plant was used to calm an upset stomach, cure insomnia, control fear and depression. Henbane was not only used as calming antidote but like mandrake, was also used in love potions as an aphrodisiac.

Herbs such as myrrh, frankincense, cassia, thyme, opium, juniper, aloe, castor oil and fennel are mentioned in medical papyri. Garlic was very popular as it helped in the digestive process, induced vitality and strength while dispelling evil spirits. Garlic and onions were believed to induce endurance and were consumed regularly. Raw garlic was taken as a remedy for respiratory ailments. Honey and milk were pre-scribed for respiratory and throat ailments. To calm a persistent cough and moisten dry lungs, a very common problem in the dry climate of the desert, a concoction of dried figs, dates, aniseed, honey and water was simmered into a thick mixture and taken as an effective remedy. Tannic acid from the acacia nut helped heal burns and coriander was pre-scribed for stomach illnesses as it was thought to contain digestive properties. Henna and saffron were used to mend small wounds.

The medicinal potions included such ingredients as blood and fat of an animal, powdered bones, hooves and horns dissolved in water, milk, beer or wine. Milk and wine were specifically thought to contain medicinal qualities on their own. Treatments were inserted into a body cavity and ointments made of honey or fats along with special diets were often prescribed. Natron was used as an effective cleanser, disin-fectant and healing agent.

The mud of the Nile was incorporated into potions which was believed to rapidly heal wounds. The Nile River was believed to possess healing and rejuvenating properties. However, one must wonder about the hygienic properties of the Nile.

Hedge your bets

These prescriptions usually had to be accompanied by the proper magical spell. Physicians divided the body into 36 parts, each of which was governed by a specific demon. When the correct demon was at-tacked, the body was rid of its evil influences. In addition, healing gods were assigned to all regions of the human body and, when summoned, would cure the individual. Thus, while preparing the medicine, the physician chanted specific spells and prayers.

Heka played a monumental role in the medical practices as magical spells, charms, amulets, potions and incantations were applied. Medicinal prescriptions were inscribed on papyrus, which the patient was instructed to swallow.

Unexplainable diseases were believed to be caused by evil spirits invading the body inflicted by a demon or an angered god. By vocalizing certain magical words or names of gods in their specific tone, a priest/doctor/magician healed the sick and dispelled the evil demons believed to inhabit the body. Such healers were known as *Sunu*, a title synonymous with "doctors." Some physicians who specialized in certain medical areas or branches were retained by royalty .

And if that doesn't work

The powerful goddess Sekhmet and her many aspects was also worshipped as a "Patroness of Physicians," and as "Mistress of Healing." She is credited with curing epidemics, as her destructive qualities were applied in the banishing of illnesses and diseases. However it was also believed that Sekhmet, when angered, brought plagues upon man. Doctors known as Priests of Sekhmet were trained in the arts of healing and skilled in curing the diseases she inflicted upon mankind.

Evidence on a stela from Uast reveals that Khonsu was also credited and worshipped as a healing god. It was Khonsu who rid the Princess of Bekhten of the demons causing her illness during the reign of Ramses the Great. Auset is also a healing deity as she healed with her magic and brought back her husband, Ausar to life.

Douao and Weret were healing gods associated with diseases of the eye.

Tehuti was associated with healing as he restored Heru's eye back to health after his battles with Set. Tehuti authored a compilation 42 scrolls dealing with law, education, philosophy, theology, geography, history, writing, astronomy and astrology. Six additional books dealt with medicine and the entire collection came to be known as the *Her-*

metic Books as Tehuti became equated with Greek god Hermes.

Some say that the modern symbol for prescriptions, "Rx", is derived from the Eye of Heru as symbolic of health and wholeness — although it is generally accepted to be the abbreviation for the Latin word for "recipe."

The medicinal practices of the day contained many strong astrological elements. The day was divided into hours which fell under a specific stellar influence. Medical papyri instructed the physician as to the designated times at which to administer the correct cure, antidote or treatment. The timing of an operation was determined by observing when the appropriate celestial harmonies corresponded to the particular illness.

Predictions of life and death were prognosticated in the magical papyrus entitled the *Tables of Democritus*. In this ancient form of numerology, the moon's course and number of thirty day periods which elapsed since the illness began were recorded. If the number of days left over fell in the upper section of the tables, the patient was expected to recover. If it fell below, he was not.

32. THE CALENDAR

In the beginning, the sky was sectioned into 36 parts that came to be called *decans* (Greek for the number ten). These were stars that rose above the horizon ten days before the next decan rose. Each lunar month (or *abd*) was divided into three decans. Decans were known as *sebau shepsu*, meaning noble stars. The months were grouped into three seasons of four months, adding up to 360 days. Five holy days were added, as described below, to complete the lunar year.

The seasons, Akhet, Peret and Shomu, corresponded to the cycle of the Nile and the agricultural phases of the land. During Akhet, inundation occurred, at Peret the crops emerged and in Shomu, the harvest took place. Each lunar month was in turn divided into three weeks of ten days each. From this division, the 24-hour day was born, with 12 assigned for the day and 12 for the night. However, in Egypt and elsewhere at the time, the hours were not standard in length; rather, they were reckoned as 1/12 of the period of daylight or darkness, which varied according to the season.

For administrative purposes the months were indicated by their seasons, from one to four — for example, the fourth month of summer was called Shomu IV. However, in a religious context they were referred to by the specific deities to which they were dedicated. The

Copts preserved the names of the 12 ancient Egyptian lunar months as follows:

Akhet I	Tehuti
Akhet II	Paopi
Akhet III	Het Heru
Akhet IV	Khoiak

Peret I	Tobi
Peret II	Mekhir
Peret III	Phamenoth
Peret IV	Pharmuthi

Shomu I	Pakhon
Shomu II	Paoni
Shomu III	Epep
Shomu IV	Mesore

The five Epagomenal days, in honor of the births of Ausar, Heru, Set, Auset and Nebet-Het, were added to complete the lunar calendar. On these five holy days, no work was done; it was a time of celebration and festivity. The birth date or Epagomenal Day dedicated to Set was considered unlucky, while that of his consort Nebet-Het was considered neutral because of her loyalty to Ausar, Auset and Heru, whose birthdays and anniversaries were regarded as promising.

This lunar calendar was based on the moon's 29- or 30-day cycle, from one new moon to the next. It served well for agricultural and religious purposes as well as allowing the dating of events. This "original" calendar was said to have been established by the lunar deity, Tehuti.

The solar calendar was adopted c. 2900 BC and started with the rising of the brightest star, Sopdet (Sirius). Each year, before rising on the eastern horizon, Sopdet disappeared for 70 days — it hid beneath the sun's rays, only to rise again in the east, just before the sun, heralding the annual event of the Nile flood. This took place around June 20 and was called *Peret Sopdet*, "The Emergence of Sopdet," and it brought on the first month of Akhet. The beginning of the New Year was known as *Wepet Renpet*, "Opening of the Year"; it was a most important and joyous astronomical event of great ceremonial relevance. Auset's temple at Iunet was constructed to observe the heliacal rising of Sopdet. By averaging the days between each Sopdet cycle (Sothic Cycle) or return, the 365 day year or civil calendar was determined.

Based on the dates when Sopdet's rising occurred (records exist from many different years), scholars have been able to correlate the dates of specific pharaonic reigns with the calendar in use today. Censorinus, a Roman writer and historian, fortunately recorded the simultaneous event of the rising of Sopdet and the Nile in 139 AD. This enabled later historians to calculate previous positions and risings for Sopdet and to deduce that the solar calendar came into use around 2773 BC.

The earliest recorded date based on Sopdet's rising is in the 7th year of the reign of Senwosret III, of the 12th Dynasty: the 16th day of the 4th month of winter (Peret). From this information the date has been determined to correspond with what we call 1870 BC, with a margin of error of 1 to 5 years, depending on where in Egypt the observation was made. Another significant recording is from the 9th year of the reign of Amenhotep I, of the 18th Dynasty: the 9th day of the third month of summer (Shomu). That date has been calculated as falling somewhere between 1554 and 1534 BC.

The solar year, derived from the lunar, was also divided into three seasons of four months each, with every month consisting of three weeks of ten days, plus five, totaling 365 days. This became the civil calendar, used for the administration of the country, while in farming and everyday life, the lunar calendar was retained. The two calendars were eventually incorporated for the purpose of scheduling religious events and lunar festivals that had to be coordinated with the astronomical cycles and agricultural phases.

However, a discrepancy developed between the two calendars, as the lunar system fell behind the solar calendar at a rate of one day for every four years. This resulted in festivals being celebrated at the wrong time. The experts calculated that they would have to wait 1460 (365 x 4) years for the heliacal rising of Sopdet to coincide with the first day of the Nile's flooding again. Thus, c. 2500 BC, another lunar calendar was implemented. This was based upon the civil year where an extra, 13th, month was inserted every two or three years to compensate for this lapse.

As early as the Old Kingdom, all three calendars were in use: the original lunar calendar for agricultural purposes (which depended on the phases of the moon and season), the solar calendar for administrative functions, and a lunisolar calendar for religious purposes, to establish the proper time to hold ceremonies. All this stellar knowledge contributed to forming the basis of the calendar still in use today.

During 239 BC, King Ptolemy III Euregetes introduced the current method of correction by use of a leap year, every four years, to stabilize the monthly positions. This correction was published by the Egyptian priests as the *Decree of Canopus.*.

In 46 BC, Julius Caesar commissioned the astronomer Sosigenes, from Alexandria, to help reform and improve the lunar calendar in use in Rome. Sosigenes advised Caesar to abandon the lunar calendar altogether, and proposed that the months be arranged on a seasonal basis using the Egyptian solar year of 365.25 days. To re-align the calendar with the seasons, Sosigenes proposed that two intercalations be implemented in 46 BC. The first was an extra month inserted between February and March. The next intercalation consisted of two months added between November and December. These intercalations extended the year to 445 days. No doubt the Romans referred to 46 BC as the "year of confusion!" After these one-time adjustments, Caesar dropped the intercalations, retained the Epagomenal Days and established seven months of 31 days, four months of 30 days and one month of 29 days, to which an extra day was added every four years. In 44 BC, the Roman Senate changed the names of the 7th and 8th months from "Quintilis" to "July", after Julius Caesar, and from "Sextilis" to "August", after Augustus. A further adjustment subtracted a day from February and gave it to August, so that Augustus would have as many days in his month as Julius had. Thus the Julian Calendar was established, and it was used until the 16th century.

As the year of the Julian calendar was slightly over 11 minutes longer than the solar year, the difference led to a gradual change in the seasons, which accumulated to 10 days. By 1580, the spring equinox fell about 10 days earlier than it should have.

In 1582, Pope Gregory XIII reformed the Julian Calendar. Under the advice of his astronomers, he had ten days dropped from October, as a one-time adjustment. By doing this, the next equinox was restored to its proper date and the calendar years corresponded more closely to the solar year. To further correct the discrepancies of the Julian calendar, Pope Gregory XIII added an extra day to February in century years divisible by 400, such as 1600 and 2000. The Gregorian calendar therefore was about two weeks ahead of the Julian calendar. This modernization was quickly picked up by most of the world; however, some countries were slow to adopt it. Great Britain used the Julian calendar until 1752. Russia only switched to the Gregorian calendar in 1918 (which is why the Great October Socialist Revolution now falls in November), and Turkey switched in 1928.

In the early days of civilization, astronomy and astrology were one. The motion of the stars and planets were observed and attempts were made to correlate these changes with "facts on the ground": planetary movements were thought to be predictors of major events such as eclipses, floods, epidemics, earthquakes, wars and famine.

The fact that the ancient Egyptians devised the calendar and were able to predict the most important annual event — the Nile's inundation — proves their knowledge of astronomy. Records were kept and rectilinear horoscopes have been discovered dating as far back as 4200 BC.

It is generally accepted that the Chaldeans (Babylonians) originated the art of astrology. However, research has suggested that they may have learnt it from the priesthood of Egypt. Sir Isaac Newton hypothesized that this must have taken place when the Ethiopians invaded Egypt during the 3rd Intermediate Period (1087-712 BC) or (more likely) during the Late Period (712-332 BC.) As Egyptians fled the invading Ethiopians and immigrated into the land of Babylon, they would have brought with them the study of the stars, introducing it to the Chaldeans — who immediately embraced the new science and took it further.

A Greek horoscope has been discovered with a notation crediting the ancient Egyptians with the creation of (and devotion to) astrology, adding that they handed down their knowledge through generations. However, there seems to be no record of individual astrological charts as we know them today, until the Ptolemaic Dynasties, when horoscopes became very much in vogue.

Temple priests known as ("Overseers of the Hours"), *Imy Unut*, consulted star charts. Their name could very well be the origin of the word "minute." From their temple rooftops, these astronomers observed, measured and recorded time by the passing of the stars; they devoted themselves to studying the stellar bodies and searching for signs. In the systematic construction of their temples, the floor represented the earth, sacred pools symbolized the seas and rivers, and the arched ceilings embodied the heavens. The planetary movements, their order, rising and setting were carefully noted. This was of utmost importance as the timing of the temple rituals was determined by stellar movements. It was believed that the priests were privy to the answers and the secrets of the universe, and so astronomy/astrology became an integral part of their religion.

The symbol for astrology was a palm branch. In Egyptian stellar processions, it was carried by *Horoscopus*, along with an hourglass symbolizing time. Horoscopus was the name of the priest representing stellar wisdom. All astronomer priests had to be fully versed in Tehuti's wisdom and had to be able to recite the four books of astronomy (from the collection of 42 books he authored). The fours texts described the positions of the fixed stars, the illumination of the sun and moon, the conjunctions and eclipses as well as the rising and setting of other heavenly bodies. This collection of writings has never been discovered, but reference is made to the scrolls in several papyri.

The 18th Dynasty scribe named Nakht, whose tomb gave us such wonderful illustrations of musicians at work, was also a trained stargazer at the temple. His duty was to chart the information of the stars and their effect upon the seasonal changes of the earth. The great Imhotep was also well versed in the science of the stars. During the Late Period, he was deified not only as the father of architecture and of medicine, but of astronomy as well. Petosiris was also known for mastering the art of Egyptian astrology. He was chief administrator of the Temple of Khnemu and High Priest of Tehuti.

The oldest astronomical diagram of Egypt is found on the ceiling of the tomb of Senenmut, Queen Hatshepsut's confidant, advisor and architect of the 18th Dynasty. A mural in the tomb of Ramses VI (20th Dynasty) reveals the arched body of Nut, goddess of the sky and heavens, swallowing the sun each evening and giving birth to it again the following morning.

The Egyptians divided the sky into 12 sections, each assigned a name and a form. In 1250 BC, Pharaoh Ramses II (also known as an astrologer), fixed the four cardinal points of the compass using the cardinal signs of the zodiac: Aries, Cancer, Libra and Capricorn. When Ramses II departed this world in 1223 BC, his body was placed in a sarcophagus adorned with astrological symbols, which also surrounded his tomb at the Temple of Amen at Karnak.

As mentioned in the previous chapter, each month was divided into three decans, a system still used by today's astrologers; the decans were stars that were observed to rise above the horizon ten days before the next decan rose. These movements were crucial in calibrating the timing of religious ceremonies. Lists of planetary decans inscribed upon coffin lids of the Middle Kingdom show that the Egyptians were familiar with the concept of the zodiac (Greek for "band of animals") thousands of years before the Greeks. The illustration shows 36 stellar configurations not related to Chaldean, Greek nor modern signs of the zodiac. However, it was the Greeks who popularized astrology; their interpretations are imbued with Egyptian symbology and mythology. The first representation of the signs of the zodiac as we know them today, albeit combined with Chaldean and Greek constellations, comes from the Zodiac of Denderah dated to the 1st century BC. The Temple of Denderah is an astronomical wonder; the circular zodiac that adorns the ceiling of the grand temple is believed to show the solar eclipse of 51 BC. Along with the signs of the zodiac, Sopdet (Sirius) and Sah (Orion) are sculpted on the portico of the grand temple.

Sopdet remained hidden beneath the sun's ray for 70 days before rising each year. This is the same number of days taken for the preparation and mummification rituals of the wealthy before they were laid to rest, in preparation for their rise to immortality. It was believed that, as the planets and stars rose and set, all Egyptians could also rise again and become united with the heavenly bodies after earthly death.

Sopdet and Sah were so bright, they had to be divine. Auset became immortalized in Sopdet and Ausar in Sah. Southern stars such as these had specific orbits and were named *ikhemu weredu* or "stars that never rest," as they were never still, they rose and set. Every eight years, Sopdet rises simultaneously with Venus, symbolizing the sacred marriage of Ausar and Auset. The heavenly bodies, known as "flowers of the night" or "flowers of the sky," were regarded as gods and souls. These were the spirits of the departed ones who dwelled in the sky (which was also referred to as the "field of reeds").

The circumpolar or northern stars were known as *ikhemu seku,* or the "imperishable ones," as they remained fixed in the sky and never rose nor set. These heavenly bodies were held in special reverence as they were believed to embody the special souls of those who had attained eternal perfection. On the ceiling of the burial chamber in the tomb of Seti I is one of the oldest zodiacs illustrating the stars that never set. It is dated c. 1280 BC and shows the twelve hours of the night and the heavenly constellations represented in human and animal form.

Stars were known as *sebau* and their symbol was a five-pointed star, the same symbol as for the concept of learning and, interestingly, for the Kingdom of the Duat. Besides the luminaries, the Sun and Moon, the ancient Egyptians recognized *Sebeg* (Mercury), *Seba Djai or Benu* (Venus), *Heru Descher* (Mars), *Hor-Upesh-Pet* (Jupiter) and *Hor-Ka-Pet* (Saturn). Khonsu and Tehuti, as lunar deities, represented the moon; however, Tehuti as a god of communication and learning came to embody Mercury as well.

The planet Pluto can be assigned to Ausar and Anpu as gods of the underworld and transformation. Heru, the avenger, is identified with the active planet, Mars. His counterpart, Het-Heru, the cow-goddess, is embodied in the sign of Taurus, the bull. Serqet, the scorpion goddess, is associated with the sign of Scorpio and Hap can be equated with Aquarius, the water-bearer. The first sign of the Zodiac, Aries, might well be called the "opener of the Zodiac"; and the glyph for this sign is indeed the same as the symbol of *pesh-en-kef,* the instrument used in the funerary "Opening of the Mouth" ritual. Ma'at clearly personifies the sign of Libra, the scales of justice. Libra is the sign of the descendant or setting sun in the horoscope and its symbol is the same as the hiero-glyph for *Akhet*, meaning horizon. The planetary ruler of Libra is Venus, and its astrological symbol is almost identical to the ancient Egyptian ankh, representing everlasting life. The entrance into the descendant realm, the land of the setting sun, or west, was regarded as the gateway to the underworld. Gemini was embodied in the twins, Shu and Tefnut, while the lion-headed goddess Sekhmet personified the attributes of the sign of Leo. Amen is immortalized in Aries, the ram, and Khepera personified the sign of Cancer.

The sun was embodied in Ra, the solar god and supreme deity who traveled the sky in his sun boat. Ra's solar temple was situated in Iunu (Heliopolis, in Greek, the "City of the Sun"). It became a preeminent center for the study of astronomy. The sun was especially honored as it was regarded as the source of all the power that controlled the Nile. In addition, as the sun rose and set, it became symbolic of rebirth.

The moon also embodied the concept of renewal and rejuvenation as it grew from a new moon (or *psdn*) to a full moon and repeated the cycle each month. Its monthly waning and disappearance symbolized Set's stealing of Heru's lunar eye. The moon's return was attributed to Tehuti repairing and restoring the Eye of Heru; and the symbol representing a full moon was the Eye of Heru.

Eclipses were sacred and were held to symbolize Apep swallowing Ra and his solar barque as it traveled through the night sky. Nebet-Het was revered as the goddess of eclipses and her songs, with her sister Auset, sang of the union between the sun and moon during *neshenu* (eclipses) — which must have been awe-inspiring events for the Egyptians as their beloved life-giving sun vanished from sight.

From the decans, the Egyptians were also first to divide the day into 24 hours. Lists providing the positions of the stars during the twelve hours of the night, at fifteen-day intervals, were discovered in the Valley of the Kings. This 20th-Dynasty illustration was found in the tomb of Ramses VI and is especially unique as it is drawn in the shape of a seated man.

Water clocks and sundials were used to measure time. One water clock belonging to Amenhotep III was in the form of a water-filled alabaster vase that emptied as time passed.

Astronomy and astrology reached a peak during the Ptolemaic Era, as Alexandria became a major center for the study of the stars. Astrology then was combined with the symbology of Egypt, the mathematics of the Greeks and the philosophy of the Chaldeans. Unfortunately, the Alexandrian astronomical and astrological texts were destroyed in a fire by Christian zealots in the 5th century AD.

Nectanebo II was a great pharaoh/astrologer/magician. According to legend, when Olympia, Princess of Epirus and wife of King Phillip II of Macedonia, was about to give birth in 356 BC, Nectanebo II stood by her side making stellar observations; he urged her to hold the child within until an auspicious hour when the heavenly bodies were favorably aligned. Apparently she succeeded, for she gave birth to Alexander the Great. Olympia herself proclaimed that her son was the divine child of Amen, as Hatshepsut had claimed for herself over a thousand years earlier. There is some speculation as to whether Nectanebo II himself was the true father of Alexander the Great. Among his myriad accomplishments, Alexander the Great drove the Persians out of Egypt and established the final dynasty there.

As this great era closed with the Roman invasion of 30 BC, 3000 years of spectacular pharaonic rule came to an end. However, the spirit of ancient Egypt has truly endured and achieved its divine goal of immortality.

Further Readings

Andreu, Guillemette. *Egypt in the Age of the Pyramids.* New York; Cornell University Press, 1997.

Brewer, Douglas J. and Emily Teeter. *Egypt and the Egyptians.* Cambridge, UK; Cambridge University Press, 1999.

Brier, Bob. *Ancient Egyptian Magic.* New York; William Morrow and Co., 1980.

Budge, E.A. Wallis. *The Gods of the Egyptians.* New York; Dover Publications, 1969.

Budge, E.A. Wallis. *Egyptian Magic.* New York; Dover Publications, 1971.

Casson, Lionel, et al. *Ancient Egypt; Great Ages of Man.* Alexandria, VA; Time Life Books, 1965.

Johnson, Paul. *The Civilization of Ancient Egypt.* London; Weidenfeld and Nicolson, 1999.

McMahan, Ian. *Secrets of the Pharaohs.* New York; Avon Books, 1998.

Spence, Lewis. *Ancient Egyptian Myths and Legends.* London; Dover Publications, 1990.